T0326947

Romanticism
at the
End of History

Jerome Christensen

Romanticism at the End of History

The Johns Hopkins
University Press
BALTIMORE AND LONDON

© 2000 The Johns Hopkins University Press
All rights reserved. Published 2000
Printed in the United States of America on acid-free paper
9 8 7 6 5 4 3 2 1

The Johns Hopkins University Press
2715 North Charles Street
Baltimore, Maryland 21218-4363
www.press.jhu.edu

Library of Congress Cataloging-in-Publication Data
will be found at the end of this book.
A catalog record for this book is available from the British Library.

ISBN 0-8018-6319-8

For Stanley Fish and Neil Hertz,
who taught me to read

Some of his students — not many, not even most, but one a year, say — did get incensed about the past. He had a case at present, that ginger-haired boy, MacSomething . . . , who became quite enraged by the failure of good (as he saw it) to triumph over evil in History. Why hadn't x prevailed? Why did z beat y? He could see MacSomething's puzzled, angry face staring back at him in classes, wanting to be told that History — or at any rate historians — had got it wrong; that x had in fact gone into hiding and turned up years later at w; and so on. Normally, Graham would have ascribed such reactions to — what? — immaturity; or, more specifically, to some local cause like a churchy upbringing. Now he wasn't so sure. MacSomething's rage against the past involved complex emotions about a medley of characters and events. Perhaps he was suffering from a retrospective sense of justice.

— Julian Barnes, *Before She Met Me*

Contents

Acknowledgments

My thanks to *Critical Inquiry*, *South Atlantic Quarterly*, Purdue University Press, and AMS Press for permission to include revised versions of essays that first appeared in their pages.

I am grateful to Willis Regier and Douglas Armato for their initial interest in this book and to Jacqueline Wehmueller, Maura Burnett, Celestia Ward for seeing it through to publication, and to indexer Barbara E. Cohen. Frank McConnell made the book better by honoring me with a shrewd, candid, and sympathetic reading.

In many respects this book caps sixteen deeply rewarding years as a member of the English Department at Johns Hopkins University, where what Stanley Fish called "the life of the mind" is truly honored. I want to express esteem and affection for my colleagues, who have sustained that spirit over the years: to Leo Braudy, Allen Grossman, Stanley Fish, Avrom Fleishman, Lee Patterson, Ronald Paulson, John Plotz, Mary Poovey, and Larzer Ziff. My administrative service to the department was made immeasurably easier by the marvelous talents and unfailing good humor of Susie Herrmann, Graduate Coordinator, and Peggy McKenzie, Administrative Assistant. And last but most, I want to applaud the scores of smart, passionate graduate students who, in seminar after seminar, made Gilman 148 the best place in the world to teach.

Romanticism
at the
End of History

Introduction

> *Bru:*   Do you know them?
>
> *Luc:*   No sir. Their hats are plucked about their ears,
> And half their faces buried in their cloaks,
> That by no means I may discover them
> By any mark of favour.
>
> *Bru:*   Let 'em enter. [*Exit* Lucius]
> They are the faction. O Conspiracy,
> Shamest thou to show thy dangerous brow by night,
> When evils are most free?

— Shakespeare, *Julius Caesar*, 2.1, 72–79

This is a book about Romantic hope. The following essays use British Romanticism to negotiate the difference between a writing life lived in a postrevolutionary, preindustrial, preprofessional age and one lived in a highly differentiated and minutely organized society in which those who are likely to read the various texts of the writers called Romantic are institutionally situated and subject to disciplinary protocols all but unimaginable to the writers they esteem. That difference cannot be fully theorized, for the impulse to theorize is implicated in the phenomenon under consideration. I take it that the best reason for negotiating the difference between the Romantics and their contemporary readers is not to define a historical discourse, to compass an intellectual horizon, or to quarantine an ideology but to use the poets to identify a good way of living in the ongoing practice of making a living. This undertaking will involve a blurring of the distinction between Romantic and Romanticist that has been the pride of the practitioners of ideology critique during the past fifteen years. "A good way of living" is the best way for me, I suppose, but not just for me, I claim, because there is no moment of self-consciousness available to the institutionalized practitioner of literary studies that is not recursively involved in a practice of reading, writing, and teaching, of purposively engaging other minds bent on other purposes — no moment of knowledge not ethically circumstanced. Romantic ethics, I argue, is a secondary imagination, a re-creation of the given in the light of our best conceptions of good use. Thus I take it as my responsibility to develop not only the way in which Romantic ethics can be applied to the service of critique but also the way in which ethics can be practically applied as a policy within postmodern culture and especially within the university, where I make my living.

Historicists will not sympathize with my procedure here. These essays endeavor to fend off sympathy, the historicist's preferred technology for channeling the past. Being antihistoricist does not entail a denial of history but a rejection of the inevitability of history, then, now, and for the future. History is what happened, not what had or has to happen. Unlike the historicist, dead set on decoding the iron logic of past events, the Romantic fully credits the possibility of accidents and readies himself or herself to take advantage of swerves or lapses from the norm as opportunities for change. Novelists, like actuaries, endeavor to master accidents according to the regime of the probable. Poets and essayists court accidents; they induce what Wordsworth calls the "regular impulses of mild surprise" that freshen poetic meter or the routine of publication into something more than mere rhythm. Promoting and practicing a Romantic ethic involves a prudent idealism: not the claim that consciousness can bring about change on its own — as if, after deconstruction, we could in good faith claim that consciousness is its own place or has its own way — but the recognition of an agency with an indisputable capacity to do things or get things done and which may or may not act on behalf of institutions, institutions that, in turn, may or may not be good in their aims and ends. Romantic idealism involves a principled frustration with the way things have turned out and a deliberate impatience to turn them right.

I ask my readers to imagine what the *Edinburgh* reviewer of 1802 imagined, that Romantic poets were conspirators against the order of things whose designs have not yet been realized. Imagine poets as the unacknowledged conspirators of a future in which poets will openly rule. As a conspiracy against the given, Romanticism is primordially and persistently open to unforeseen consequences, one of which is Romantic criticism, which is not a subspecialization of philosophy but a species of the poetic imagination. Imagine that, as an engaged reader of Romantic poetry and prose, you are complicit in that conspiracy. Such imagining I take not to be a utopian dream but an ethical practice and a political aspiration. To imagine the poets in this conspiratorial guise, with their "hats plucked down upon their ears," is to activate, as Shakespeare did in his depiction of the faction set against Caesar, the power of anachronism as the potent icon of the past's incapacity to coincide with itself, to seal itself off as period or epoch or episode with no or necessary consequences for our time. Anachronism is the herald of the future as yet unknown.

Such formulations resonate with some and repel others. It is true that the future of the Romantics — inextricably bound up with the future of poetry — is, because unforeseen, without the kind of sociological mass that gives a Marx or a Weber his gravitational power. Yet a conspiratorial theory of Romantic poetry can, I urge, be justified by its ethical application. It renders the ineffable not as the unspeakable secret of the gothic or the phenomenal overload of the sublime but as the artisanal tact of the good collaborator. Conspiratorial intimacy is a breathing together — an occasion of mutual implication that, fortunately, is not capable of being rendered in language that all who run may read. The contemporary moment of discursivity rules out breathing bodies (call them "poems," which are bodies *only* because they breathe) in favor of supersaturated sets of statements from an expired past. Historically constructed, Romanticism remains under construction in the history that we are making. Indeed, the notion that persons — poet and poet, poet and critic, teacher and student — collaboratively make history continues to be Romanticism's gift to the common as well as to the academic reader. It is blessedly uncertain what, exactly, follows from that premise; nevertheless, knowing that *something* will, we should use that knowledge as best we can to achieve agreed upon ends.

These essays cluster around three dates — 1798, 1802, 1815 — dates that conform to distinct if not impermeable kinds of time: wartime, truce, and peace.

Wartime is the most durable and intense kind of time engaged here. During the years of conflict with the Revolutionary, the Consular, and then the Imperial governments of France from 1792 to 1801, from 1803 to 1814, and then again in 1815, wartime, as it was compellingly predicated by the great counterrevolutionary trump of Burke's *Reflections on the French Revolution,* consolidated dailiness in Great Britain and became the natural condition of the nation. Truce occurred in 1802, when a fragile suspension of hostilities was effected by the controversial Treaty of Amiens. The time of peace began with Napoleon Bonaparte's announcement of his abdication in 1814, then was eclipsed by the meteor of the Hundred Days, and then was restored following Waterloo and the final incarceration of Bonaparte in 1815.

With the launching of the counterrevolution, wartime became a period in which grouping occurred as a compulsory mobilization of people by the state into a totality, whether as audience, nation, or social class. Despite the soothing tales told by the natural historians of the Scottish enlightment, who narrated the slow progress of the social composition as it elaborated itself over the centuries, the fact that societies will unravel and that the people so atomized will often violently group in unprecedented large numbers forcibly imposed itself on the minds of the politicians and poets at the end of the eighteenth century. Conservatives such as Burke endeavored to domesticate this mobilization through the cultural trope of the theater. To an extraordinary degree, this strategy succeeded. But the cost of its political success was a transformation of theatricality itself from the prescriptive codes of performance and reception that had underwritten the career of Garrick to the calculated excess of Van Loutherberg's spectacles of light and of Pitt's spectacles of power. As Burke himself attests, the proscenium would not hold.

Wartime, as all-engrossing spectacle, does not exist for frontline soldiers mired in the intimate, blind, and chronically tactical space of the battlefield; it is concocted for those whom, in "Fears in Solitude," Coleridge calls "spectators and not combatants," those who "read of war, / The best amusement for our morning meal!" Wartime becomes modern as it becomes spectacle; and because modern war is spectacle it is always to some extent a cold war, conducted by means of strategic representations of remote conflict and waged at home on behalf of some citizens and against others. Attendance at the Shakespearean theater may explain why cultivated Britons shed tears when kings die. But modern wartime, which is not an event but a condition of eventfulness — that is, the simulation of dailiness within an imposed totality — is inconceivable without journalism. Journalism as practiced by Coleridge's *Morning Post* constituted the discursive superstructure and the material infrastructure that was the chief instrument of British time-making, an operation that Byron in *Don Juan* called "gazetting." In the 1790s, a climate of turbulent semiosis in which every well-placed sign was potentially what Coleridge called the "watchword of a faction," newspapers became the indispensable, suddenly hot vehicle for transmitting poetry as well as propaganda. Bonaparte's famous observation that "three hostile newspapers are more to be feared than a thousand bayonets" not only attests to the power of journalistic technology in wartime, but it also justifies Coleridge's own Napoleonic delusions as the chief leader-writer for one of the top British newspapers.

Wartime is an intense sequence of events marked by a punctual, declared beginning and experienced as being of inevitably limited though practically indefinite duration. By *intense*, I mean that in wartime reported incidents of conflict acquire a pronounced episodic structure that, in the reporting — like a romance in its recounting — effectively implicates the noncombatant auditor or reader in its narrative unfolding. I take Coleridge's "Reflections on Having Left a Place of Retirement," "Fears in Solitude," and "Christabel," as well as Wordsworth's "Salisbury Plain" and "Ruined Cottage" to be exemplary texts in that regard. Wartime puts extraordinary pressure on those partitions between the spaces of the private and the public, the individual and the society, that English liberal philosophy had so carefully erected during the constitutional slumber in which Britain had gloried since 1688.

Although compellingly eventful, wartime episodes cannot assume their just order of significance except in terms of a historical narrative that cannot be responsibly undertaken, let alone convincingly completed, until the war ends. In *Power and Paranoia: History, Narrative, and the American Cinema, 1940–1950*, his illuminating study of the strange fortunes of Hollywood narratives during World War II, Dana Polan argues that "the war shows the possibility of a period in which narrative perspective can only be incomplete, in which retrospection can only fall out of alignment with history perceived as an unfolding narrative. During a war there is no full position outside of history that would enable a complete and secure retrospection." Wartime thus moots both the idealist's aspiration to escape from history and the materialist's claim to explain it. As Burke was the first to demonstrate, and as Coleridge was among the first to perceive, reflection on war during wartime is just another way of making war. In wartime the question put regarding the future is, When? And when the future is dressed up as something besides a mere ending, it is most often figured not in terms of vigorous reform but as retirement, as the luxurious banality of the return to the refuge of a quiet home.

If we have an eye to accounting for change in the years between 1789 and 1815, we need to discriminate between two wartimes. The first period, roughly from 1790 until 1802, the period of Pitt's ascendancy, was characterized by the deployment of what Coleridge called "the watchword," which he defined as "some unmeaning term" that "acquires almost a mechanical power over [a man's] frame." The *watchword* may have been a catchall term of abuse like *aristocrat*, with which the popular assemblies could short circuit debate, or like *Jacobin*, with which a technician of the totality such as Pitt could galvanize a political reflex in a susceptible populace. Or it may have been something like "the exponent or symbol held forth by metrical language," which, according to the historicizing Wordsworth of the 1800 preface to *Lyrical Ballads*, excited readers' expectations — a kind of excitement that his modest lyrics were designed to counter. It was during the second wartime that the possibility of a new kind of sign, the massive and concrete lure of the world picture, emerged to answer the ambitions of artists and emperors. We might locate the apprehension of that shift right around the self-coronation of Bonaparte as Holy Roman Emperor, an act of orbital closure monumentalized by Jacques Louis David, former engineer of revolutionary watchwords. The instauration of the world picture is, in Heidegger's terms, the act of "a strong hand, which brings a world into being, [of] a genius who gives the measure and draws up the guidelines for everything that is." The advent of a new world picture entails a transformation of what will happen when wartime ends, from the mundane realignment of parties and the redress of grievances to the appearance of a New Man — whether that new man be Bonaparte or Byron, the philosophical poet of the *Biographia Literaria* or the "passive hero" of *Waverley*.

A truce makes suspension official and formalizes transition as a specific kind of time. Truces cannot last forever. Although a passage to another kind of time, there is in principle no way to know whether a truce will lead to the instauration of peace or the renewal of war. Amiens was a truce of mutual convenience between the Addington administration and Bonaparte. It also suspended hostilities between the British center right and the British center left and thus for the first time effectively distilled the partisans of war and the partisans of peace, independent of the antiquated opposition between Whig and Tory. Among other incidents both public and private, the truce was marked in Great Britain by the writing of the "Immortality Ode," the publication of the inaugural number of the *Edinburgh Review,* and the reporting of the strange case of the seduction of the innocent Maid of Buttermere by the treacherous bigamist Alexander Augustus Hope, also known as Headfield, also known as Hatfield. A truce is that time when a different time appears that is not yet the future expected. Because truce has no grounding in anything but convention, it is a peculiarly rhetorical time, its period, like the circumlocuting prose of Coleridge's self-analysis, is a suspension of objectives, its form supplied by metaphor ("breathing place" or "threshold") or extended analogy (a "landing-place" along the unending spiraling staircase of a ruined or renovated castle or estate). A truce defines the present as the portal through which a certain version of the past will pass and become the future.

Neither peace nor war, among some people truce invites the suspicion of cabals cloaking intrigue under the letter of plain speech in order to shape the future to some unknown end; among others the truce invites the imagination of, the hope for, a future that will be not merely *when* the war is over but a *new* kind of common time. The possibility of a common time beckons to some because during the truce grouping appears underdetermined to all. If, as Linda Colley has argued in *Britons: Forging the Nation*, it was the war against the French that forged the British nation, it is worth asking now, as it was asked during the Treaty of Amiens's suspension of the war, What then during this syncope of the blood could possibly have been holding the nation together? Wordsworth equivocates between blank verse and irregular Pindarics. Coleridge forthrightly offers three options: fear, hope, and memory. And, announcing his apostasy from the days of glad political movements, Coleridge reports that this truce is a time when the seduction of hope will prove false.

Peace is when the war is over, a kind of time which is aftermath, a time of demobilization, a time when groups seek to be determined, when the crowd takes to the streets and the silent soldiers seek their voice. Peace, the future presupposed by wartime, itself presupposes no future of its own. If the discourse after Waterloo is marked by the medicalization of the past as a time of diseased thought and action, then peace, as Coleridge and Scott would identify it, is a time of extended convalescence, which anticipates no return of robust, belligerent health. The end of war, which is the condition for a retrospect on its unfolding as a narrative of violent ruptures and collective delusion, coincides with the foreclosure of a future that is anything more than that condition of normal change which Immanuel Wallerstein has described as the characteristic temporal modality of modern liberalism.

The historical advent of aftermath made it possible for Coleridge, Constant, Scott, Wordsworth, and Byron to think the posthistorical. And the arrival of aftermath again, here and now — whether conceived in political terms, as the expiration of ideological struggle that defined the Cold War, or in artistic terms, as convalescence from the long era of bitter conflict called modernism, or in philosophical terms, as the perplexity about legitimating the exercise of political will in a world in which the market is subject to no conditions it does not contrive — has made it possible to think the posthistorical again. We ought to think of it not as a time that condemns us who have materialized here to imprisonment in a duration for which the future is merely virtual. Rather, educated by the Romantics, we ought to think of the posthistorical as a *kind* of time, the generic image projected by the powerful and their clerks.

My interest in this kind of time flows from the odd *ricórso* of contemporary liberals such as Francis Fukuyama and Richard Rorty. Although their versions of what liberalism is and what liberals do diverges dramatically, Fukuyama and Rorty converge in their return to the Romantics as guarantors of the posthistorical, as if they were returning home to a polite debate after a long and arduous war. My working hypothesis is that a renewed attempt at discriminating Romanticisms under the rubric of the posthistorical will suggest a taxonomy of the varieties of liberalism as they twine their way from the nineteenth century toward the millennium. Compare the corporate liberalism of Coleridge, who seized the opportunity of peace to begin his long and ultimately successful campaign to acquire for critics and criticism an established, self-regulating exemption within the nation, with the bureaucratic liberalism of Scott, who imagined the exercise of the writer's office as the formal precondition for national security.

I have referred to three dates. A fourth should be added: whatever year counts as contemporary with the publication and reception of this book. In the final chapter I undertake to apply Romantic ethics to the predicament of the humanities in the university at a time when the claims of corporatism have become as pervasive as the air we breathe. This chapter takes me well beyond the scope of my professional expertise in an attempt to formulate a policy of cryptoliberalism that will motivate, if not guide, a reconsideration of the kind of work that humanists ought to be doing. At its most ambitious this policy revives a theme that ought to be familiar to readers of the Romantic poets: that Romanticism is an ethics of imaginative, collaborative work and that any Romantic ethics is also a poetics, which provides the model for how work ought to be organized in human terms.

Chapter One

The Romantic Movement
at the End of History

> We profess it in our Creed, we confess it in our lives.
> — Jeremy Taylor, *Holy Living* (1727)

I profess Romanticism, I romantically confess. And if I choose a pre-theoretical, prerevolutionary epigraph from an eighteenth-century divine to enfranchise this essay, rather than a phrase from a timelier master, such as Paul de Man or M. H. Abrams, it is because I want to use Jeremy Taylor as Samuel Taylor Coleridge chronically used him, to stage a resistance to theory, to ward off revolutionary utterance, and to keep melancholy at bay. In Taylor's terms, professing romanticism is what I do on each occasion of classroom teaching or of publishing an article in a specialized journal or a book at a university press. My creed, of course, is not to Coleridge, to Byron, or to Wordsworth. I do not commit belief to what is loosely called a canon, but to that discipline which the institutions of education and publication collaboratively authorize and reproduce and which in turn certifies the felicity of my professions. If, as Taylor states, confessing is a matter of living, living ought to be imagined as that structuring activity that Anthony Giddens calls *practical consciousness*: an ensemble of repetitive maneuvers, signature gestures, and obsessive themes.[1] Living is for servants and for critics — for those who do not have *texts* in Edward Said's sense of the term, but only what Coleridge calls *personalities*.[2] This practical, pretextual consciousness assorts the idiosyncratic and the routinized into a compromise formation, something romantic, something like a biographia literaria, something which may be at odds or at evens with an institutional warrant. It depends.

I want to address how confessing romantically bears on the profession of Romanticism and to argue that its bearing matters. This chapter presupposes that Romanticism is not an object of study, neither the glorious expression nor the deplorable symptom of a distant epoch and peculiar mentality, but a problem in identification and in practice. As a

Christian divine, Jeremy Taylor sought to induce a harmony between creed and life in himself and for others. Romantic writers grandiloquently profess to wish for such a harmony (*poet* is the name that Coleridge gives to the achieved ideal), even as they prosaically confess that what our creeds profess and what our untimely lives confess do not often synchronize.

The advantages of that discrepancy clarify in the light of the "end of history" argument as it has been influentially advanced by Francis Fukuyama in his interrogatory 1989 article "The End of History?" and his subsequent declarative book *The End of History and the Last Man*.[3] Three features of Fukuyama's "universal history" of the triumph of liberalism are salient here. First, in line with his all-too-clerical affirmation of the power of ideology to make history, Fukuyama identifies the end of history not with a momentous incident or a sovereign decision but with the prescribed end of what he calls "ideological evolution," consummated in the freshly consolidated global hegemony of the liberal state. For the sake of developing a Romantic argument, I am prepared to accept both aspects of that claim: that history is (or rather was) ideological contestation; and that ideological conflict has ended. I conclude that if one is looking for something with the strength to challenge the commercialist hegemony here at the end of history one should look for something nonideological, something one cannot find, something like a "black and empty area" vacant of figures from the past.

The second arresting feature of Fukuyama's argument is its unembarrassed repetitiveness. Fukuyama freely acknowledges as his precursor Hegel, who announced the end of history in 1806. And Hegel was not alone, probably because he was somewhat premature. Not Europe in 1806 but Europe in 1815 is the better analogy with the worldquake of 1989. The contemporary scene of imperial breakup, ethnic crackup, and commercialist mop-up closely, even eerily, parallels the European aftermath of Waterloo, when commerce first conquered conquest. Just as 1989 found its voice in Fukuyama's celebration of "the triumph of the Western idea" over Soviet collectivism and the completion of the dialectic of history in liberal society, so did 1814–15 find its spokesman in the anglophiliac Benjamin Constant, who, in *The Spirit of Conquest and Usurpation*, celebrated the triumph of British liberty over Napoleonic tyranny and the advent of perpetual commercial prosperity. Let's say that Fukuyama is right. Let's say that Constant and Hegel were right. What do three rights separated by 175 years add up to? Well, history. A history that is indistinguishable from posthistory, because it is a history in which, despite the stirring spectacle of wars and revolutions, the same truth has been proven time and time again, and in which no real change has occurred.

Thus the third feature of Fukuyama's universal history: its relentless synchronicity. A fundamental belief in a prevailing synchronicity encourages Fukuyama, like Richard Rorty, to indulge the notion of the history of philosophy as a series of conversations with dead authors. He can imagine that he enters into intellectual exchange with Hegel and that, in his passage through *The Phenomenology of Spirit*, he can come upon the chapter on lordship and bondage and recognize liberalism's glory. The "end of history" argument is an "always already" formation of considerable elasticity. Although Fukuyama begins by speaking of ideological evolution, he must really mean ideological elaboration, because all change has always already occurred. A pallid scientism, "evolution" imputes a kind of necessity to the discursive process, subjects change to predictability, and allows the evidence of "real change" to be stigmatized as monstrous, anomalous, or, worse yet, anachronistic. Constant was succinct. Writing in 1814 after the abdication of the usurper, he could not only trumpet the end of the era of conquest but also announce that under the reign of commerce, should some savage fool attempt to conquer, usurp, or dictate, he would "commit a gross and disastrous anachronism."[4] Constant got it right, indeed: only a few months after the publication of his book Bonaparte returned to France and for a hundred days anachronistically suspended the conventions by which monarcho-liberalism ruled. And therefore Constant got it wrong, for the assumption that an anachronism was a mere nothing that would expire in its appearance proved vain. Although an anachronism does not count in the way that clocks and bank tellers count, the *commission* of anachronism romantically exploits lack of accountability as the emergence of unrecognized possibility.[5]

Posthistorical liberalism's disdain for the anachronistic is exceeded only by a fear of it, the same affect that fuels the postmodern drive to abolish the possibility of anachronism. It is because Fredric Jameson, the best Marxist theorist to engage postmodernism, shares many of the evolutionary assumptions of the neoliberals (the word *revolution* does not appear in the index to his *Postmodernism, or, The Cultural Logic of Late Capitalism*) and adheres to the epochal model of tidy synchrony ("the postmodern must be characterized as a situation in which the survival, the residue, the holdover, the archaic, has finally been swept away without a trace")[6] that his utopian agenda looks less like a challenge to postmodernism than another elegant variation. Jameson's utopia is insufficiently Romantic. Considered as a set of doctrines, Marxism does not trouble Fukuyama's reverie, but the emergence of Marx under the Hegelian sun and his Romantic commission of the anachronism of *Das Capital* in the middle of the nineteenth century emphatically should.

Immanuel Wallerstein has proposed a useful taxonomy of the dominant ways that historical change has been represented since the Enlightenment. The emergence of the condition of "normal change" in eighteenth-century Europe was answered, he argues, by the formation of three institutions: "the ideologies, the social sciences, and the movements." Wallerstein identifies three ideologies: liberalism, which he calls the "natural ideology of normal change"; conservatism, which upholds the prerogatives of traditional arrangements; and Marxism, which imagined change "as something realized not continuously but discontinuously" and which held that "the world had yet to realize the perfect society."[7] Here's Fukuyama's scorecard: Marxism is defeated, conservatism absorbed, and liberalism, the "natural ideology of normal change," triumphant.

Although that verdict has been contested by the losers, such an outcome means neither payoff nor penalty for Romanticism, as Jameson indirectly acknowledges: "(I must here omit yet another series of debates, largely academic, in which the very continuity of modernism as it is here reaffirmed is itself called into question by some vaster sense of the profound continuity of romanticism, from the late eighteenth century on, of which both the modern and the postmodern will be seen as mere organic stages)" (*Postmodernism*, 59). This chapter (indeed, this book) will more or less cross and recross the space of that omission: here I will settle for "largely academic," alter "profound continuity" to "intermittent insistence" and discard the cliché of "organic stages." I shall proceed on the assumption that if we want to discover what possibilities for change remain open now, we might inquire into the untimely then, back at the beginning of the nineteenth century, when history first ended. Posthistorical historiography suggests that Romanticism, which, at least in the British instance, has led a kind of phantomized political existence, crossing among professions conservative, liberal, and Marxist, may, as phantom, confess a political life that is a virtual alternative both to what rules and to what would have inverted ruler and ruled. I orient myself in this episode of the argument in relation to Coleridge's *Biographia Literaria* for contrary reasons: written in 1815, it is decidedly a Waterloo composition with the Constantian ambition of proclaiming a new dispensation; yet, because it was afflicted by near catastrophic miscalculations in the printing office, the book was not published until 1817 and thus appeared as an anachronism, a ghost at the banquet it had set.

British Romantic writing, I argue, does not belong with the ideologies but with what Wallerstein calls the "movements," those political associations on the run which attempted to organize "spontaneous antisystemic impulses" into a "politics of social transformation" (*USS*, 21). Neither sect nor school, the British Romantic writers who straggled onto the scene between 1798 and 1802 formed what E. J. Hobsbawm has called a "primitive" or "pre-political" social movement.[8] I shall later take advantage of the reemergence of the prepolitical in a post-Jacobin and post-Napoleonic Britain to suggest analogous possibilities for a posthistorical America. Matthew Arnold preferred "prematurity" to "primitiveness" when he made his canonical diagnosis that Byron and Wordsworth "had their source in a great movement of feeling, not in a great movement of mind."[9] Arnold pits mind against feeling with the aim of stopping Romantic movement altogether; and he was successful insofar as he can be credited with growing precocious writers into Victorian worthies, freezing them as eminent pictures at the Oxbridge exhibition. Arnold's verdict has the unintended consequence, however, of aligning premature Romanticism — turbulent feeling as yet unsubjected by a regulative idea — with Marx's definition of communism: "Communism is for us not a stable state which is to be established, but an *ideal* to which reality will have to adjust itself. We call communism the *real* movement which abolishes the present state of things."[10] We call Romanticism the real movement of feeling which challenges the present state of things, including that consensus that would bury it in the past, whether by omission or by labeling it an ideology. We do so in the faith that what was premature then may help revive the possibility of prematurity now — if not by forcing the spring at least by heralding to quicken it.

Not long ago Jerome McGann stigmatized Romanticism as a version of what Marx called the German Ideology, which "turns the world upside down and sees it from a false vantage because its own point of reference is conceptualized within a closed idealistic system."[11] McGann alludes to Marx's famous metaphor of the camera obscura: "If in all ideology men and their circumstances appear upside-down, as in a *camera obscura*, this phenomenon arises just as much from their historical life-process as the inversion of objects on the retina does from their physical life-process" (*GI*, 14). Given that ideology is inversion, the critic's responsibility is clear: he must labor to turn the world right-side-up and restore it to its truth.

Roughly speaking, two takes on ideology prevail. The first, shared by Fukuyama and McGann, regards ideology as a set of ideas that you and people like you hold. In that view, ideology is opinion dressed to kill. Others conceive of ideology as a set of representations that holds us, that, according to Louis Althusser, "hails or interpellates concrete individuals as concrete subjects" — concrete subjects being concrete individuals who "work all by themselves."[12] In the Althusserian view, because ideology has no history (or, as Fukuyama would have it, because its history is "universal"), it need have no "end" (there is no truth to restore). Nonetheless, there are limits to ideology's scope, for there remain "individuals" out of range of its call. Where things work, ideology *is*; where things do not work, ideology is not; and where ideology is not, *cause*, paradoxically, is. Or, as Jacques Lacan aphorizes (thinking of Kant, thinking of Hume) "there is cause only in something that doesn't work."[13] For Althusser, "art," like Constant's "anachronism," names one of those things that, like an idiot boy or an ancient mariner or a female vagrant, does not work but does somehow, occultly, *cause*.

Given Lacan's aphorism, it is notable that Marx's artful image of how ideology works does not itself work. Paul Ricoeur has observed that the "unfortunate image" of the camera obscura "is a metaphor of the reversal of images, but it proceeds as a comparison involving four terms. The ideological reversal is to the life-process as the image in perception is to the retina." But what an image on the retina is remains a puzzle, for, as Ricoeur concludes, "there are images only for consciousness." There may be an image *in* itself, but because there is no image *for* itself, Marx's analogy fails to close and, in so failing, alludes to something like a supervisory consciousness. Ricoeur goes on to echo Althusser's charge "that the inverted image belongs to the same ideological world as the original. As a result, he claims, we must introduce a notion quite different from inversion, that of an epistemological break."[14] I suggest that what appears as something like consciousness is a *movement* that disrupts the closure of the optical model and makes Marx's camera obscura metaphor unworkable for the systematic purposes to which Marxists have put it.

W. J. T. Mitchell has observed that "Marx's use of the camera obscura as a polemical device for ridiculing the illusions of idealist philosophy [begins] to look even more ungainly when we recall that Locke had used it as a polemical device — in exactly the opposite way."[15] Ungainlier still, for if the inversion of the camera image belongs to "the same ideological world" as the original, what are we to make of the common cause of Karl Marx, avowed materialist, and Samuel Taylor Coleridge, alleged idealist? Here is Coleridge's footnoted denunciation of the habits of the contemporary reading public from Chapter 3 of the *Biographia:*

> For as to the devotees of the circulating libraries, I dare not compliment their *pass-time* or rather *kill-time,* with the name of *reading.* Call it rather a sort of beggarly daydreaming, during which the mind of the dreamer furnishes for itself nothing but laziness and a little mawkish sensibility; while the whole *materiel* and imagery of the doze is supplied *ab extra* by a sort of mental *camera obscura* manufactured at the printing office, which *pro tempore* fixes, reflects and transmits the moving phantasms of one man's delirium, so as to people the barrenness of an hundred other brains afflicted with the same trance or suspension of all common sense and all definite purpose. (*BL*, 1:48 n)

Although both Marx and Coleridge use the camera obscura to illustrate the mechanical projection of inverted images of reality, it is the so-called romantic idealist who refers the mechanism to a system of commodity production. Mitchell likewise adjusts Marx by weaning the camera obscura metaphor away from its Lockean parent, invoking instead the nineteenth-century technological context of photography in order to suture Marx's characterization of ideology with his analysis of commodity fetishism. In Mitchell's account,

> the commodity is a "fantastic" form — literally, a form produced by projected light; these forms, like the "ideas" of ideology, are both there and not there — both "perceptible and imperceptible by the senses." The difference from the images projected by the *camera obscura* is that the fantastic forms of the commodity are "objective character[s]" in the sense that they are projected outward, "stamped upon the product of . . . Labour." The evanescent, subjective projections of ideology are imprinted and fixed the way a printing press (or photographic process) stamps the "characters" of typographic or graphic imagery. (*Iconology*, 189–90)

If Marx echoes Locke, Coleridge, who never saw a photograph, anticipates not only Marx but Mitchell as well by making the connection between ideology and commodity production in the context of an imaginary apparatus that looks like nothing so much as the apparatus of the imaginary we moderns know as the cinema. Projecting his light forward as if a light bestowed, the index of the distance that Coleridge travels beyond Marx is his failure precisely to historicize his camera obscura. That failure is marked syntactically by his failure properly to refer. Are the delerial "moving phantasms" phantasms that empathically move (sad ghosts) or phantasms that seem to physically move (the flickering image on a movie screen)? If the phantasm, an untimely and unaccountable life, is the figure of anachronism, Coleridge's "moving" really moves — and romantically commits that anachronism to the future.

Whether or not you buy such a fantastic claim, once the fantastic has been reinscribed in the Marxian mechanism (classically by Walter Benjamin), it is difficult to see how Coleridge's "gothic" use of the camera obscura substantively differs from the "mental operation of materialist reversal and demystification," which, according to Jameson, is "alone the feature by which 'materialism' as such can be identified" (*Postmodernism*, 358). That may be because the image of the camera obscura works *as* a camera obscura, turning upside down reality and dream, idealist and materialist, Coleridge and Marx, Jameson and Fukuyama. Althusser's lesson — which he abstracted from *The German Ideology* but which the Russian masses suffered hard time to learn — would seem to hold: the more the world is turned upside down, the more it stays the same. Such a world seems suited to Fukuyama's clerical spin: from the perspective of universal history, once you wipe off the actors' greasepaint, all change, no matter how professedly apocalyptic, is normal change. In such a world the camera obscura's "mechanism of inversion" is not only what Mitchell calls it, "a figure for the formal pattern of revolution and counterrevolution," but also a figure for the reduction of revolution and counterrevolution to mere formality, historical change to the elaboration of some pattern, whether simple, like inversion, or fractally complex. Most readers will find Fukuyama's moral comforting. No surprise. But some will be unreasonably angry at the message and suspect the messenger. And that's interesting.

In the *Biographia Literaria* Coleridge engages the relations between the mechanism of inversion, the possibility of change, and unreasonable anger in his analysis of the reception of *Lyrical Ballads*. He invokes *Macbeth* to epitomize the predicament of the readers of Wordsworth's Preface, who suffer an "unquiet state of mind" and who wonder "at the perverseness of the man, who had written a long and argumentative essay to persuade them, that 'Fair is foul, and foul is fair.'" Explaining

his explanation, Coleridge appends a complicated footnote that diagnoses and performs the Romantic Movement:

> In opinions of long continuance, and which we had never before
> been molested by a single doubt, to be suddenly *convinced* of an
> *error,* is almost like being *convicted* of a fault. There is a state of
> mind, which is the direct antithesis of that, which takes place
> when we *make a bull. The bull* namely consists in the bringing to-
> gether two incompatible thoughts, with the *sensation,* but without
> the *sense,* of their connection. The psychological condition or that
> which constitutes the possibility of this state, being such dispro-
> portionate vividness of two distant thoughts, as extinguishes or
> obscures the consciousness of the intermediate images or concep-
> tions, or wholly abstracts the attention from them. Thus in the
> well known bull, "*I was a fine child, but they changed me*"; the
> first conception expressed in the word "*I,*" is that of personal
> identity — *Ego contemplans*: the second expressed in the word
> "*me,*" the visual image or object under the form in which it imag-
> ined itself previously to have existed — *Ego contemplatus.* Now
> the change of one visual image for another involves in itself no ab-
> surdity, and becomes absurd only by its immediate juxta-position
> [sic] with the first thought, which is rendered possible by the
> whole attention being successively absorbed in each singly, so as
> not to notice the interjacent notion, "changed" which by its in-
> congruity with the first thought, "*I*" constitutes the bull. Add only,
> that this process is facilitated by the circumstance of the words "*I*"
> and "*me*" being sometimes equivalent, and sometimes having a
> distinct meaning; sometimes, namely signifying the act of self-
> consciousness, sometimes the external image in and by which the
> mind represents that act to itself, the result and symbol of its indi-
> viduality. Now suppose the direct contrary state, and you will
> have a distinct sense of the connection between two conceptions,
> without that *sensation* of such connection which is supplied by
> habit. The man *feels,* as if he were standing on his head, though he
> cannot but *see,* that he is truly standing on his feet. This, as a pain-
> ful sensation, will of course have a tendency to associate itself with
> the person who occasions it; even persons, who have been by pain-
> ful means restored from derangement, are known to feel an invol-
> untary dislike toward their physician. (*BL,* 1:72–74 n)

Coleridge develops a correspondence between Wordsworth as wise
physician and the reviewers of *Lyrical Ballads* as ignorant, ungrateful

patients. Feeling as if they have been turned upside down by Words-worth's argument, the reviewers blame the "painful sensation associated with this revolution in feeling on the author, as patients are wont to blame even that physician who has restored them from derangement." Wordsworth's Preface thus made discursive sense where there had been only outlandish poetic sensation, but at the cost of transforming everyday sense into the stuff of dream — rough magic guaranteed to antagonize the custodians of conventional wisdom.[16]

Now suppose the direct contrary. Suppose that the "bull," "I was a fine child, but they changed me," anticipates Coleridge's own criticism of Wordsworth's ambitious "Immortality Ode" in the second volume of the *Biographia*. In Coleridge's acknowledged source, the Edgeworths' "Essay on Irish Bulls," the authors feature this resentful expostulation: "I hate that woman, for she changed me at nurse." "Change" here signifies "exchange": "our Hibernian's consciousness," the Edgeworths comment, "could not retrograde to the time when he was changed at nurse; consequently, there was no continuity of identity between the infant and the man who expressed his hatred of the nurse for perpetrating the fraud."[17] Coleridge queries Wordsworth's "bull" likewise. He has in mind the eighth stanza, which addresses the "six years' / Darling of a pigmy size":

> Thou, whose exterior semblance doth belie
>   Thy Soul's immensity;
> Thou best Philosopher, who yet doest keep
> Thy heritage, thou Eye among the blind,
> That, deaf and silent, read'st the eternal deep,
> Haunted for ever by the eternal mind, —
>   Mighty Prophet! Seer blest!
>   On whom those truths do rest,
> Which we are toiling all our lives to find,
> In darkness lost, the darkness of the grave. . . .

In "what sense is a child of that age *philosopher?*" Coleridge later asks. "In what sense does he *read* the 'eternal deep?' . . . These would be tidings indeed; but such as would pre-suppose an immediate revelation to the inspired communicator, and require miracles to authenticate his inspiration. Children at this age give us no such information of themselves; and at what time were we dipt in the Lethe, which has produced such utter oblivion of a state so godlike?" (*BL*, 2:138–39).[18] Words-worth's embedded fiction of a Letheward hand corresponds to the Irish-man's fanciful notion of a malignant hand that changed him at nurse.

Coleridge's "I was a fine child but they changed me" distills the dependence of Wordsworth's notion of change as alteration on an unreasoned synonymity with exchange as substitution. Coleridge's note thus warns the readers of the *Biographia* — Wordsworth chief among them — that Coleridge's antithetical criticism, designed to set Wordsworth's feet back on the ground of true principle, would likely provoke the poet's "involuntary dislike" — which notoriously proved to be the case.

Now suppose we mix in the quotation from *Macbeth*. As physician is to patient, so, it would seem, are the fair-fouling witches (Wordsworth) to Macbeth (reviewers), who, his world overturned, murders the king and usurps the throne. But it is a peculiarity of this matrix that analogies do not multiply symmetrically; they chiasmically cross. In the analogy of Coleridge's note, Macbeth's "involuntary dislike" ought to have been directed against the hags who persuaded him that fair is foul and foul is fair, not against Duncan, the rightful king. Macbeth's "mistake" leads to the primitive violence that Constant calls "usurpation" and that, at the outset of Chapter 4, Coleridge identifies as the predominant trait of the "commanding genius." History progresses to contain that violence by preventing such mistakes, which entails rationalizing wild inversion by subjecting it to the tropes of substitution and condensation. Consider Coleridge's logic: if we take the split between witches and king as the difference between those who know and the one who authorizes, then the modern physician is *the one who can authorize because he knows*. Historical progress, as Coleridge represents it, has the hallmark of what Freud calls "transference." Not only have "new editions or facsimiles of the impulses and phantasies [been] aroused and made conscious during the progress of analysis; but they . . . replace some earlier person by the person of the physician."[19]

Coleridge's note thus assesses the therapeutic possibilities of inversion in the framework of a transition from the feudal era of Macbeth to the modern moment of the professional physician — a transition that reforms the violently discontinuous change of usurpation as the normal change of remediation. History thus provides a new answer to the question that Macbeth puts to the doctor who comes to treat his maddened Lady: "Canst thou minister to a mind diseased?" *Macbeth*'s doctor must answer no; the modern psychiatrist professes yes. But even for the latter, ministration occasionally misfires. Although the transition from usurpation to remediation would seem to be an unambiguous good, the persistence of the "involuntary dislike" — what Wordsworth calls "Obstinate questionings / Of sense and outward things" — is evidence of the holdover of untransferred affect, a movement of feeling that taints the efficiency of the inversion. Although the physician has the credentials to summon spirits from the vasty deep of the unconscious, he still cannot guarantee that they will heed his call.

That the professional authority of the physician remains as dubious for the modern as monarchical authority had been for Macbeth suggests to the romantic mind that despite history's progress nothing fundamental has changed: mistaken ideologies fall as the professions rise in a process of substitution without alteration. Progress through Coleridge's topsy-turvy note induces the same moral. Characteristically, Coleridge has shaped his footnote as a chiasmus (sensation: sense :: sense: sensation), a figure indifferent to the cause of truth but well-designed to work like a camera lens to invert perception. Both physician and philosophical critic profess to cure. And maybe they do, generally. Yet Coleridge's mimicry of the accredited physicians' therapeutic technique might very well trigger an outburst of hostility toward the critic. The obtrusiveness of the rhetorical scheme in the production of the cure confesses to a sophistical virtuosity in the manipulation of tropes that compels one to change one's opinion, virtuosity that only simulates the dialectic that impels one to knowledge of the truth. Like the posthistorian's mimicry of evolutionary change, such gimmicks seem to turn the world upside down only to return us to where we always were. If the camera obscura illustrates that the ideological reduces to the rhetorical, the impression of rhetorical virtuosity here implies that the remedial is underwritten by the coercive: compulsion is applied to the patient reader to recognize himself as subject. That compulsion is not overt, as it is in the cases of the divining witch and the commanding king; it is bound up with the pretense inherent in every profession, whether credentialed or not.

That enabling pretense is the chief theme of Coleridge's numerous attacks on the professions.[20] For Coleridge, a person must always profess to profess — or, to put it in Jeremy Taylor's terms, professions inevitably confess the pretense of their claims to autonomous power. Such confession lives as the compulsion that invariably backs the bid to transfer and that may either reflect the absence of institutional support for the profession to cure (as in the case of the sophist) or register the dissembling of the institutional basis of the professional claims to cure (as in the case of the physician/psychiatrist). Either way, the perception of the intimate conjunction between pretense and compulsion is sufficient to trigger a hostile movement of feeling. However arduous, this particular note of Coleridge's hardly qualifies as a critique of professions; for although its rhetorical structure effectively parodies the dialectic of the cure and detonates antagonism, the intention of the note is ultimately as opaque as the formal scheme of the double-crossing chiasmus — which is to say, its movement of dislike appears involuntary, like an elementary sense of injustice.

Twentieth-century readers are less familiar with this discharge of affect under Coleridge's phrase "involuntary dislike" than under Freud's "negative transference." Nonetheless, the concept had long inhabited the British liberal tradition under the names "negative liberty" and "the right of resistance." J. G. A. Pocock has distinguished between the republican, civic, and virtue-based tradition, in which possession of real property grounded a citizen's autonomous political existence, and the liberal, juristic, rights-based tradition. In the latter, the law alone confers on a citizen his liberty, which is a right to be safe from political interference but which presupposes no part in the imperium. The citizen's legally constituted rights are acquired and exercised through his "role in possession, conveyance, and administration of things," and because those rights are ultimately things as much as any other thing, individuals could be said to have been "invested with rights [so] that they might surrender them absolutely to the sovereign."[21] If the type of republican resistance is an act, the liberal right to resistance is a species of property as exchangeable as any other.[22]

According to C. B. Macpherson, nineteenth-century liberalism internalized the "precapitalist" tension between the republican and the juristic traditions as the distinction between economic liberalism, which stresses the "maximization of utilities," and democratic liberalism, which stresses the "maximization of powers." The democratic ethic prescribes that each person cultivate his "potential for realizing some human end, necessarily includ[ing] in a man's powers not only his natural capacities (his energy and skill) but also his *ability* to exert them."[23] Rather than maximize powers, liberal society, obedient to an economic imperative, has consistently promoted a "net transfer of powers," which it executes by allowing some to deny others access to the instruments with which they might develop their natural capacities.

In Macpherson's account, Freud looks like an economic liberal, concerned to maximize utility, not power. When, in his essay "The Dynamics of the Transference," Freud asks how it comes about "that the transference is so pre-eminently suitable as a weapon of resistance," his aim is disarmament. He divides in order to conquer. First he distinguishes positive from negative feeling, then he divides positive feeling into "friendly or affectionate feelings as are capable of becoming conscious and the extensions of these in the unconscious. Of these last,"

Freud inevitably adds, "analysis shows that they invariably rest ultimately on an erotic basis." It must be so because "to begin with we knew none but sexual objects," and only feelings that have objects are recognizable and subject to the cure. He argues that "the transference to the physician is only suited for resistance in so far as it consists in *negative* feeling or in the repressed *erotic* elements of positive feeling." The "or" registers an uncertainty about what exactly these negative feelings are — whether they are what they seem, or whether they are "ultimately" a repressed element of something else. What the feelings are puzzles because what the feelings do is *move*. They elude inspection: "The unconscious feelings strive to avoid the recognition which the cure demands; they seek instead for reproduction, with all the power of hallucination and the inappreciation of time characteristic of the unconscious. The patient ascribes, just as in dreams, currency and reality to what results from the awakening of his unconscious feelings; he seeks to discharge his emotions, regardless of the reality of the situation."[24] As the psychoanalyst tries to turn feelings, which move under their own power, into desires, which must posit objects, random discharge becomes anger. "Involuntary dislike" is the movement by which the "unconscious feelings strive to avoid the recognition which the cure demands" and the net transfer of power that it entails.

Psychoanalysis, according to Freud, works to "rid the patient of a *cliche* or stereotype which perpetually repeats and reproduces itself as life goes on" ("Transference," 106). Here is the last, terrible sentence of Freud's essay: "It is undeniable that the subjugation of the transference-manifestations provides the greatest difficulties for the psychoanalyst; but it must not be forgotten that they, and they only, render the invaluable service of making the patient's buried and forgotten love-emotions actual and manifest; for in the last resort no one can be slain *in absentia* or *in effigie*" (115). To cure means to bring up occult, conspiratorial, pointlessly reproductive emotions, to recognize them, and to subject them to the guillotine of analysis, thereby adjusting the patient to the ideological world that Freud calls "real life."

What Freud called "real life" contemporary liberalism has come to call the "posthistorical." Fukuyama's universal history tries to reclaim the philosophical vagrants and neurotics of the past (e. g., Hegel and Nietzsche) for the "liberal descent" by adjusting them to a narrative that legitimates the way things are. He supplements the classical, Hobbesian definition of man as driven by the threat of scarcity, fear of death, and an insatiable desire for accumulation, with a Hegelian conception of man as motivated by a "totally non-economic drive, the struggle for recognition." Hobbes is the scion of economics, Hegel the scion of the political; and it is the clerical profession of a universal history to wed them. To seal that bond Fukuyama redescribes affect that is not perceptibly acquisitive as inchoate feelings which seek, not, as in Freud, avoid, recognition. Inexorably (epistemology is destiny), the so-called universal struggle for recognition becomes redescribed again as a universal "*desire* for recognition" (*EH,* 152; emphasis added). By identifying the so-called totally noneconomic drive as desire, Fukuyama surreptitiously renders it as *already economic* because it is susceptible to the promise of satisfaction, which generates those reciprocal exchanges that maximize utility. Fukuyama thus vindicates Macpherson's taxonomy of liberalisms by attempting to engineer the net transfer of power from political men and women to economic man all at once by means of a massive redescription of struggle as desire. But the maneuver, however witty, is without consequence: nothing changes. Anger, outrage, involuntary dislike, and obstinate questionings persist. The power of Freud's account of human motivation inhabits his reluctant acknowledgment of the intransigence of that which resists the cure. For Freud a drive is a drive, not a desire manqué. Nothing resists Fukuyama's redescription, and, as most liberal economists will tell you, nothing is got for nothing.

If Freud circumscribes Fukuyama, Coleridge's account of his early instruction in English composition characterizes Freud. In the *Biographia* he recalls the lessons in Shakespeare and Milton that cost him so much "time and trouble to *bring up,* so as to escape [his teacher James Bowyer's] censure." Drilled in the rigorous logic of poems, Coleridge learned that "in the truly great poets . . . there is a reason assignable, not only for every word, but for the position of every word." Diction fell under the purview of a hanging judge:

> In our own English compositions . . . he showed no mercy to
> phrase, metaphor, or image, unsupported by a sound sense, or
> where the same sense might have been conveyed with equal force
> and dignity in plainer words. Lute, harp, and lyre, muse, muses,
> and inspirations, Pegasus, Parnassus, and Hippocrene, were all an
> abomination to him. In fancy I can almost hear him now, exclaim-
> ing, "*Harp? Harp? Lyre? Pen and Ink, boy, you mean! Muse, boy,*
> *Muse? your Nurse's daughter, you mean! Pierian spring? Oh 'aye!*
> *the cloister-pump, I suppose!*" (*BL,* 1:9–10)

Such was the learning of English composition at Christ's Hospital at the end of the eighteenth century. And such, still, is moral education, at least according to Michael Oakeshott, who argues that "a morality . . . is neither a system of general principles nor a code of rules, but a vernacular language. . . . What has to be learned in a moral education," Oakeshott argues, "is not a theorem such as that good conduct is acting fairly or being charitable, nor is it a rule such as 'always tell the truth,' but how to speak the language intelligently."[25] Because the conversational standard of the vernacular has never been simply a diction, given or found, but always a jurisdiction, answerable to the imperative of what Benedict Anderson has called "the revolutionary vernacularizing thrust of capitalism,"[26] which peremptorily determines native intelligence by censoring unruly, demotic speech as gibberish (a tale told by an idiot boy) or jargon (an explanation given by a laborer),[27] there is no practical difference between moral and political education or between political education and legal judgment.[28] For Bowyer, as for Oakeshott, each fact is a "verdict" (Oakeshott, 2). "Certain introductions, similes, and examples," Coleridge recalls,

> were placed by name on a list of interdiction. Among the similes, there was . . . the example of Alexander and Clytus, which was equally good and apt, whatever might be the theme. Was it ambition? Alexander and Clytus! — Flattery? Alexander and Clytus! — Anger? Drunkenness? Pride? Friendship? Ingratitude? Late Repentance? Still, still Alexander and Clytus! At length, the praises of agriculture having been exemplified in the sagacious observation, that had Alexander been holding the plough, he would not have run his friend Clytus through with a spear, this tried, and serviceable old friend was banished by public edict in secula seculorum. (*BL*, 1:10)

Coleridge's boyish stereotype reproduced promiscuously.[29] Because it belonged nowhere, the Alexander and Clytus *topos* could be discharged anywhere. Bowyer interdicted this demotic frenzy by commanding banishment. But, as Freud knows, interdiction is not transference and banishment is not slaying. Having been put away as if it were the thing of a child, Alexander-cum-Clytus nonetheless thrusts back into Coleridge's biographical composition, where, in the very excess of his proscriptive zeal, Coleridge involuntarily transforms judgment into stereotype and, resisting the transference he wills, tips piety into parody.

As Freud argues, and as my medley of writers illustrates, willful resistance to the cure involves an "inappreciation of time," which manifests itself in the refusal of the patient to meet the requirement that "he shall fit these emotions into their place in the treatment and in his life-history" (Freud, 114). As fugitive feelings resist recognition, so they resist being narrativized into the formation of an identity, whether of "a person," "a people," "a nation," "a consumer," "a social class," or, in the case of Coleridge, "a philosophical critic." From the liberal perspective shared by Fukuyama and McGann, inappreciation of narrative time looks like a conservative refusal to recognize history. But for the Romantic, inappreciation of time is neither position nor attitude but the willful commission of anachronism, the assertion of the historical as that which could not be over because it has not yet really happened.

Coleridge said much the same thing in his unpacking of the term *Jacobin*:

> The word implies a man, whose affections have been warmly and deeply interested in the cause of general freedom, who has hoped all good and honourable things both *of* and *for* mankind. Jacobin affirm[s] that no man can ever become altogether an apostate to Liberty, who has at any time been sincerely and fervently attached to it. His hopes will burn like the Greek fire, hard to be extinguished, and easily rekindling. Even when he despairs of the cause, he will yet *wish*, that it had been successful. And even when private interests have warped his public character, his convictions will remain, and his wishes often rise up in rebellion against his outward actions and public avowals.[30]

Coleridge's definition unlinks emancipatory ardor from French principles.[31] Attachment to liberty means resisting the cure of historicization, being locked into synchrony with what the vernacular says can be said. Blind to the vicissitudes of parties and programs, *Jacobin* names a wish that can be fulfilled only in a future toward which, in rebellion against the way things are, the ardent soul moves.

Because *Jacobin* nevertheless imparts the taint of the foreign and ideological, I prefer the term *demotic*. The distinction between vernacular and demotic may be roughly apportioned in terms of the difference between two kinds of disturbance that troubled the social landscape of Great Britain in the 1790s and the early years of the nineteenth century: the riot and the insurrection. A riot involved the hostile, occasionally violent action of a crowd against property or authority, but the rioters observed a traditional protocol which did not, according to John Bohstedt, "normally challenge the arrangement of local power." Even in the revolutionary 1790s the authorities responded moderately because "they recognized the rioters as members of their own community."[32] The same authorities who countenanced rioting used *Jacobin* to describe the agent of a disturbance who was unrecognizable according to the traditional norms. That agent has, by and large, remained invisible to historians. One might be inclined to blame that invisibility on the ideological investments of individual historians,[33] but the resistance to historicization inhabits the historical field, for to be an agent of insurrection meant and means resistance to becoming an object of study, whether by William Pitt or by J. C. D. Clark. As Roger Wells has shown in exacting detail, those agents may have been actual strangers or persons whose motives were unclear, such as Mr. Hatfield, the notorious "seducer" of the Maid of Buttermere (see Chapter 5 below), or persons whose motives were too clear and patently ideological. The agent also might have been no "person" at all, just the occulted and anachronistic appearance of the "grip, password, sign, countersign or travelling password," handed, muttered, or scrawled.[34]

If, as Susan Stewart argues, "graffiti" are considered obscene because such wild autographs are "utterances out of place," the intricate oaths, furtive handshakes, and cryptic hails of insurrectionaries are signs out of time.[35] The holdovers of tradesmen's rituals and memorials of failed revolutionary projects, they are, however, no more nostalgic than a Wordsworthian epitaph, for they save the place of a possible future by performing a social movement without a social vehicle. Unlike the devices of masons, such "signs" do not certify membership or indicate status but betoken an affiliation that is transitive but not transferable and that is illegible according to what, in the Preface to *Lyrical Ballads*, Wordsworth calls "preestablished codes of decision." Insurrectionaries can be distinguished from rioters by consciousness, by regional origin, by class, or by anything else you like. They themselves begin to distinguish themselves from rioters as soon as they begin to produce their means of resistance, a step that is conditioned only by their symbolic resourcefulness. Demotic utterances challenge traditional systems of social control not with pikes and pistols but by the uncanny repetition of stereotypes circulating without respect to region or kind, resisting protocols of recognition but soliciting acknowledgment of one stranger by another, from United Irishman by United Briton, from United Briton by Yorkshire weaver, from Yorkshire weaver by Lake poet.

The propagation of demotic utterances identifies a species of what Eric Hobsbawm has called "primitive social movements," which historically have been characterized by a ritualistic formalism of ceremonies and symbolism. In the nineteenth century two kinds of organizations shared those features: "secret revolutionary societies and orders . . . and trade unions and friendly societies." (*PR*, 153). As "primitive" suggests, Hobsbawm (whose study appeared in 1959, well before history expired) consigns such archaic groups to a prepolitical stage of development. In the prepolitical (to adapt the Marx of the Eighteenth Brumaire) form exceeded content; in the revolutions to follow, Hobsbawm implies, the content would exceed the form. The problem that Hobsbawm never confronts — the problem that dogs every engagement with insurrectionary Great Britain after the coronation of Bonaparte — is the *return* of the prepolitical, a formalism which, because it recurs, cannot be branded as primitive and which, because it is involuntary, cannot be stigmatized as sentimental. The return of the prepolitical or (romantically to equivocate Raymond Williams's famous distinction) the emergence of the residual is Romantic formalism on the move. Because it is practiced without good reason in the aftermath of utopian dreams, that movement might be called the politics of hope.

Hobsbawm is inclined to criticize British repressiveness of the postrevolutionary era not for its reactionary ferocity but for its redundancy, for he concludes that "the belief of early nineteenth-century British governments in the necessarily subversive nature of initiations and secret oaths was mistaken. The outsiders against which the ritual brotherhood guarded its secrets were not only the bourgeois' and not always the government's." Yet he adds that "only insofar as all working men's organizations by virtue of their class membership, were likely to engage in activities frowned upon by employers or the authorities, did the initiation and oaths bind their members specifically against these. There was thus no initial distinction between, as it were, legitimately and unnecessarily secret societies, but only between the fraternal activities in which their members were ritually bound to show solidarity, some of which might be acceptable to the law while others were not" (*PR*, 158). The government's evident overreaction testified not only to a class bias but also to the fact that the initial indistinction between the legitimately and the unnecessarily secret societies that was induced by transitive repetition of stereotypes constituted a shared volatility of purpose which was insurrectionary without regard to ideology.

That explains why Coleridge's poetry of the late nineties, which in its supernatural, preternatural, and conversational modes resonates with suggestions of omens and signals ("Frost at Midnight"), strange visitations and conspiratorial understandings ("Christabel"), mysterious symbolism (*The Rime of the Ancient Mariner*), insistent metrical schemes and arbitrary anachronisms (choose your favorite), did nothing to diminish his reputation for radicalism. It explains why such blatantly bullish ballads of Wordsworth as "We Are Seven," "Simon Lee," "The Idiot Boy," and "The Thorn" could, despite a lack of revolutionary content, so deeply unsettle a common reader, as Coleridge canonically attests in Chapter 17 of the *Biographia Literaria*. The production of stereotypes ("Oh misery! oh misery! / Oh woe is me! oh misery!"), which initiated strangers into imagined communities far from the metropolis and unaccountable to the nation state, was dangerous and was branded as such by the whiggish *Edinburgh Review*. In its inaugural issue of 1802, which appeared four years after *Lyrical Ballads* but at a time when, as Roger Wells demonstrates (*Insurrection*, 220–52), insurrectionary activity had strongly revived, the *Edinburgh* (see Chapter 4, below) both adopted the Enlightenment pose of debunker of conspiratorial theories of the French Revolution and yet succumbed to making hysterically sarcastic charges of "sect" and "conspiracy" in its review of the activities of the Lake poets. The issue was not Jacobinism—despite half-hearted attempts, Francis Jeffrey, the editor in chief, would ultimately agree with the contemporary practitioners of ideology critique that none was detectable—but a species of insistent formalism, which, because its ideological mission was inapparent, seemed the pretext for a secret code that could only be defended against by condemning it as sectual (Jeffrey's favored ploy) or sexual (the Freudian recourse).

The Edgeworths' "Essay on Irish Bulls" may be taken as another example of the way the legitimately and the unnecessarily secret could be confused. In the bull the joke is always on the Irishman, and the Edgeworths are at pains to argue that he is unfairly victimized by the prejudice that the bull exploits. Yet the Edgeworths' project, to prove that the bull is not a "species of blunder *peculiar* to Ireland," was finally motivated less by a desire to rescue the Irish from English ridicule than a desire to dissipate the English suspicion that there is some kind of essential character or form of thought that binds together the Irish, rejecting English reason, inassimilable to polite society.[36]

The "depeculiarization" of Irish speech, which meant translating the demotic into the vernacular (Maria Edgeworth's glossaries, like Walter Scott's, prosecute that end), carried forward the Enlightenment project of homogenizing mankind in the guise of the bourgeoisie and, as Mitchell has argued, of restricting character to what can be stamped on a commodity. Yet that strategy could only be partially effective, for insurrectionary signs solicited acknowledgement while eluding recognition by mobilizing borrowed and disposable stereotypes.[37] The difference between the character of the commodity and the character of the demotic is the difference between a trademark, copyrightable and subject to exchange, and what Marx, in *The German Ideology*, calls a "form of activity." The difference is between using a printing press and being one. That difference can be illustrated by George Cruikshank's demotic "The New Man of the Industrial Future," which is both the figure of a figure capable of reproducing stereotypes and a stereotype that I reproduce (fig. 1).

The difference between the character of the commodity and the demotic can be further elucidated by a romanticized Marx (I have substituted "resistance" for "subsistence"):

> The way in which men produce their means of [resistance] depends first of all on the nature of the actual means they find in existence and have to reproduce. This mode of production must not be considered simply as being the reproduction of the physical existence of the individuals. Rather it is a definite form of activity of these individuals, a definite form of expressing their life, a definite *mode of life* on their part. As individuals express their life, so they are. (*GI*, 7)

Excepting that by "actual means" Marx means "material conditions" and we mean "symbolic conditions," the Marxian passage captures the way insurrectionaries work with the stereotypes they have on hand, repeating them in a transitive form of activity that binds men and women together in an insurrectionary mode of life, the politics of Romantic hope.

What was truly peculiar to the insurrectionaries was this form of activity. Hobsbawm comments that "the fantastic nomenclature of the brotherhoods was totally non-utilitarian unlike later revolutionary organizations which have normally attempted to pick names indicative of their ideology or programme" (*PR*, 166). "Non-utilitarian" should not be translated as "aesthetic." That the nomenclature was nonutilitarian simply means that it did no work, like the bull. Because it did no work, professed nothing, it was therefore without value. It could not be inverted or transferred, dialecticized or evolved. But because it did not work it remains a cause in the way that Lacan speaks of cause — a cause untransferred to history's narrative and therefore untouched by history's end.

This cause is rather like the strange creatures captured in the Burgess Shale, which were mistaken by their discoverer and recently reinterpreted by H. B. Whittington. For the evolutionary model embraced by

Fig. 1. George Cruikshank, "The New Man of the Industrial Future," from
William Hone, *The Political Showman — at Home! Exhibiting His Cabinet of
Curiosities and Creatures All at Once* (London, 1821). Courtesty Special Col-
lections, Milton S. Eisenhower Library of the Johns Hopkins University.

Fukuyama, Jameson, and Hobsbawm, which moves confidently from the archaic to the postmodern, from the prepolitical to the posthistorical, I would substitute one closer to that proposed by the Romantic paleontologist Stephen Jay Gould in *Wonderful Life*. There Gould meditates on the implications of the scandal that Whittington's reconstruction of the residue of the anomalous multicellular creatures visited on evolutionary biology's faith in the "Cone of Increasing Diversity." He urges the application of the thought experiment called "replaying life's tape" as a means to adjudge the necessity of the way things have turned out. In the cases of the defunct species *sidneyia*, *marella*, and *opabina*, replaying life's tape argues for the contingency of their extinction, and therefore the contingency of all that followed.[38] Replaying life's tape confesses the same contingency in the failures of demotic forms of social life, of Romantic movements, to succeed. But replaying the tape is only a thought experiment with organisms, which cannot in truth be revived by Gould's song. Because the resources of the demos were and are symbolic, no such barrier cuts the path between then and now. The demotic cause lives just because it did not succeed; the Romantic Movement is inescapably anachronistic because it is the politics of the future and always will be, or at least until something better comes along. And as contingent analogies between phrases of address (grips, passwords, meters, motifs, commonplaces) bound each to each in transient but strong commonalities then, so now as then. Sensitive to the strength of willful analogy in forging a common cause, I ask you to acknowledge that Coleridge's cliché of "Greek fire" marks the demotic heat in Wordsworth's contemporary reference to those "embers" in which there is "something that doth live" and to affirm that that vital cliché threads through the political unconscious to link Wordsworth's irrepressible insurrectionary glow by analogy with the volcanic *Prometheus Unbound*, with the fantastically explosive *Don Juan*, as well as with the fire of the Greek Revolution and, perhaps, the 1992 insurrection in Los Angeles.

In *City of Quartz*, his superb rendering of the postmodern endzone of Los Angeles, Mike Davis recalls one memorable instance, when,

> during a [civil rights] protest at a local whites-only drive-in restaurant, when the timely arrival of Black gang members saved them from a mauling by white hotrodders. The gang was the legendary Slausons, [who] became a crucial social base for the rise of the local Black Liberation movement. The turning-point . . . was the festival of the oppressed in August 1965 that the Black community

> called a rebellion and the white media a riot. Although the "riot
> commission" headed by old-guard Republicans supported Chief
> Parker's so-called "riff-raff theory" that the August events were the
> work of a small criminal minority, subsequent research . . . proved
> that up to 75,000 people took part in the uprising, mostly from
> the stolid Black working class. For gang members it was "The Last
> Rumble," as formerly hostile groups forgot old grudges and
> cheered each other on against the LAPD and the National
> Guard. . . . Old enemies, like the Slausons and the Gladiators . . .
> flashing smiles and high signs as they broke through Parker's in-
> vincible "blue line."[39]

From the thin red line poised against uprisings of ragged Yorkshiremen
in 1802 to the thin blue line in Los Angeles in 1965 — and again in
1992. It is no doubt irresponsible of Davis to embellish his account of
the Watts Rebellion, which lacked any recognizable ideology with such
Jacobin stereotypes as the "festival of the oppressed"; and it is no doubt
irresponsible and inappreciative of time, that is, Romantic, to stereotype uprisings in different lands and different epochs in order to draw
analogies with no workable plan in view except to suggest that although we may have seen the end of history, we have certainly not seen
the last rumble. Or the last Romantic Movement.

Or so I wish. Fredric Jameson might judge the term *political unconscious* misapplied in the service of that wish. And yet, if we cultivate a
strategic inappreciation of time, we can take advantage of Jameson's
own studied vagueness about what exactly the "political unconscious"
is in order to broaden the Romantic Movement. Queerly enough, this
means fostering the fraternization of Jameson and Pocock. The former
is a Marxist; the latter identifies himself as "a non-Marxist interested in
finding circumstances under which Marxist language can be employed
with validity" (Pocock, *Virtue*, 44). As a Romantic, I am both a non-
Marxist interested in employing Marxist language and a nonhumanist
interested in finding circumstances under which civic humanist language can be employed with validity. Jameson's version of Marxism
shares with Pocock's reconstruction of civic humanism the insistence
that "everything is 'in the last analysis' political."[40] Yet for civic humanism the belief that "men were by nature good and political" was a belief
only about *men*, and even then not about all men — only those enfran-
chised by ownership of real property (Pocock, *Virtue*, 43). That would
not do. And it did not do. As the exhaustion of civic humanism's capac-

ity to command belief among men and women was the historical pre-condition for Pocock's scholarly narrative, so, much earlier, it enabled Coleridge to launch his illiberal and transcendental project of identify-ing real property with self-consciousness.

As Coleridge proceeds along his "dim and perilous way" in the *Bio-graphia* he not only encounters metaphysics' hit parade of contradic-tions but also senses an unsettling insistence of a feeling of injustice among the unenfranchised: the women, artisans, and others included in that phrase of convenience, "the general reader." When Coleridge turns to answering those critics in the reviews who falsely attribute irritability to men of genius, he imputes this irritability to a "class" of minds that, cold by nature, seek warmth in a crowd:

> Cold and phlegmatic in their own nature, like damp hay, they heat and inflame by co-acervation; or like bees they become restless and irritable through the increased temperature of collected multi-tudes. . . . The passion being in an inverse proportion to the in-sight, *that* the more vivid, as *this* the less distinct; anger is the inevitable consequence. The absence of all foundation within their own minds for that, which they yet believe both true and indis-pensable for their safety and happiness, cannot but produce an un-easy state of feeling, an involuntary sense of fear from which nature has no means of rescuing herself but by anger. (*BL*, 1:31)

That analysis of the reader's bullish predicament does not describe class consciousness but mass movement. The reader suffers generalization and the imposition of a social psychology because she lacks a sure foundation for that which she cannot help but believe she needs for her safety and happiness. The lack in each makes for the irritation of all. This amalgamating arrears — an inverse proportion of insight and pas-sion, need and means, belief and grounds — produces unease, "an invol-untary sense of fear," and that movement of the mass called anger.

Coleridge would have publicly avowed that those things the general reader understands as "true and indispensable" are illusory. He insists on the importance of a "foundation within their own minds" because he will not concede that the public can even have its own mind without the kind of foundation that his deductions will disclose and Words-worth's poetry will propagate. Commentator after commentator on the *Biographia* agree that Coleridge never lifts the veil on his "vantage ground," however. Diagnosis without a remedy, Coleridge's social psy-chology involuntarily justifies a mass of readers bound by an anger that springs from the institutionalized inversion of sense and sensation, sensation and sense, manipulated by those who permit access to the tools of social reproduction only at the cost of a transfer of power that would make such access inconsequential.

Coleridge could discover this rebellious wish for justice breaking through the public avowals of conformity because it was there all along—not lodged in the rocks and streams and trees of "real property" but in the unsteady "ground" of the political unconscious, where what matters plays the politics of maneuver and thus remains unmasterable by the ideological eye. According to Coleridge's teaching, the material impenetrability of those whom authors and booksellers aim to generalize as readers is "a mode of resistance; [for the admission of impenetrability] places the essence of *matter* in an act or power, which it possesses in common with *spirit*" (BL, 1:129). The impenetrability of the mass is an act in common, but it is a commonality without traditional determinants or articulable purpose. The mass resists in a heavily dialecticized, darkly proverbial, lavishly stereotypical, and insistently repetitious, demotic speech which falls short of the vernacular and cannot be counted on for useful labor. The conservative Oakeshott has found a home in so many liberals' footnotes because he simply affirms what no conservative or liberal can deny, that "only individuality matters." That truism can be revived as Romantic truth if, following Coleridge's lead, we put the stress not on "individuality" but on "matters." In the liberal vernacular individuality signifies as the lure with which society induces the transfer of that power without which individuality signs itself as cipher.[41] But individuality can matter only if it matters in common. In practice, individuality does not oppose common purpose; individuality is the common purpose.

On the way individuality commonly matters Coleridge is precise: "This principium commune essendi et cognoscendi, as subsisting in a WILL, or primary ACT of self-duplication, is the mediate or indirect principle of every science" (BL, 1:281). That every science requires a mediate principle is a plausible claim; and it is fitting that the transcendental science would name what is common to knowing and being as "will"; but it is a surprise that Coleridge does not write "the" will, that self-determining faculty which guarantees freedom, but "a" will—as if it were not quite recognizable, as if it were *any* will. Richard Flathman has identified a political stance called "willful liberalism," which he has wedded to a conception of "strong voluntarism" anchored in Thomas Ockham's designation of the will as that which "marks the commencement of action but equally the terminus of explanation and understanding of its having commenced." Bent on extending liberalism's range, Flathman leaps forward and across the Channel from Ockham to embrace Nietzsche's familiar affirmation of the will to power as a modern version of Ockham's voluntarism.[42] But if we linger in the Britain of the early nineteenth century, the story gets more complicated. For one thing, it is hard to ignore the ideological freight borne by "voluntarism," whether considered as an ethical potency embodied by the philanthropist William Wilberforce, a loyalist political commitment solicited by the Castleragian apparatus of state repression, or a cozy social disposition lathered on the unlettered by Hannah More. For another, in the *Biographia* strong voluntarism as Flathman describes it — spontaneous, ungrounded in real property or in God's consciousness, without warrant or franchise — appears at the end of the metaphysical line as perfectly indistinguishable from a strong involuntarism, a founding discrepancy that cripples the liberal project of securing self-possession.

Only a conception of the will as strongly involuntary ("in" as the token of repression) explains the scandal of Coleridge's ascribing to the will the primary act of "self-duplication." The self comes to itself in a doubling of itself, which could only happen to what Freud calls a cliché or a stereotype. Nothing authorizes a will. Self-identical with an act of self-duplication, the primary act of the will could be said to plagiarize the self — could be said, that is, were there any original self who could hold copyright and prefer charges before the bar of reason. Described in terms of the literary culture in which any book must make its way, the will is less an act of plagiarism than a primordial and continual challenge to the hypothesis of a right to copyright.

Hedged by clauses, sentences, and entire paragraphs lifted from Schelling, Coleridge's phrasing of the will is one of the few locutions in his labored advance to the theory of the imagination that can be said not to be someone else's — though to call the assertion of a primordial involuntary act of self-duplication Coleridge's *own* statement would be vertiginously ironic. Schelling's ponderous deduction of the sovereignty of consciousness offers a dainty lure to the aspirant to bona fide philosophical criticism: although Coleridge could never convince himself of his own self-possession, he could nonetheless guiltily attest its truth by stealing its signs from others. Theft proves property right; and scribal plagiarism is a form of subjection to what John Horne Tooke, reformist etymologist, called "the dominion of speech." So, although Coleridge's willful phrase does not seem fully his own, neither does the juridical category of "plagiarism" quite fit the way it fails to work. Out of synch with Schelling, with all of Coleridge's public avowals, and with all the zeitgeisted legitimations of a sovereign consciousness juridically sustained, the phrase erupts as a discursive version of the speech act that Tooke stigmatized as the closest to a sheer act of will, the interjection.

"The dominion of Speech," Tooke writes,

> is erected upon the downfall of our interjections. . . . Voluntary interjections are only employed when the suddenness or vehemence of some affection or passion returns men to their natural state; and makes them for the moment forget the use of speech: or when, from some circumstance, the shortness of time will not permit them to exercise it. And in books they are only used for embellishment, and to mark strongly the above situations. But where Speech can be employed, they are totally useless; and are always insufficient for the purpose of communicating our thoughts. And indeed where will you look for the Interjection? Will you find it amongst laws, or in books of civil institutions, in history, or in any treatise of useful arts or sciences? No. You must seek for it in rhetorick and poetry, in novels, plays, and romances.[43]

If the dominion of speech depends on the downfall of the interjection, the upsurge of the interjection (and you know that there is no telling when an interjection — whether apostrophe, or parenthesis, or, yes!, typographical mark — will surge up), like Coleridge's willful assertion of self-duplicative will, challenges that dominion by a strong marking of times and places where communication fails, where transference stalls, and where the conventional criteria of value — use and exchange — lapse. Interjections which have lost their place "in rhetorick and poetry, in novels, plays, and romances" assert a decisive if indeterminate difference from the law, from civil institutions, and from history; and they make that assertion not according to any adjudicable right but as an affective, Romantic movement against the present state of things. And not case by case (there is no law governing these matters) but instance by instance.

The first interjection was not uttered by Coleridge but by Cain — Coleridge's contemporary, as Coleridge is ours. Lord Byron explains his dramatization of Cain's act in the historical present:

> Cain is a proud man — if Lucifer promised him kingdoms &c. — it would *elate* him — the object of the demon is to *depress* him still further in his own estimation than he was before — by showing him infinite things — & his own abasement — till he falls into the

frame of mind — that leads to the Catastrophe — from mere *internal* irritation — *not* premeditation or envy — of *Abel* — (which would have made him contemptible) but from rage and fury against the inadequacy of his state to his Conceptions — & which discharges itself rather against Life — and the author of Life — than the mere living.[44]

Cain's murder is first a violent discharge; it is an act against Abel only secondarily. Cain's act is violent because it is speechless — and speechless not as deficit but as interjection, which, because it is "insufficient for the purpose of communicating our thoughts," effectively marks the inadequacy of a state in which all communication takes its tithe by transferring power from the living to the author of life. Immune to the sublime as staged by deity or devil, Cain discharges his rage because he suffers what Byron calls a "fit of dissatisfaction" with the dominion of speech, whether that speech is uttered by God or echoed by Satan's inversions ("Thou art my worshipper: not worshipping / Him makes thee mine the same" [1.1.316–17]). Cain's movement of soul resists sacrifice urged in the name of communication, whether it be the sacrifice of individuality enacted by the prayerful gatherings of the Adamic family or the pious bloodletting on the altar by which Abel transfers the dead weight of his labor to the author of life.

Cain early complains of his postlapsarian lot: "I judge but by the fruits — and they are bitter — / Which I must feed on for a fault not mine" (1.1.78–79). the murder of Abel, however, *is* Cain's fault, not God's, Cain's willful act, not His. Cain becomes Cain as he willfully becomes what Eve wittily calls the "incarnate spirit of death" (3.420). But Cain's act is expeditiously patented as incarnate sign by the appearance of the angel commissioned "to mark upon thy brow / Exemption from such deeds as thou hast done" (3.498–99). The mark forecloses a cycle of mimetic violence. Slavoj Žižek's Lacanian formulation illuminates divine justice: "The crucial point here is the changed symbolic status of an event: when it erupts for the first time it is experienced as a contingent trauma, as an intrusion of a certain non-symbolized Real; only through repetition is this event recognized in its symbolic necessity — it finds its place in the symbolic network; it is realized in the symbolic order." The mark repeats and contains the interjection of Cain as a symbol which "announces the advent of the Law."[45] If the fault be Cain's, the responsibility is God's. Such is theodicy. In Byron's literal interpretation of the myth, the mark of Cain is the impression of a divine copyright, which, by *coup de main,* transfers responsibility for the authorship of Cain to the divinity without any imputation of fault. Fault is mere interjection, an act without symbolic value. Fault strangely shifts the state of things, and is remembered as an irrational, incommunicable, and anomalous discharge — what the good call evil. After Cain history will become the monotonously normal change of begettings and perishings, imbued with purpose (or such is the liberal wish) by the copyright of the contingent, the prescribed subjection of events to law. *Cain* lessons us that recognizable repetition is what god-given liberalism means by normal change. And it affirms the axiomatic truth of liberal society: normal change could not be without copyright.[46]

Hannah Arendt makes a case for Cain's interjection when she argues that "under certain circumstances violence — acting without argument of speech and without counting the consequences — is the only way to set the scales of justice right again." As *Cain* shows, one of the unforeseen consequences of violence may be to reveal that the scales of justice never have been balanced. And in *Cain*'s light Arendt's caution that "rage and violence turn irrational only when they are directed against substitutes" (*On Violence*, 65) does point a moral: although justifiably enraged with God, Cain irrationally attacks Abel. But the moral does no good. No matter how much God deserves assault, because he is the Real, the author of life sealed off from the living, there can be nothing but irrational violence. Cain's historicity is his existential conviction that history has ended before justice can be established. The advent of the posthistorical is the proof that history has never happened for me or for those who are like me because, like the Nottingham weavers in 1818 and like the Rostock steelworkers in 1992, we movingly reproduce the stereotype of Cain. The real injustice of Cain's posthistorical existence is that under the dispensation of the law no rage can be directed against anything that is not a substitute, the reprint of some original, incontestable script. As in the double-plotted story that Fukuyama tells, so for *Cain:* history, whether authored by Hegel in 1806 or by God some years before, began as the advent of its end — normal change, endless substitution, case after damned case — an end which, after the blood and thunder rhetoric of a Marx or a Christ, it is our right liberally to recognize. But for Cain, "history" so conceived is the very name of injustice.

The demotic Cain makes vernacular history workable by moving out of the Old Testament narrative. It is the great infirmity of the romantic mind to attempt to follow him, to gather Coleridge, Wordsworth, Byron, Shelley, and Marx into the party of Cain. Leigh Hunt's review of

Cain sounded a cautionary note by recalling "the Cainites, a sect who sprung up in the second century merely out of the perplexities of this single story, and who found it so contradictory to their ideas of justice, that they ran, out of resentment, into a great absurdity. They supposed the God of the Old Testament to be a real malignant principle, who had sown discord in the world, and subjected our nature to a thousand calamities; upon which they concluded, that it was their business to oppose him in every one of his injunctions."[47] If the first interjection — a violent outburst against the system of divine justice — was Cain's, the first ideology, formed as the inversion of God's truth, belonged to the Cainites, who responded to the singularity of Cain's story by locking themselves into the very opposition that in Byron's account Cain had himself repudiated. Again Arendt is apt: "This violent reaction against hypocrisy, however justifiable in its own terms, loses its *raison d'etre* when it tries to develop a strategy of its own with specific goals; it becomes 'irrational' the moment it is 'rationalized,' that is, the moment the re-action in the course of a contest turns into an action, and the hunt for suspects . . . begins" (*On Violence*, 66). Wallerstein's account of the bureaucratization of the movements during the course of the nineteenth century bears Arendt out. The romantic alternative to what Byron calls "the politics of paradise" cannot be found in the cell, nor in a union hall somewhere east of Eden.

Hunt acknowledged that Lord Byron may "give occasion to the weak and the hypocritical to charge him with something of this Cainite spirit." He did not err. Numerous hostile reviews echoed the *Gentleman's Magazine*'s identification of Byron as a type of Cain, whose "series of wanton libels upon the Supreme Being" would earn the poet Cain's stigma, an "immortality of infamy." The reviewer reported "that the publication of [*Cain*], as was naturally to be expected, has given offence to a person of the highest rank in this country, and that in consequence of his repeatedly expressed disgust of the atrocious tendency of the work, it is now *suppressed*, and will never more be reprinted."[48] Unreprintable by Byron, each copy of the first edition would then become an "incarnate spirit of death." The reviewer's indignation may seem excessive. After all, Cain was said to have killed his brother; Byron had murdered no one. Yet the reviewer's sense of right adumbrates a redescription of Cain's crime for commercial society: the punishment of suppression fits the crime of reckless printing — a speechless act of willful self-duplication.

Although his logic was impeccable, in the course of events the reviewer proved wrong. There was no noble lord to squelch reprinting. In truth, it was because of *Cain*'s atrocious tendency that *Cain* was reprinted as widely and wildly as it was. "In truth" because in the judgment of the law. Here is Lord Chancellor Eldon deciding on the plea for an injunction against the booksellers who were pirating *Cain*:

> Where an action of damages will lie in a Court of Law for the piracy of a work, it will lend its assistance to aid the defective remedy which such a proceeding affords; for it is obvious that publication after publication might take place, which you could never otherwise hunt down {by proceeding in the other courts}. But when the work is of such a nature that an action for piracy will not lie, then this Court will not grant an injunction to protect the copyright. {Now this publication, if it is one intended to vilify and bring into discredit that portion of scripture history to which it relates is a publication with reference to which . . . the party could not recover any damages in respect of a piracy of it. . . .} All I am now called upon to say is, whether I entertain a reasonable doubt on the character of the book; and I trust I shall not be considered unreasonable when I say I do entertain such a doubt. {There is a great difficulty in these cases, because it appears a strange thing to permit the multiplication of copies, by way of preventing the circulation of a mischievous work . . . but that I cannot help: and the singularity of the case, in this instance, is more obvious because here is a defendant who has multiplied this work by piracy, and does not think proper to appear. . . . It is true that this mode of dealing with the work, if it be calculated to produce mischievous effects, opens a door for its wide dissemination, but the duty of stopping the work does not belong to court of equity, which has no criminal jurisdiction and cannot punish or check the offence} (*LBC*, 15–16).

If God's mark sealed the trauma of Cain by copyrighting it, making it symbolize divine authorship even of the radically contingent, Lord Byron's perverse variation on God's story willfully repeats Cain's act and goes him one better by undoing the author's own right. The trauma reappears, like a discharged sailor on the threshold or a Greek fire on the hearth, as a "strange thing." *Cain* compels the law to do the strange thing of reasoning itself irrationally to permit the atrocious tendency to prosper and the libel against justice to go forth and multiply in acts of bloodless violence called piracies. And this with the strongest of legal prohibitions against such hateful speech. Byron's deed, though wholly an involuntary expression of hostility (in publishing *Cain* Lord Byron never planned to abandon his claim to fame and profit), was nonetheless politics most practical because it was effectively directed against the state's support of property right itself. What is strange about the case is that nothing appears before the law except the strange thing and that the strange thing occurs as a textual movement, anomalous yet fraught with consequences. The piratical defendants refuse to be recognized before the bar and nonetheless win a case that is, however, not "theirs," neither in *propria persona* nor as representatives of a class. No appearance, no speech; no speech, no ideology. The defendants cannot appear because they do not speak the vernacular but subsist, speechlessly and commonly, "in a WILL, or primary ACT of self-duplication." The refusal of the defendants to be recognized is the conjectural mark of a mass resisting the cure of physician and judge, the trace of a movement against and beyond the jurisdiction of the law, where the pirate crew willfully multiplies its lawless stereotypes.

By the time of Arnold, the pirates had been recruited into the service of the empire, and the Romantic notion of justice had become a sentimental idealism; in the 1960s it once again sounded revolutionary; in the 1970s and 1980s things soured as stern-lipped academics, fortified for history's long haul by strong doses of Marx, denounced Romantic hope as an ideological refuge embraced by apostates to the true cause. Now that the long haul has been aborted, and Marx's beautiful theory has withered, the Romantic Movement marks time as the reviving possibility of change that is not merely normal, the hope for justice that is not merely the confirmation of property rights. The Romantic Movement sounds along its dim and perilous way as the willful commission of anachronism after anachronism linked by bold analogy. By promiscuously replicating stereotypes that resist recognition and transfer, the Romantic Movement rejects the imperial epochalism of the posthistorical as the sign of the naturalization of injustice. At one point in his writings on ideology and literature, Raymond Williams wisely warns against what he calls "premature historicization." Until there is justice, all historicization is premature. Until there is justice, the timely slogan of Romantic politics will not be "always historicize," but "now and then anachronize."

Chapter Two

The Color of Imagination
and the Office
of Romantic Criticism

In his marginalia on the works of the early modern chemist Hermann
Boerhaave, Coleridge queries this bit of legend:

> The emperor *Ferdinand* III. says he, did himself change three
> pounds of mercury into two pounds and a half of pure gold; and
> this by means of a single grain of tincture. This notable transmuta-
> tion was perform'd at *Prague*; and a medal was struck of the same
> gold, in memory thereof.

> Had Ferd. III. no political design in spreading the belief of the
> chryso-poietic powers?[1]

Most contemporary readers would regard Coleridge's question
about political design as rhetorical and scoff at the interest in chryso-
poiesis ("gold-making") as typical Coleridgean mystification. But even
if we accept that all designs are political, it does not necessarily follow
that all politics is designed. In this chapter I want to explore the ways in
which Coleridge, as well as the criticism that takes its antiprofessional
bias from him, sets about making gold by employment of what phar-
macologists and genealogists alike name "tincture."

The hook on which I would hang this picture is Wordsworth's
phrase from the Preface to the *Lyrical Ballads* "the coloring of imagination." The phrase has its place in Wordsworth's thesis that "the principal object . . . proposed in these Poems was to choose incidents and
situations from common life, and to relate or describe them, throughout, as far as was possible in a selection of language really used by men,
and, at the same time, to throw over them a certain coloring of imagination whereby ordinary things should be represented to the mind in
an unusual aspect."[2] Although in the *Biographia Literaria* Coleridge
painstakingly scrutinizes the doctrine of diction advanced in the first
clause, he virtually ignores the tinctural office ascribed to the imagination — one might guess because it fundamentally contradicts his con-

ception of the imagination as a coadunating or esemplastic power. That hypothesis does not, however, account for Coleridge's subsequent description of "the poet's imagination" as "a state which spreads its influence and colouring over all that co-exists with the exciting cause."[3] The echo enriches rather than dispels the contradiction; it looks like Coleridge hangs on to the notion despite the contradiction, perhaps because it satisfies needs not subject to argument.

Coleridge was not bowing to authority. Colorists have not been held in high regard by those whose regard matters. Joshua Reynolds's complaint in his *Discourses* was well known: "Well coloured pictures are more in esteem, and sell for higher prices, than in reason they appear to deserve, as colouring is an excellence, acknowledged to be of a lower rank than the qualities of correctness, grace, and greatness of character."[4] If Reynolds is like Kant in his derogation of color, he is closer to Pierre Bourdieu in the reasons he gives. As if reluctantly bowing to a higher necessity, Reynolds suavely shifts the ground of discrimination from aesthetics to commerce. More precisely, he interprets a painting's color as the shifter among aesthetic, social, and commercial concerns. With Reynolds in mind, the manifest tension between Wordsworth's interests in selecting real language and in coloring that language looks less like an awkward inconsistency than a shrewd articulation of the common speaker and the common reader in a single recursive operation. By coloring the poetry he selects, the poet can induce the vulgar speaker to pay to read what he or someone just like him once said. Whatever impels the reflexive movements of the individual mind, the reflux of reader on speaker is mobilized by a tincture that heightens routine in order to make it marketable. If the cultural moment of realism can be described as a collective mirror-stage for the emerging middle class, Wordsworth's Romantic project differs. He drastically discounts the role of the reflected, identifiable figure in favor of the lure of the tinctured image. Gazing into a glass glazed by a canny romancer, the reader of Wordsworth is not formed but enhanced.

There is a precedent for this approach in David Hume's explanation of the agreeableness of representations of melancholy events. In "Of Tragedy," Hume decides that what "raises a pleasure from the bosom of uneasiness" is the "very eloquence with which the melancholy scene is represented. . . . The impulse or vehemence, arising from sorrow, compassion, indignation, receives a new direction from the sentiments of beauty. The latter, being the predominant emotions, seize the whole mind, and convert the former into themselves, at least tincture them so strongly as totally to alter their nature."[5] For Hume as for Wordsworth, delight is the effect of a change in directions and the conversion of some low impulse, such as the urge to vent one's rage, into a higher, purer emotion, instinct with its own pleasure. The sublimational process closely resembles alchemical tincturing as defined by Paracelsus: "Tincture, therefore, is the noblest matter with which bodies, metallic and human, are tinged, translated into a better and far more noble essence, and into their supreme health and purity. For a Tincture colours all things according to its own nature and its own colour." Paracelsus's emphasis on the nobility of tincture has its parallel in Hume's inclusion of himself in the select company of those "few critics who have had some tincture of philosophy" (Hume, 217).[6] To adopt a philosophical relation to tragedy as a dramatic kind is directly analogous to being elevated into a tragic relation to human suffering: nobility is a matter of contemplation — what Burke would call "reflection" — not of action.

According to Hume's tinctural hypothesis, reading literature or listening to oratory or attending the tragic theater, however flattering, is never merely narcissistic, the meager pleasure of the mirror. Wordsworth commonsensically extends Hume's reasoning: if you want ordinary people to buy poems in which ordinary people speak (and, as Hume knew, nothing — not the fate of Medea, not the catastrophe of Oedipus — is so melancholy as the monotonous reiteration of tales of everyday life), you should color and thereby heighten their low or real language. Give the ordinary reader an enhanced or colored image of himself. One reading of Hume's consequences fuelled the eighteenth-century version of what Jonas Barish has called "the anti-theatrical prejudice": if a person's emotions can be raised by coloring, why not his or her social status? Applied to social ends, color could and would be interpreted loosely. As the Quinceys found, a *De* added to the family name would tincture it sufficiently that a mercantile background could plausibly mesh with aristocratic pretensions. The Jacobin festivals of the first years of the Revolutionary Republic, in which uniform color schemes were imposed on the participants in the spectacle, adapted the same principle — not to raise social status, however, but to accomplish the contrary end of removing signs of status from the social.

Wordsworth takes things further. As Coleridge anxiously perceived, he argues that the theater, although sufficient, is not necessary to such social disorientation; what theater does well reading does better. Or worse: defending against Wordsworth's consequences, Coleridge argues that reading "real language" is not really reading because it involves social aspiration (in the postrevolutionary world, a kind of implicit action) — as opposed to the clericized, contemplative engagements with Spenserian, Shakespearian, Miltonic, or Wordsworthian language proper, which ideally put one in one's place. To enter, by whatever vehicle (the circulating library or the daily newspaper had proven to be as potent as Drury Lane), what De Quincey called the "new class of readers" is decisively to evacuate the social class into which one has been born. Crucially, however, this exodus does not deliver one into a new, improved social class. It is not class aspiration as such that disturbs Coleridge but the fact that the "new class of readers" is imaginary; it corresponds to no class in the world. The tease performed by Wordsworthian theory and circulating libraries alike arouses readers into a state of high irritation with no satisfaction forthcoming — a condition not firmly distinguishable from that "unfeigned uneasiness" which, according to Hume, tragic art is meant to cure. Color fades, the philosophical critic teaches; anxiety is long.

The contours of this social and cultural predicament emerge fairly clearly in a review of several books on madness by the *Quarterly Review* in 1816. The reviewer deplores the pervasive fashion of nervous diseases:

> Let the farmer's wife tell us, since she gave herself up to all the indulgences of the tea-table, and sent her daughters to the boarding school to be manufactured into misses, how the fiend ennui, from small beginnings, has swelled into gigantic bulk, and breathed contagion through the family. The present agricultural distresses have in some measure repressed the power, if not the desire of this class, to soar into the superior ranks of life; but all the freshness and delightful simplicity of rural happiness is gone! it has withered under the pestiferous blight of these miserable and mistaken notions of the actual constituents of real felicity. We were almost upon the point of saying, the apothecary is the only individual who has been benefitted by the conversion of cultivators of land into cultivators of arts and sciences. Let us not be understood to express ourselves in favour of feudal oppression, when we venture to hint that the present habits of society have rather too strong a tincture of democratical freedom for the well-being of individuals.[7]

The reviewer does not, of course, intend to let the farmer's wife actually tell "us" anything. That she can be imagined as speaking is alarming enough. Appalled, the reviewer announces the demonic triumph of a vision heralded by the newborn *Spectator,* which, in its tenth number, projected great changes in social behavior as the condign consequence of small adjustments in domestic space and time: the arrangement of the "tea equipage," the allotment of glances at periodical papers. Writing in the wake of Continental Revolution and in the rising tide of reformist agitation, the *Quarterly* reviewer has developed a jeweler's, almost a Blakean eye for incommensurability: any adjustment in "the actual constituents of felicity" — any tincture — can be imagined to produce what De Quincey, who confesses how he strategically tapped the expertise of apothecaries to prepare the tincture of laudanum requisite for wholesale conversion, called "an apocalypse of the world within."

Inasmuch as the *Quarterly's* analysis is rather more than less naked in its service of entrenched class interests, it will not startle anyone to hear it called ideological. I want to narrow my usage of that term, however, by offering a definition of ideology that both fits the phenomenon above and characterizes the political discourse that prevailed in Great Britain from roughly 1745 until 1832. Several aspects of the *Quarterly's* commentary are salient. The reviewer identifies a moment of massive social change as metaphorical transfer — the exchange of cultivation of the land for cultivation of the arts and sciences — and argues that the ill effects illustrate the limits of metaphor: one form of cultivation cannot be transmuted into another without producing psychic and social deformation. Although this argument prosecutes the standard Tory critique of the generalization of exchange value by political economy, it notably accepts the enabling condition of ideological debate, that whether or not one can, in good moral and mental health, exchange land for luxuries, there can be no return to the life — good or bad — that one has left: "the simplicity of rural happiness is gone!" Political economy may have failed to convert a concrete, value-infused existence into a mechanical system of wealth production ruled by the laws of the market; but it has succeeded in extinguishing the referent. Post-Enlightenment ideology in Great Britain was public discourse generated by and sustained in the acknowledged obliteration of the referent.

That extinction was carried out on multiple fronts, both discursive and nondiscursive, in the eighteenth century. Among its manifestations are (1) the annihilation of strength, considered as a causal quality of the object, carried out by Hume in the *Treatise of Human Nature*; (2) the correlative dissipation of the notion of intrinsic value formulated by Adam Smith in *The Wealth of Nations*; (3) the dissolution of the affective force of the beautiful by Edmund Burke in *A Philosophical Enquiry into Our Ideas Concerning the Sublime and the Beautiful*; (4) the quelling of the oratorical voice as a source of civil authority, officialized by the introduction of stenographers into the House of Commons; and (5) the genocide performed against the Highland Clans, of which Ossianism is the chief, ambivalent cultural testimony.

Something lost, someone gains. According to the *Quarterly* reviewer, the misfiring of the metaphor of cultivation has produced a new thing, a nervous disorder — an ailment that, in turn, supports the profitable enterprise of the old order of apothecaries. But because, according to the *Quarterly,* modern disease is the result of a "strong tincture of democratical freedom," the distress the apothecary relieves looks suspiciously like a distress he, or someone resembling him, has caused. The apothecary offers a remedy for a disease he has not only diagnosed but induced — perhaps by throwing a certain democratizing color of imagination over people's real language or lives. A concept of historical change that entails the extinction of the referent requires the existence of an agent, even if it is a metaphorical apothecary whose job it is to convince people that metaphors can take the place of realities. Whether the apothecaries' dose is poison or remedy depends on one's inevitably partisan — that is, colored — perspective; the apothecary profits either way.

The apothecary, whether inhabiting Plato's Athens, Shakespeare's Verona, or De Quincey's London, is a time-honored scapegoat. Here, suspicions about apothecaries reflect the *Quarterly's* concern about its own participation in the phenomenon it decries:

> As the law now stands, every *soi-disant* practitioner of medicine is competent to the signature of a certificate declarative of insanity. Let the power of signing such certificate be confined to the hands of a legitimate prescriber, that is, to one who has either obtained a diploma from some medical university or who is a member of the College of Surgeons. . . . There are many of this profession, who are miserably deficient in every qualification but that of impudence; and we believe that, according to the present constitution of the law, both as it applies to the practice of medicine and to the statutes of lunacy, there are no means of distinguishing legally between one and the other description of men. (414)

The attack on the diagnostic credentials of the "*soi disant* practitioner of medicine" is issued by a diagnostician who has no authority to sign for his own cultural prescriptions. The insistent emergence of the figure of the apothecary in the pages of the *Quarterly* reflects not only a concern about the permeability of the boundaries between social classes and mental states but also an uneasiness about the professional status of the critic who exercises his talents for hire in the reviews. Professionalist controversy at the beginning of the nineteenth century (as at the end of the twentieth) erupts most fiercely at those points where the abolition of the referent, such as madness, health, life, or the poor, has become dramatically clear and oddly irrelevant. As the critic invokes the apothecary both to explain and to take the blame for a social and psychic debility which it has been the assignment of every post-Addisonist periodical essayist, whatever his party, to promote, so professionalist discourse takes advantage of a world (well) lost to construct a new service class that is the articulate looking glass for the imaginary class of nervous readers. This transitional class multiplies offices, each with its code of recognition, each professing the authority to delimit a domain of expertise and to create and distribute benefits. To the *Quarterly* writers and other men of letters in the early nineteenth century, men who were writing in advance of the establishment of any academic or commercial system of certification, falls the tricky task of persuading their contemporaries that by reading they have been made sick and by reading, properly tinctured, they can be healed.

The task may be tricky, but it does have its rewards. In his notes to the work of the early modern chemist Hermann Boerhaave, Coleridge observes: "Of all the Chrysopoets Carpus is the truest — he did indeed make gold out of Mercury, so that he declared he did not know the end of his own wealth — but it was by discovering first Mercurial Salivation for *the new disease*, Syphilis." Coleridge's comment is not a demystification of chrysopoiesis or alchemy but a practical example of his belief that "the Alchemists may perhaps be decipherable into intelligible notions."[8] The phenomenon Coleridge would save is not a formula for turning mercury into gold but a technique for producing wealth out of knowledge. Like the modern apothecary, the Renaissance alchemist handsomely benefitted from a fashionable disease. Carpus made it. Unlike, say, the modern Burke, who was able to go Carpus one better by both inventing a new disease, Jacobinism, and prescribing its remedy, but who, to his bitter resentment, was never able even to say that he had enough wealth.

Much of Romantic practice was devoted to making archaic notions intelligible, as Burke did, while avoiding the ravage of Burke's disappointment in the returns. De Quincey, for example, was highly sensitive to the predicament and highly ingenious in his attempts to extricate himself from it. In *The Logic of Political Economy* he attempted to rehabilitate scholastic logic with the historicist assumption that the eclipse of scholasticism was only circumstantial: "Losing its *professional* use, scholasticism lost its main functions and occupation." Like alchemy in Coleridge, scholasticism reemerges in De Quincey as a metaphor to shape inchoate notions of professionalism. The renewed usefulness of alchemy and scholasticism figures the possibility of success within industrial society for those *soi-disant* unproductive laborers otherwise made redundant by political economy. Specifically for De Quincey, the revival of scholastic logic promises to resuscitate use value by solving the fundamental conundrum of economic theory: "whether (and how) it is feasible to use a sameness as to make it do the *office* of a difference" (my emphasis).[9] The keyword *office* binds the value of economic theory to professional use and weds professionalism to simulation. Sameness fulfills the role of difference, professes difference, but sameness remains the same. It is as if a theory about the production of wealth could, effortlessly, theoretically produce wealth. But how can sameness be made to do what difference has always done? De Quincey's answer—in *The Logic of Political Economy,* in *The Confessions*—will be by tincturing it.

De Quincey could make this problem his own because it already had been solved by Coleridge. Here I shall rely on Arden Reed's vivid and convincing allegorization of the primary and the secondary imaginations according to their meteorological dispositions in his book *Romantic Weather.* What makes Reed's meteorology pertinent here is the homology between the figurative systems of the weather and those of the pharmacy in Coleridge's text (a representative crossover occurs along the chain: contingency, cloud, smoke, bewilderment, intoxication, drug, habit, necessity). According to Reed, the primary imagination occupies the position of the sun, which is the grounding, vital condition of perception but whose unmediated radiance would scorch the world into the bleakness of customary form. The dissolution, dissipation, and diffusion of the secondary imagination volatilize custom and work as what Reed calls a "parallel obstacle" to the light of the primary imagination. By obstruction and inhibition, the secondary imagination varies light and makes life possible. This passage from *Religious Musings* epitomizes Coleridge's meteorology:

> The veiling clouds retire,
> And lo! the Throne of the redeeming God
> Forth flushing unimaginable day
> Wraps in one blaze earth, heaven, and deepest hell.

The sun of primary imagination enables us to see, but, unmediated, that blazing sight conflagrates all difference; the secondary imagination enables us to see the sun—albeit through a covering of mist, figuratively.

Reed proposes a revision of the conventional opposition that groups the imaginations, primary and secondary, as symbolic and opposes them to the allegorical fancy. It is, he says, "at least as plausible to link allegory with both the secondary imagination *and* fancy, since all three establish a distance and difference between the sign and its referent."[10] De Quincey's speculation allows us to retain the conceptual force of Reed's insight and preserve the surface articulations of the text. Following De Quincey (who is following no one but Coleridge here), we can say that fancy "is" difference and that the secondary imagination is the sameness of the imagination performing the *office* of difference, professing difference for the sake of a sameness that it both upholds and endangers. Or, to put it in the terms that Coleridge chooses to describe his contribution to the *Lyrical Ballads*: "my compositions, instead of forming a balance, appeared rather an interpolation of heterogeneous matter." The Coleridgean concept of heterogeneity never fails to serve a transcendent, irreducible homogeneity. The sameness of the poet considered in his ideal perfection is assured by the apostate poet-turned-critic's performance of the office of difference. The truly, authentically, essentially different is the referent abolished in order that the poetic ideal might manifest itself over the historical horizon and that the profession of criticism might institute itself in the social, political, and cultural flux of post-Napoleonic Britain.

We might synthesize some of the concepts and metaphors deployed in Wordsworth's Preface and Coleridge's *Biographia* by reformulating the official Romantic critical position: the heterogeneous or the secondary is a cloud-coloring of imagination thrown over the real, primary sun of the imagination in order that the truth of poetic genius might be displayed in all its glory. Coleridge's illustration appears in Chapter 4 of the *Biographia*:

> During the last year of my residence at Cambridge I became acquainted with Mr. Wordsworth's first publication, entitled *Descriptive Sketches;* and seldom, if ever, was the emergence of an original poetic genius above the literary horizon more evidently announced. . . . It not seldom [however] justified the complaint of obscurity. In the following extract I have sometimes fancied that I saw an emblem of the poem itself and of the author's genius as it was then displayed:
>
>> 'Tis storm; and hid in mist from hour to hour,
>> All day the floods a deepening murmur pour,
>> The sky is veiled, and every cheerful sight;

Dark is the region as with coming night;
And yet what frequent bursts of overpowering light!
Triumphant on the bosom of the storm,
Glances the fire-clad eagle's wheeling form;
Eastward, in long perspective glittering, shine
The wood-crowned cliffs that o'er the lake recline;
Wide o'er the Alps a hundred streams unfold,
At once to pillars turn'd that flame with gold;
Behind his sail the peasant strives to shun
The West, that burns like one dilated sun,
Where in a mighty crucible expire
The mountains, glowing hot, like coals of fire.

The poetic Psyche, in its process to full development, undergoes as many changes as its Greek namesake, the butterfly. And it is remarkable how soon genius clears and purifies itself from the faults and errors of its earliest products; faults which, in its earliest compositions, are the more obtrusive and confluent because, as heterogeneous elements which had only a temporary use, they constitute the very ferment by which themselves are carried off.

Coleridge is not perfectly clear about what he means by "emblem" — whether the extract, in its movement from mist to sunlight, represents the transition of the poet from throttled to full power or whether the extract is itself representative of Wordsworth's obscure genius at the time. A developmental interpretation won't fit — not least because as emblem of Wordsworth's dawning genius Coleridge selects a setting sun. Moreover, the coordinates of the image itself are violently dualistic, the contrast between east and west, water and sun, aggressively marked. The scene changes in a manner that Paul Sheats has characterized as Revolutionary but that is also enigmatic: dark with mist, the sun glares forth with the darkness of excessive light.[11] Nor is the mist, the sign of Coleridgean heterogeneity, carried off by its own ferment; the cloud cover is annihilated by the burst of light. *Everything* is heterogeneous to this untinctured sun: although contextualizing alchemical metaphors are invoked ("turned," "crucible"), the elements and the world are obliterated, not transmuted.

Coleridge is constitutionally unable to identify an emblem of Wordsworth's genius without painting himself into the picture. Here the Coleridge-surrogate is the peasant spectator of the apocalypse who cannot take the heat. What makes the identification plausible is not only the parallel between the peasant's abject position and Coleridge's typical posture before blazing Wordsworth (see, for example, "To William Wordsworth") but also his pathetic attempt to hide behind the sail of his boat, as if, in proleptic parody of Coleridge's statesmanlike theory of the symbol, he hopes to turn its death-dealing, allegorical opacity into a benign translucence. The peasant is both an admonition — beware exposure to the rays of Wordsworth! — and a mediation: as surrogate, the peasant is the moon to the Coleridgean reader, reflecting the light that neither he nor anyone can directly tolerate.

When Coleridge rewrites this passage from *Descriptive Sketches* in the 1797 poem "This Lime-Tree Bower My Prison," he alters the relations among the particulars. The Wordsworthian or primary position retains its solar privilege and power, but the Coleridgean position has been split between a speaker, who, fortunately flawed, has a good excuse for shunning the sun's radiance, and a little black boy figure called "gentle-hearted Charles," who, all unknowing, is exposed to the divine fire. I shall not pursue all the colorful nuances of the solar imagery here, but the famous conclusion is quintessentially Coleridgean:

> My gentle-hearted Charles! when the last rook
> Beat its straight path along the dusky air
> Homewards, I blest it! deeming its black wing
> (Now a dim speck, now vanishing in light)
> Had cross'd the mighty Orb's dilated glory,
> While thou stood'st gazing.

This is the same sun as that in *Descriptive Sketches*, but with a difference. The rook — substituted for the fire-clad, wind-hovering eagle — lowers the imperious argument of the Wordsworthian sun by throwing a certain coloring of imagination over it. The bird's officious crossing saves the sun as a phenomenon for Charles, enabling him to hold his ground and his gaze. If the black wing of the rook does perform the office of difference by tincturing, we would expect, from Hume and Paracelsus, an elevating conversion to occur. It does. The black wing not only connects the speaker with the gazer, but by threading its way through the light it also sutures the sun to the gazer's eye. "Mighty orb" refers not only to the primary sun but to an eye become soliform, transfigured into the subjective condition of the sun's objective radiance: "Never," avows Coleridge in Chapter 6 of the *Biographia*, "could the eye have beheld the sun, had not its own essence been soliform." Gentle-hearted Charles has become a seer blest. Mighty prophets, we see, are made, not born. The poet's double cross of the sun (he blesses or crosses what has already crossed) both assures that the rook's office of difference does not violate the same — it deems that this is a suture without a cut — and expands it to include all those dappled things that might otherwise be heterogeneous. The coloring of the imagination — here not a mist but a vanishing line that in its dim blackness seems to have no color at all — recreates the sun as the image of the eye that sees it and educates the gazer into his essential divinity.

What goes for prophets, we have been told often enough, goes for poets as well. So it is fair to ask how this poet was made. Where and when did he learn to become so quintessentially Coleridgean? How came he to dare cross the sun? And what is his interest in doing so? The answers lie in Wordsworth. Look at another extract from Wordsworth, this time from *Evening Walk*, written earlier than *Descriptive Sketches*:

> Hung o'er a cloud, above the steep that rears
> It's edge all flame, the broad'ning sun appears;
> A long blue bar it's aegis orb divides,
> And breaks the spreading of it's golden tides;
> And now it touches on the purple steep
> That flings his shadow on the pictur'd deep.
> Cross the calm lake's blue shades the cliffs aspire,
> With tow'rs and woods a 'prospect all on fire;'
> The coves and secret hollows thro' a ray
> Of fainter gold a purple gleam betray;
> The gilded turf arrays in richer green
> Each speck of lawn the broken rocks between;
> Deep yellow beams the scatter'd boles illume,
> Far in the level forest's central gloom;
> Waving his hat, the shepherd in the vale
> Directs his winding dog the cliffs to scale,
> That, barking busy 'mid the glittering rocks,
> Hunts were he points, the intercepted flocks;
> Where oaks o'erhang the road the radiance shoots
> On tawny earth, wild weeds, and twisted roots;
> The Druid stones their lighted fane unfold,
> And all the babbling brooks are liquid gold.

Chrysopoiesis — the making of gold. This passage, which follows upon the dizzying contemplation of a Piranesian stone-quarry, completes a meditation on labor, utility, and value as it concludes the daylight section of the poem by producing the dazzling apparition of wealth. Any reader of Geoffrey Hartman on Wordsworth would see that in the inhibition of the apocalyptic tides that are released with such splendor in *Descriptive Sketches* and such terror in the *Prelude*'s "Dream" we have a passage that is quintessentially Wordsworth. Any reader of Thomas Weiskel would recognize here the lineaments of the positive or poet's sublime. But all readers ought to acknowledge that the egoistic investments that both Hartman and Weiskel require to psychologize their Wordsworths do not appear: a sun does.

This sun does not invest; it spends. Not a meteorological effect but an imaginative cause, the blue bar, the most natural artifice in the world, is the formal element that enables the sun's benefaction; sublimely ignorant of its setting, it gilds rather than floods. By dividing the sun the blue bar makes the orb recognizable as a sign, an aegis, but it does not separate signifier from signified. This is not the bar of repression: what is above is exactly the same as below (an effect seconded in the image of a "shadow" flung across a "pictured deep"). The bar does not repress because the bar is not merely a line: color blues it. The blue bar is a certain coloring of imagination primordially thrown over the native logos of the sun, the tincture that breaks forth its evening light as the dawn of gold.

This extract from *Evening Walk* is not so much an emblem of Wordsworth's genius as a demonstration of the genius of the emblem — its power as tinctured image. There is difference, made and making. And what makes difference, as the "aegis" indicates, is for Wordsworth a genealogical rather than a pharmacological question. The "aegis" sun of *Evening Walk* traditionally falls under the professional expertise of the herald, for whom tincture has a different significance than it does for either alchemists or metaphysicians. Along with figure, tincture is one of the two fundamental modes of genealogical signification. Heraldic theory cannot *be* without settling the issue of their priority. Alexander Nisbet, whose *System of Heraldry* was the dominant authority on these matters during the eighteenth century, delivers his opinion with due gravity:

> I lay it down as a principle, that a shield of one of the aforesaid tinctures only, without any figure, cannot be called a coat of arms, or an armorial bearing, no more than a red coat or a black hat, arms; and no more than a piece of virgin-wax can be called a seal, or a sheet of clean paper an evident, for two tinctures are absolutely necessary, at least, to form a coat of arms; and when two tinctures meet in one shield, (though there be no proper or natural figure), there appears a partition or terminating line, which makes a figure, however small; and is sufficient to make an armorial bearing.[12]

As the *Quarterly* reviewer intuited, tincture is democratic; anyone can wear a red coat or a black hat. Heraldry is dedicated to preserving the same by exercising its office of difference: identifying hereditary marks of distinction. The emergence of the figure identifies the person, act, and family by which one gets one's bearings in a world of undifferentiated color. Like the Coleridgean rook that crosses the sun in "This Lime-Tree Bower," the figure humanizes the grounding glare.

But that is to speak figuratively about what is not yet a figure in Nisbet's account: all that can be posited is the appearance of a partition, a dividing line, which is not the appearance of the identifiably human but the liminal emergence of distinction as the irreducible presence of class. The discovery of distinction is the *unum necessarium* that makes the aegis a design and, insofar as it carries over into the extraordinary privilege attributed to line over color, the privilege of those who can find themselves in the line. One of those so privileged by the partitive transformation of the crest into what Coleridge calls an "intelligible notion" is the herald. The line Nisbet posits literally performs the office of difference because the discovery of class, which coincides with the repression of color by line, makes a class — the official class of classifiers. And because the interest of the herald so neatly coincides with the principle of partition, it is impossible to imagine that line as *just* a line. Lines have no bearings unless they have an interest for the perceiver, and interest is colored indifference. The elemental fact of visibility repressed in the herald's account and revealed by Wordsworth's aegis is that line can only appear insofar as it is already tinctured.

At this stage we might conclude that Coleridge learned to revise *Descriptive Sketches*, devised the line he would follow as poet and critic, by hearkening back to an earlier Wordsworth poem and an earlier Wordsworthian crossing of the primary sun. But that genealogy does not yet explain the repression of *Evening Walk* in favor of *Descriptive Sketches*. By using "repression" I commit myself to showing that the blackness of the Coleridgean line is not merely the opposite of white (as, say, a rook crossed by blessing is the chiasmic opposite of an albatross killed by a crossbow) but that blackness is a "certain coloring of imagination."

April 1798. "Fears in Solitude":

> Oh! blasphemous! the Book of Life is made
> A superstitious instrument, on which
> We gabble o'er the oaths we mean to break;
> For all must swear — all and in every place,

College and wharf, council and justice-court;
All, all must swear, the briber and the bribed,
Merchant and lawyer, senator and priest,
The rich, the poor, the old man and the young;
All, all make up one scheme of perjury,
That faith doth reel; the very name of God
Sounds like a juggler's charm; and, bold with joy,
Forth from his dark and lonely hiding-place,
(Portentous sight!) the owlet Atheism,
Sailing on obscene wings athwart the noon
Drops his blue-fringed lids, and holds them close,
And hooting at the glorious sun in Heaven,
Cries out, 'Where is it?' (79–86)

Obviously, the owlet's flight metaphorizes the sophistry, hypocrisy, casuistry — call it professionalism — that is a Coleridgean target early and late. Eerily, the owlet's eye figures the Wordsworthian sun of *Evening Walk*. Obscenely, it displays that sun's primordially figurative status — the image's displacement of the natural, true sun from its proper place. The connection hangs on a certain coloring: the blue-fringed lid suspends the owlet's eye between the blue-barred sun of *Evening Walk* and the divinized, sutured orb that concludes "This Lime-Tree Bower." Wordsworth's "sun" has mockingly cut itself off from the source of light, fount of life and value. By its own eye inspired, the owlet does not see. The hooting blindness does not obliterate the referent, however; the owlet thwarts the sun by parodically duplicating it. This perversion empowers. The owlet goes where owlet has never gone before; it demonstrates what should not be shown: that difference can perform the "office" of sameness.

Why should Wordsworth's "sun" return here, in April 1798? Coleridge's subtitle invokes the climate of fear aroused by rumors of a planned French invasion. But he also writes in the fretful backwash of his acceptance of an annual subsidy of £150 from the Wedgwood brothers that has freed him from the "professional bias" of the ministry and enabled him to extend his "tether" to the Alfoxden home of the Wordsworths. The hysterical attack on those who, pressed between the injustice of the Test Act and the need to support their families, were less scrupulous than Coleridge could now afford to be, suggests that the gift has not brought him peace. Indeed, the only extant letter from April ignores the French; it treats with Joseph Cottle regarding the publication of Coleridge's and Wordsworth's tragedies and a collection of

Wordsworth's verse. Not only does the threat posed by the monstrous Bonaparte coincide with the prospect of greater intimacy with "The Giant Wordsworth," but it comes at a time when Coleridge was negotiating for a publication he had identified as an "evil" in a March letter to his conservative brother George. In that exculpatory letter (which begins with a paean to the convalescent powers of tincture of laudanum) Coleridge repudiates "the *filthy garments* of vice" (red shirts? black hats? tricolor ribbons?) worn by democrats in favor of the "decorous" habits of aristocrats and commits himself to a "long meditation" on the "quantity & the nature of the Evil," which he regarded as "the only means of preventing the passions from turning the Reason into an hired advocate."[13]

By April Coleridge's conversion has been ironically confirmed. He has turned from meditating "evil" to practicing it. A good portion of the Wedgwood annuity has been invested in tincture of laudanum. Saved from hired advocacy of the gospel, Coleridge has become an unpaid literary agent for Wordsworth. He has turned from preaching the gospel to publishing a poet who, without giving thought to money, raises gold like dew. The professional anxiety that erupts in "Fears in Solitude" reflects the anxiety of someone who has exchanged his position in the world for a coloring with no clear design: no profession, no bias at all. As the great metalepsis of Wordsworth's poetry, which originates in the moment the sun sets behind the horizon, projects no future, so the Wordsworthian aegis — unmerited, unaligned — designates no livery: the owlet's blue-fringed lid is the figure of the lack of context; it marks the ineradicable difference between Wordsworth and Coleridge, between poetic making and the practice of a literary career.

Practically speaking, atheism means that the conditions of profession repudiate the value of that which is professed, as the Wordsworthian effusion of gold wipes out the notion of wealth. Imagine you are a reader of Wordsworth — that reading Wordsworth is not only what you do but the way you define what your doing means. Imagine, that is, that you are Coleridge. *Evening Walk* presents you the problem: if gold falls in the forest and there is no one there to pocket it, is it wealth? Is it wealth or is it not mere difference in all its gaudily transitory gilding of the sameness of things? We are extricated from the conundrum because, in contrast to the pointed indifference of the shepherd in the scene, Coleridge was able to receive, pocket, and invest Wordsworth's gold, to convert genial sameness into wealth by throwing over it a coloring that would make it do the office of difference. Coleridge profited from Wordsworth's example by adopting the magic of his technique while repressing its atheistic and democratic provenance. By foregrounding the obliterative sun of *Descriptive Sketches* he refers Wordsworth to an origin and sets a task for himself to perform: to make Wordsworth's obscure genius visible.

Not blue, the color of office is black. Recall Hazlitt's account in "My First Acquaintance with Poets" of Coleridge's arrival by coach in Shrewsbury, in January of 1798, "to succeed Mr. Rowe in the spiritual charge of a Unitarian Congregation there." Mr. Rowe "could find no one at all answering [Coleridge's] description but a round-faced man in a short black coat (like a shooting jacket) which hardly seemed to have been made for him. . . . Mr. Rowe had scarce returned to give an account of his disappointment, when the round-faced man in black entered, and dissipated all doubts on the subject, by beginning to talk."[14] Graced by the Wedgwood subsidy, Coleridge had exchanged ministerial office for the role of a peripatetic philosopher. But even had Coleridge not versified the fearfulness of the solitude into which the fulfillment of his wishes delivered him, there is good evidence that the transfer from pastoral duties to cultivating arts and letters misfired. Coleridge did not change his clothes. He remarks on the significance of his clerical habit in his exuberant report to his wife of the response he excited in a group of boisterous Danes on the crossing to Hamburg in September of 1798: "My name among them was Docteur Teology — (i.e. Theology) — & dressed as I was all in black with large shoes and black worsted stockings, they very naturally supposed me to be a Priest. — I rectified their mistake — what then? said they — Simply I replied, *un Philosophe*." Later in the passage Coleridge feels obliged to dissipate the preconceptions that "*the continental sense* of the expression" *un Philosophe* conveyed to his companions. Not "simply" *un Philosophe* but a philosopher on the way to becoming a philosophical critic, Coleridge is executing an office of difference in a livery of his own device. Although Coleridge may appear an odd bird, poor Yorick, a philosopher without a system or a minister without portfolio, during the musical and linguistic "Bacchanals" on deck, he is performing his secret ministry of desynonymization while his actual portfolio, the seasick Wordsworth, is stowed safely below.

What is above decks is as telling as what is below, however. Coleridge's crossing becomes no less allegorically significant if one itemizes what the packet manifests: a ship from England with a group of drunken Danes presided over by an ambiguously philosophical character dressed in black who is en route to a university in Germany. Hamlet's "suits of woe" have become Coleridge's robe of office — an office which, Wordsworth notwithstanding, includes the export of Shake-speare, and particularly of *Hamlet*, to Germany. The merchant of Shakespeare travels light; he does not pack texts, he peddles a world-view by demonstrating how the world can uncannily be staged — that is, *lived* — according to a Shakespearean design. Coleridge conveys this symbolic freight to Germany, where he will exchange it for philos-ophy — which is exemplary in Germany not merely because it is tran-scendental but because it has the institutional support that Coleridge will pursue for his English hybrid, philosophical criticism.

There is, then, a continuity between Coleridge's project of critical tincture and the ideological discourse I defined earlier. Coleridge per-forms a double reading of Wordsworth: he derives his chrysopoietic technique from the true emblem of Wordsworth's genius, his native difference, in *Evening Walk;* but the transformation of that gold into wealth, of technique into capital, depends on the repression of both emblem and derivation in favor of a Wordsworth whose shine is always the same, though sometimes obscure — who needs Coleridge. Cole-ridge's profession of desynonymization, his transformation of chryso-poiesis into not only an intelligible notion but also an effective practice for him and for a new class of critics, depends on his ability to obliterate its referent, the blue-barred sun, and to make the color of *his* line imperceptible — that is, official, like the black ink on this page. Cannily, Coleridge employs the Wordsworthian sun from *Descriptive Sketches* to do the work of Revolutionary annihilation for him. Moreover, if it seems irresistible to say that the obliterated sun is the referent both for the glorious image from "This Lime-Tree Bower" and for Coleridge's critical profession, it is necessary to add that the blue-barred sun is first made a referent by that obliteration, which precisely annihilates the prima facie supplementarity that is the genius of the Wordsworthian image — its thoughtless expenditure. That annihilation coincides with the repression of the materiality of the image and the imagination: the divided bar breaks; but Coleridge blackly professes to "deem" and to "bless."

What Coleridge has done for himself in his time we can do for ourselves in ours: make Wordsworth work for us. In the remainder of this chapter I controvert some of the enabling pictorialist assumptions of Romantic New Historicism in order to indicate how the coloring imposed by Wordsworth's imagination may serve as an icon answer-able to the predicament that is alternatively termed the postmodern or the posthistorical. The fundamental issue, I take it, is whether Romantic poetry is dead to the world, immured in its time, or is yet potently, richly available for use.

The best New Historicist criticism on Wordsworth has been written by Alan Liu. His early essay, "Shapeless Eagerness," which later became the capstone to his book *Wordsworth and the Sense of History*, provides a salient example of the pictorialism of that school, a pictorialism that I contrast with a dehistoricizing, formal quality of the Wordsworthian imagination — its color — which Coleridge perceived and effectively applied to ends he designed. Liu analyzes the tension between what he calls Wordsworth's "enactive" and "epitaphic" poetry in the "Revolution" books of the 1805 *Prelude*. As he explains it, "the bulk of Books 9–10 is enactive because Wordsworth engages the reader in his younger self's perpetual confusion about the *kind* of thing the Revolution is and the kind of language appropriate to describe it." He argues that "such shapelessness — really an excess of shapes — reduces the distance between the reader and the 'I' on the page." Liu contrasts an enactive episode with a stabilizing, "memorial" moment, which "really records the poet in the act of mourning for — and simultaneously celebrating — the death of his revolutionary self."[15] For Liu the moral of the story is the inadequacy of any derivative genre to frame the historical event of the Revolution. In his recourse to the epitaph Wordsworth denies history by depositing it in the past.

Liu measures the young Wordsworth's passage through the field of Revolutionary history according to a series of rapid shifts from one "generic frame" — the travel narrative, the romance, the drama, the Miltonic epic — to another. Each frame collapses because it fails to grasp the singularity of Revolutionary time, what Liu calls its "sublimity." Revolutionary sublimity names a fundamentally pictorial experience that the young Wordsworth inevitably and inexorably misread. Liu graphically illustrates the poet's error when he corrects Wordsworth's reading of Le Brun's painting *The Repentant Magdalene*. Liu's own reading has no more than a contingent relation to Wordsworth's text, which neither proposes aesthetic judgment nor attempts extended ekphrasis. Wordsworth simply says that other objects "Seem'd less to recompense the Traveller's pains / Less mov'd me, gave me less delight than did, / Among other sights, the Magdalen of Le Brun, A Beauty exquisitely wrought, fair face / and rueful with its ever-flowing tears" (9:75–79). By a remarkable feat of the historicist imagination, Liu anchors his scenario not in what Wordsworth wrote but on what he *probably* saw during his visit. Liu novelistically situates Wordsworth in the chapel where the painting was displayed, ascribes to him a response governed by the aesthetic of the beautiful, and fancies his attitude before the painting as an imitation of a sculptural surrogate—all that to show that the painting was misread because "in fact, Le Brun's painting depicts beauty, not in the aspect of sentimental sorrow, but in the act of being emotionally ravished or violently transported" (Liu, 11).

What the painting depicts "in fact" turns out to be what it depicts according to the theory of Edmund Burke: "In Burke's terms, what the young Wordsworth has difficulty seeing is that *The Repentant Magdalene* really illustrates not so much beauty as the rape of beauty by the *sublime*." Liu draws this conclusion: "Just as the young traveler misreads Le Brun's painting, so *The Prelude* shows him misjudging the over-all type of pictorial experience political France offers" (13). The "fact" of Le Brun matches the "fact" of the Revolution. According to Liu, what Wordsworth "wants" to see is a Revolutionary country in which liberation arrives. . . . "With the soft, fluid undulations of a necklace spilling from a box." What *Liu* wants to see is "jewels, Magdalen, and light . . . being liberated not by gentleness but by cataclysmic, 'masculine' revolution"—in short, the Revolution as sublime (10). Liu's proof of Wordsworth's error depends on evidence from Burke, from Reynolds, from Richard Wilson's *Destruction of Niobe's Children*, and from popular belief that the Le Brun painting "was a masked portrait of Louise de la Valliere"—evidence that, by overdetermining figural representation, violates the frame of aesthetic contemplation with a sublime force that is virtually history itself. The Le Brun image, then, functions for Liu as the conspectus of a world picture, which in its sublimity displays and activates the Revolutionary event that Wordsworth misapprehends. It is crucially the case that even if the painting's formal design is overridden by an unframable event, in the last, sublime analysis, the painting remains a picture that can be read wrongly and read rightly. Ultimately for Liu and for Romantic New Historicism, what is unframable can only be grasped in terms of a picture itself framed and framing.[16]

In Liu's critical narrative the poem comes upon the epitaphic as accidentally as the youthful Wordsworth (in the rendering of the older poet) came upon the discharged soldier—himself an uncanny representation of the epitaphic. The refusal to credit the poet with a purpose answers to Liu's appetite for poetic failure. He wants a poem to be completely subject to a history that it thoroughly denies.[17] Liu's zeal to prove failure curiously highlights his own programmatic failure to identify exactly who the poet is, to distinguish between the remembered

and the writing Wordsworth. The latter makes his shadowy appearances, surely, but as something more like the projection of the critic/
reader than as the deliberate agent of those poetic effects that the critic
abstracts from the "flow" of the two books. Note the convergence of
the writer and represented reader in the following critical account of
the depiction of 1794 Wordsworth standing over the grave of his former teacher William Taylor:

> Reading the stone, the 1794 Wordsworth then recalls Taylor's
> own self-epitaphic words, "my head will soon lie low," and goes
> on in turn to spin what is really an epitaph for himself. If Taylor
> were now alive, he says, he would have loved him. . . . It is the na-
> ture of the self-epitaph to trigger a further stage of self-epitaphic
> consciousness in the reader standing over the tombstone. Such
> self-consciousness seals off enactive history, causing a sudden shift
> of perspective by which a self caught up in the deluge of event can
> see itself in the past tense. . . . Epitaphic history creates such a sen-
> sation of finish that even the present becomes *as if* past. (Liu, 25)

"Recalls," "goes on," "what is really," "he says" — in Liu's analysis the
past becomes *as if* present as a result of the substitution of the present
tense for the past tense that in 1805 Wordsworth himself employed to
represent his younger (1794) self. In the very act of defining epitaphic
history, Liu demonstrates that it is as fully enactive as those episodes
from which he aims to distinguish it, for the substitution of present for
past tense correlates with the supplanting of the writing poet by the
analyzing critic. It is tempting to ally the epitaphic with the posthistorical; but because there is in fact nothing more than a *generic* distinction
between enactive and epitaphic in a poem where those traditional literary sovereignties called genres cannot hold, the concept of the posthistorical must apply to the whole process if it applies at all.

   If something we could call the posthistorical emerges as the result of
what Liu calls Wordsworth's denial, Liu finds something like postmodernism forced upon him by the inadequacy of Wordsworth's apparatus
of representation. "Apparatus" is apt, for there is a sense of being
before the technology in the Wordsworth of the Revolution books. Far
from denying history, Wordsworth celebrates the obstinate resistance
of the events in which he lived, moved, and had his being to the current
apparatus of representation, and not simply the street theater of London or the picture by Le Brun, but also books: "Oh, laughter for the
page that would reflect / To future times the face of what now is!"

(9:176–77) Although Liu ignores such affirmations by the poet (in this case quoting his former self), his account does inadvertently adumbrate a model of technological lag by suggesting that the reader of Books 9 and 10 experiences the movement from generic frame to generic frame as a kind of montage. "Experiences" rather than "sees" because the cinematic apparatus that might have made this montage visually patent and thus have rendered interpretation superfluous was of course unavailable to Wordsworth. When Wordsworth says of his youthful self, "I looked for something which I could not find" (9:70), "something" refers to many things, and one of them is a motion picture camera.

That Wordsworth did not explicitly say, "I need a movie camera," does not mean he was in a state of denial. Indeed, the inability to represent one's own situation accurately, which Wordsworth expressly affirms, has been credited as a distinctively authenticating predicament by Fredric Jameson:

> Yet this mesmerizing new aesthetic mode itself emerged as an elaborated symptom of the waning of our historicity, of our lived possibility of experiencing history in some active way. It cannot therefore be said to produce this strange occultation of the present by its own formal powers but rather merely to demonstrate, through these inner contradictions, the enormity of a situation in which we seem increasingly incapable of fashioning representations of our own current experience.[18]

For Jameson the incapacity to fashion representations of one's current experience does not involve a denial of history but is rather the poignant, even authentic, registration of one's own historical position. I think it is fair to consider Liu's sublime Revolution as a "mesmerizing new aesthetic mode," fair too to substitute "framing" for "fashioning." Such fair trade practices deliver us to a formulation that makes Wordsworth (albeit an English Wordsworth traveling through an alien France rather than a Marxist academic spinning through a global market) our contemporary—if by contemporary we mean a fellow traveler in the peculiar space-time of what Jameson calls postmodernity, a time in part defined by an acute, Wordsworthian intuition of the incapacity of our apparatus of representation, not marked by a Coleridgean remorse over our will to represent.

Insofar as it positions him in some uncertain way as herald of our posthistorical predicament, Wordsworth's failure to represent adequately his own lived experience ought to be credited as a foresight, not stigmatized as a failure. If we believe this, it is because Wordsworth appears to have known it. He chose to represent a painting as a depiction of Revolutionary turmoil, accepting the condition that it would be misread—not only by the younger Wordsworth but also by anyone whose notion of a picture has been tinctured by earlier passages in the poem, such as the apparition of Venus in Book 4 or the Drowned Man passage of Book 5 or the entire carnival of images in Book 6. What makes Wordsworth Wordsworth is that he invites misreading rather than suffers from it, invites it in the Romantic hope that no one will suffer from the correction that a proper reading, Jacobin or Royalist, deconstructionist or New Historicist, imposes. Liu, not unsettled by the precedents of pictorial inadequacy in the poem, by Wordsworth's radical interrogation of the ontology of the image, the potency of color, and the vitality of forms, or, finally, by the poet's relentless worrying of the intricacy of framing, joining, wrighting, dismantling, and knotting in his world, took Wordsworth up on his invitation but, unfortunately, did so in the name of correction rather than the spirit of revision.

I have called Liu's essay exemplary not only because it concludes his volume *Wordsworth and the Sense of History,* by all odds the best book on Wordsworth in the last twenty-five years, but also because it represents a genre of essays in Romantic criticism that has been labeled Romantic New Historicism. Such influential essays as David Simpson's "Poor Susan" and Marjorie Levinson's "Insight and Oversight" work variations on Liu's pictorialist model.[19] Each presupposes some kind of picture, whether of London or of the Wye Valley, which Wordsworth inevitably misreads. In Simpson's case the picture is all but available for inspection. His version of the prostitute-infested London that Wordsworth denies in his account of Susan is manifestly derived from a print in Hogarth's *The Harlot's Progress.* Levinson has no such clearcut model—perhaps because the contemporary artists who depicted the Wye valley were as eager as Wordsworth to erase the marks of labor and misery from their vistas, or perhaps because her emphasis on the particular date as well as the particular place demands the imagination of something like a photograph of the scene that Wordsworth actually saw. Both versions of the pictorial reflect a naive version of historical understanding; and both are owed to the outmoded camera obscura model of ideology that Jerome McGann with unlucky influence revived in *The Romantic Ideology.* What makes the methodology naive is not only its epistemic superficiality but also its aesthetic primitivism: its reduction of the historical field into a picture of what truly is out there.

Liu's essay also lays claim to exemplarity because it performs an abstraction that torques historicism to the limits of its spatialization of the past. Liu attempts to compensate for Wordsworth's enactive flow by supplying the apparatus of a diagram that gives a visual intelligibility to the dynamics of the Wordsworthian text.

Genre	Paradigm Shift within Genre
Travel poem	Beautiful → Sublime
Romance	Chivalric → Gothic
Drama	Comic → Tragic
Miltonic Epic	Millennial → Hellish

"Each generic frame," Liu comments, "produces the same inadequate split-image of the Revolution." (Liu, 21). Liu's diagram aims to mediate between the enactive in his essay (the reproduction of the Le Brun painting) and his epitaphic verdict of "denial." The diagram's integration of stable categories, such as "genre" and "paradigm shift within genres," with arrows signifying movement exactly displays that mediatory ambition. Liu's diagram aspires to perform the function that, in Fredric Jameson's account, is, or perhaps was, the work of genre itself. In *The Political Unconscious* Jameson observes that "the strategic value of generic concepts for Marxism clearly lies in the mediatory function of the notion of genre, which allows the coordination of immanent formal analysis of the individual text with the twin diachronic perspective of the history of forms and the evolution of social life."[20] Liu's diagram aims to effect a mediation also, although the terms are different: it mediates between the occult or confused poetic text and a more accurate representation of experience that the poet was incapable of rendering. Epic may not be able to comprehend Revolution, but the diagram can comprehend Books 9–10 of *The Prelude* by memorializing the enactive and enacting the memorial.

The best account of the way an epitaphic moment can itself be "enactive" while still remaining distinctively "epitaphic," that is, a moment of commemorative reading, occurs in the final chapter of Neil Hertz's *End of the Line*, which, unlike Liu's work, highlights the distinction between seeing and reading. Hertz takes as his template the relation of Courbet and viewer to a painting in which a depicted surrogate hovers before a cavern where black rock passes imperceptibly into black water; he applies that template to the conclusion of the epitaphic Boy of Winander passage from Book 5 of *The Prelude*, "where the transfer of natural sounds and sights 'far into [the Boy's] heart' or 'unawares into his mind' is repeated in a gently animated vector within the scene itself, when 'that uncertain Heaven' is 'receiv'd / Into the bosom of the steady Lake.' If," Hertz adds, "we assimilate the poem to our diagram, it looks like this:

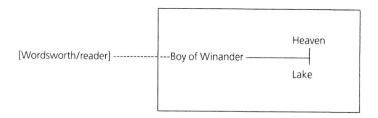

Hertz's diagram might be described as the supplement to Liu's: a kind of blowup of the epitaphic moment that follows upon and subtends the enactive progress that Liu charts.[21] Both attempt to introduce a dynamism into their diagrams: Liu by his arrows, Hertz by his dotted line. Whereas Liu understands the generic frames breaking temporally, and, indeed, regards their breaking as the narrative of Books 9 and 10, Hertz's dynamism inheres in a spatial breaking of the frame that accounts, as Liu does not, for the relation between the observing Wordsworth (here the same as the poet) and a younger, surrogate self. Of course, the supplementation of Liu by Hertz is temporal — according to the order of publication. Yet the moment that Hertz diagrams occurs some four books before the episodes that Liu analyses. It seems fair to say that a critical vision armed with Hertz's diagram might be very cautious about supplying diagrams that one can take in at a glance, in light of all the evidence that, for Wordsworth, any seeing is going to be a reading and any reading is as such a misreading, insofar as reading, unlike just plain seeing, will be duplicitous — a site of distinctions vanishing into mere difference.

Another way to put this is that Hertz acknowledges that the poem is written — a text, not a picture. Even though the text can be diagramed, the visual scheme is the contribution of the critic, not the poet. That the historicist Liu intends his diagram to be seen, whereas the poststructuralist Hertz requires that his be read, is not an incidental difference. Poststructuralist diagrams attempt to tranquilize the power of the visual while exploiting it; such diagrams are pictures of the limitations of pictures — meant to represent a process that a picture cannot. The difference in the cognitive orientation of Liu's and Hertz's diagrams reflects a fundamental divide between the theoretical allegiances of the two critics, one which Fredric Jameson incisively distinguished in *Postmodernism* as contrasting views of the historical status of the decentered subject. There is, writes Jameson, "the historicist one, that a once-existing centered subject, in the period of classical capitalism and the nuclear family, has today in the world of organizational bureaucracy dissolved; and the more radical poststructuralist position, for which such a subject never existed in the first place." Jameson adds, "I obviously incline toward the former" (*Postmodernism*, 15); indeed, it is part of his project to show the mutual implication of a historicist conception of the decentering of the subject and a *coupure* between modernism and postmodernism. But he does not condemn the alternative view. As Jameson knows, the latter view, Hertz's perspective, is not unhistorical, just nonhistoricist. Poststructuralism reads its own historical emergence in relation to a structuralism defined as both a temporally precedent theoretical posture and a timeless metaphysical paradigm. As the tone of his remarks suggests, Jameson finds it difficult to call such a position wrong. Rather, he prefers the historicist account because it gives him an opportunity to construct a critical narrative that will induce belief and perhaps entail some kind of activity, if only more criticism practiced in the same fashion as his own.

Throughout his career Jameson has been one of the most prodigious diagramers in the profession. His recourse to preference is symptomatic of a shift in his work from a confident modernism undergirded by a Marxist politics to a chastened postmodernism sustained by a probational ethics. That difference can be clearly indicated by the difference between diagrams in *The Political Unconscious* and *Postmodernism*. The favored diagram for Jameson is the structuralist *combinatoire*, which he deploys in the superb "Magical Narratives" chapter of *The Political Unconscious* as a device to integrate what he calls the three variables of the manifest text, the deep structure, and "history itself, as an absent cause." The "permutational scheme" that he devises looks like this:

FORM
    expression: the narrative structure of a genre

    content: the semantic "meaning" of a generic mode

SUBSTANCE
    expression: ideologemes, narrative paradigms

    content: social and historical raw material

After Jameson discusses the permutations, he concludes: "Thus, the *combinatoire* aims not at enumerating the 'causes' of a given text or form, but rather mapping out its objective, a priori conditions of possibility" (148).

In *Postmodernism* the *combinatoire* also makes its appearance, but no longer under the sign of objectivity. Indeed, it is after an analysis of Warhol in the context of some "fundamental mutation both in the object world itself—now become a set of texts or simulacra—and in the disposition of the subject" that he addresses what he calls "the waning of affect in postmodern culture" by way of a set of observations on Remo Ceserani's "fourfold image" of foot fetishism involving Van Gogh, Walker Evans and James Agee, Warhol, and Magritte. "Ironically" congratulating the critic, Jameson proffers that "Cesarani thereby deserves a semiotic cube of his own:

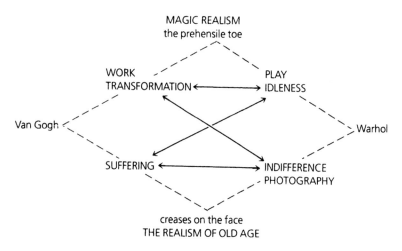

The diagram (*Postmodernism*, 10) is followed by no commentary, just a series of color plates depicting shoes and various edifices. Marxist objectivity has waned into irony. Dialectic has collapsed from an ideal objective science of history into an "impossible" Marxist discipline. Jameson justifies dialectical thinking as a bulwark against moralizing but clings to that justification with a suspiciously Arnoldian faith. The diagram, no longer capable of mediating between text and a utopian representation, has been absorbed into the gallery of postmodern figures.[22] No longer does the *combinatoire* claim to enact permutations; it depicts "a fundamental mutation," but even that depiction has no epitaphic force: Jameson's irony keenly registers the incapacity of writing an epitaph for a culture that has no kind and that shows no sign of halting its purposeless transformations—as if it were an endless romance, that is, a story whose supreme function is imaginatively and relentlessly to figure its incapacity to represent its own identity and its conclusion. When we look back to the notion of history as "absent cause," which Jameson advanced so powerfully in *Political Unconscious*, we can surmise that the insight was not a theoretical observation about the epistemic or ontological status of history as an occulted phenomenon but an early symptom of the decisive end of history, as yet unformed and unperceived.

Less dramatically, the Liu and Hertz diagrams also depict an ongoing postmodern event that might be called the dissolution of genre, considered as the mediation of individual texts with history. Consider that dissolution as a lateral process: Liu does not, cannot, identify the exact point where the object "epic" transforms into the object "romance"—the moment, that is, when the uncertain epic is received into the bosom of the steady romance. In *The Prelude* we can almost see the movement from frame to frame, but only as an optical effect, one dissolve after another, slow enough to look like what Liu calls a "split image." As I have suggested, the unrecognized ground for Liu's narrative "flow" is something like the cinema, a slow cinema—not 24 frames per second, and slower even than the silent speed of 16–18 frames per second. To diagram the cinema requires a technology that no page can mount. Our incapacity is exactly fitted to our historical predicament. After CAD, diagrams can no longer be claimed to be permutational mediations; they represent themselves as primitive technologies, the signs of a technology that will *realize*—perhaps with a mouse click— what the diagram can barely map.

The title of Liu's original essay was "Shapeless Eagerness"—a Wordsworthian phrase that he oddly deforms by ascribing "shapeless" to the objects and events that Wordsworth perceives rather than to the peculiarly inchoate affectivity of the touring youth. That transferral of agency from Wordsworth to the world of the Revolution coincides with a programmatic refusal by Liu to give the poet any credit for a nonpictorial agency that might not only anticipate Liu's own but might even advance beyond it into another region altogether. I return to the totemic phrase: "I looked for something which I could not find." One thing the young Wordsworth may have looked for is an object apposite for a shapeless eagerness, something like an uframable picture. But why conjecture? Wordsworth is quite specific in a passage, partially quoted by Liu, that overrides if not erases the Le Brun set piece:

I crossed (a black and empty area then)
The Square of the Carrousel, few weeks back
Heap'd up with dead and dying, upon these
And other sights looking as doth a man
Upon a volume whose contents he knows
Are memorable, but from him lock'd up
  (Prelude 10:46–51)

A black and empty area. A square. Framed or unframed? There are no black squares in nature. The black area is not a canvas, and though not exactly a picture, one could imagine saying, "this is not a picture, though uncannily *like* one." If the black area is like any picture, that picture would certainly not be the painting by Le Brun, which is figural, stationed in a chapel, and solicits an attitude on the part of a spectator. If like a picture, the black square can only be likened to pictures that Wordsworth could not possibly have known.[23]

With an eye to chronology we might pair it with what Arthur Danto calls "the first serious monochrome painting" of the twentieth century, *Black Square,* painted by Kazimir Malevich and exhibited in Petrograd from December 1915 to January 1916. Danto recounts that because it was "hung diagonally in a corner of a room and near the ceiling in the traditional position of the Russian icon, the association with death was irresistible to critics, one of whom wrote, 'The corpse of the Art of Painting, the art of nature with make-up added has been placed in its coffin and marked with the Black Square.' " Danto notes that Malevich disagreed with the funereal reading: "He saw it really as an erasure, an emblem of a wiping out of the art of the past, and hence of a break in the narrative of art. At one point he compares it with the Biblical flood."[24] In Malevich's account the aim of *Black Square* epitomizes the high Romantic aims often and accurately attributed to *The Prelude.* Danto's account of the semiotic status of *Black Square*'s exhibition has something to say about the status of Wordsworth's black square: placed athwart his revolutionary progress, it appears as an icon — neither simply a black square nor merely the representation of a black square — a sign with autonomous status and unexhausted significance.

To regard *The Prelude*'s black square as *like* a picture is to regard it as an impossible likeness, like something that is yet to be, something that cannot come to be except in the slow labor of a historical narrative with which this square has nothing to do. To put it in another way, the black square is a species of public art which has nothing to with the vast, populated spectacles strategically mounted by the Jacobins. The public for the black square did not yet exist in 1805 or in 1850. The public for the black square is not a historical public at all. Rather, the square can only be apprehended as the species of art it is by a post-historical public — here and now.

What I have called the impossibility of this picture is corroborated by the given name of the black area: "The Square of the Carrousel" — a real place but an impossible figure. The squared circle both suggests an unachievable ideal of completion (here ironized as the logical stoppage of the revolving or spinning mechanism by which Wordsworth has metaphorized Revolutionary terror) and specifies a figure impossible to depict and therefore to see. For that which Wordsworth calls a "sight" is strictly the metaphorical "volume" that seals his passage off from the remainder of Book 9. He does not claim to have "sighted" the square, only to have "crossed" it. Crossings, of course, are frequent and fraught movements in the poetry of Wordsworth and Coleridge, as we have seen earlier in our analysis of "This Lime-Tree Bower" and *Evening Walk*. We might add the skyey crossing of the Albatross and numerous others, most images of intensely illuminated legibility: a blue bar or black line crossing the sun. Such lines make legible a willful, sinful, or criminal inscription of the human on the natural or divine source of revelation, the primary act of imagination.

The multiple crossings of *The Prelude* are generally of a different order because they have a contingent relation to the system of the visible, whether we consider the declaration "We had crossed the Alps," the chance crossing of one of those open fields, which, "shaped like ears / Make green peninsulas on Esthwaite's Lake" (5.457–58), or Wordsworth's recollection of his recollection while making his crossing "over the smooth sands / Of Leven's ample estuary" of those pilgrims "Who crossed the sands with ebb of morning tide" (10.514–15; 522). This crossing of the black square in Book 9 eclipses the register of the visible altogether by rendering iconic the unrepresentability of the historical moment when it appears. No light glimmers on the streets of Paris. No one would know that the crossing had occurred had not Wordsworth reported it, and the reporting does not render the crossing visible. The reporting renders it iconic, the establishment of a sign that stands apart from the registers of the referential and the strictly formal. By calling the crossing of the black square iconic, I mean to insist on its status as a device rather than a representation and to invoke the one meaning of *square* that requires a crossing in order to complete its meaning. In heraldry, *square* denotes that a shield is divided by a line "in the form of a carpenter's square." That this iconic signification was, according to the *OED*, obsolete long before the writing of *The Prelude*, fortifies rather than diminishes our sense of its operation here, where the device invoked is a device unseen. Indeed, the obsolescence of the heraldic denotation both deepens the sense of a world erased and enriches the sense of anachronism by which the black square solicits the attention of the posthistorical reader, for whom, armed with the *OED*, no time or space is alien.

In the posthistorical deficit of the power of adequate self-representation, the anachronism finds its sign in the icon. What we read, then, is Wordsworth going back, recrossing a place in his past that he has already crossed in order to interpellate a future with an icon that cannot be stipulated as historically enactive or stigmatized as ahistorically epitaphic. An icon is not a phallus. Constitutive of the difference is the pathetic image of the "blighted" royalist, whose face "expressed, / As much as any that was ever seen, / A ravage out of season." The poet recalls how this man, "disarmed" of voice, shaken by fever, would read the public news, and "while he read, / Or mused, his sword was haunted by his touch / Continually, like an uneasy place / In his own body" (9.150–64). The royalist hauntingly touches his sword, in a search for something he cannot find, a corporeal absence visited on him by a history that he cannot reverse. Phallic because the royalist has become less than a man, his sword is less than a weapon, little more than a sign of castration. That little more counts the way history counts: for castration here is also a decisive obsolescence. What the royalist looks for he will never find. But for Wordsworth obsolescence is neither death nor castration; obsolescence simply means the available technology is inadequate to our imagination. Looking for something that one cannot find is looking for something in the future. And it is so: an anachronism, this uncanny passage speaks to us in a way it could not possibly have spoken to its contemporaries. The crossing of the square could and cannot be diagramed: whether one were to choose a dotted line or an arrow, the crossing, which did occur, could not be represented as having *had* occurred. The evidence of Wordsworth's return to the past, a planned obsolescence, urgently solicits an attention that could not have been provoked earlier and which gives us (nothing but) hope in the project of literary history and criticism as a practice of something more than academic interest.

That project may be evoked by juxtaposing Wordsworth's parenthesis "(a black and empty area then)" with Jameson's parenthesis on Romanticism. After canvassing the two primary accounts of the decentered subject, Jameson adds, "(I must here omit yet another series of debates, largely academic, in which the very continuity of modernism as it is here reaffirmed is itself called into question by some vaster sense of the profound continuity of romanticism, from the late eighteenth century on, of which both the modern and the postmodern will be seen as organic stages)" (*Postmodernism*, 59). The point of juxtaposing those parentheses, one framing an emptiness, one an omission, is to urge that speaking the "profound continuity of romanticism" is an indirect way of acknowledging the uncanny continuity of Romanticism as motivated by Wordsworth. As Jameson's parenthesis indicates, under the sign of postmodernism the "continuity" of romanticism/romance is a symptom of the breakdown of the dialectic that the postmodern accomplishes; indeed, the insistence of Romanticism makes it look as though that dialectic was not itself a modernist break with a past that it overcame but a parenthesis in a long story of troubles through which we are still making our way. For the Jameson of the modernist *Political Unconscious*, Romance was a genre appropriate to an archaic time of troubles and of shadowy border disputes. But in a postmodern environment, where there has been a general shift from questions of generic identity (whether of race, class, or gender) to questions of property rights, the world that we face looks like nothing but a tissue of crossings over borders constituted by corporate edict and thinly patrolled by the minions of the state.

Although Jameson has recourse to the conception of organic stages (as if anyone holds that view of Romanticism), an easier explanation for the profound continuity of Romanticism presents itself in his poignant account of the "most authentic vocation of romance in our time," which is the undertaking of "the last unrecognizable avatars of romance as a mode, [to] draw their magical power from an unsentimental loyalty to those henceforth abandoned clearings across which higher and lower worlds once passed" (*Political Unconscious*, 135). Jameson's parenthesis speaks to the fact that those clearings have not been abandoned, that, indeed, Romanticism is just such a clearing—a black square—where crossings occur, albeit not the passings of higher and lower worlds but the passings of the past that was and the future that could be. For Wordsworth, and *a fortiori* for Romanticism, the future is in the past and the past in the future; the posthistorical is in the modern and the modern in the posthistorical. Precision of terms is less important than the iconic gravity of the scheme that configures them and exhorts us to hopeful memory and memorable hope. That scheme, fully rhetorical, is the chiasmus, Coleridge's favorite trope and the one that I would apply to Wordsworth's dark icon in order to illuminate it for use. In Coleridge's hands, the chiasmus, a figure in which "extremes meet," once looked like a primitive form of the dialectic, but—now that the dialectic has itself been disarmed and has become a sword that one touches as if an uneasy place in one's body—looks like the form that dialectical hope must take in a posthistorical time.

There is no way to diagram the double crossing of the square of the Carrousel without bleaching it of its blackness. Yet as a pure rhetorical scheme, the chiasmus "the modern is in the postmodern, the postmodern in the modern" can be diagramed:

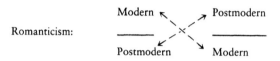

It is not clear what illumination on the chiasmus the diagram actually supplies, for the scheme is built into the figure, which is kind *as* crossing. The chiasmus is the icon of transition as such—the placeholder for a place yet to be attained. As icon, the chiasmus does not demonstrate the objective conditions by which crossings inevitably occur. It is an inducement for you to perform the crossing it schemes. If you choose. For what goes unsaid by the diagramers is the ethical option that rhetoric invariably presents. You can always stop reading.

Chapter Three

Ecce Homo
The End of the French Revolution
and the Romantic Reinvention of English Verse

> Oedipus' answer to the Sphinx's riddle: "It is a man!" is the Enlightenment
> stereotype repeatedly offered as information, irrespective of whether it is
> faced with a piece of objective intelligence, a bare schematization, fear of
> evil powers, or hope of redemption.
> — Max Horkheimer and Theodor Adorno, *The Dialectic of Enlightenment*

> The old fascination with biography, given new impetus by an
> autobiographical complacency (*Ecce Homo* underwriting Nietzsche's
> "madness"), and the old mechanism of exemplarity that was naively
> thought to be inoperative and out of use like the old myths, continue to
> function. The desire for "figurality" has never been more powerful or more
> constraining, thus forcing us — and this is the least of its consequences — to
> return once more to philosophy and to its history, to the "score" and
> scansion imposed upon it by those who thought they had passed
> beyond . . . the limits of the historical and systematic field in which the
> subject held authority.
> — Philippe Lacoue-Labarthe, "The Echo of the Subject"

The prevailing mood of the "posthistorical" among philosophers of art
and historians of social formations looks all too familiar to the student
of culture at the close of the eighteenth century. The contemporary
mentality of aftermath echoes the reassuring conviction among liberals
and conservatives alike in the late 1790s of being safely postrevolutionary. That connection has been no more explicitly spelled out than in the
historiography surrounding the bicentenary of the French Revolution
and argued with no greater sophistication and force than by François
Furet, who, focusing on the historical by casting one eye on yesterday
and another on today, resonantly proclaimed that "the Revolution
is over."

Furet could venture such a bold proclamation by virtue of adopting
what he calls a "conceptual" relation to the relevant historical material,

enabling him to break with those historiographic practices that reproduce the experience of the French Revolution by rendering it as a
spectacle that compels political identification: left or right. By rehabili-
tating the historiography of Alexis de Tocqueville and Auguste Cochin,
Furet constructed a two-track interpretive model that situated the
French Revolution within a continuous political development while
giving full credit to its explosive character — the latter interpreted as the
consequence of Rousseau's invention of a democratic ideology that
invested sovereignty and power in the undivided will of the "people."[1]
Furet elaborated Cochin's view that "the 'people' was a mental representation of power generated by the discourse of philosophical societies
that became political agents as they vied for the right to speak in its
name." From the advent of the Revolution, this representation was kept
in continual agitation by real and supposed aristocratic threats and
propelled by rivalry among factions for the "right to be the image of the
people" (Furet, 74). Robespierre won the competition; and, as "the
final incarnation of that mythical identity," he suffered his scripted fate
by becoming "the scapegoat of the guillotine" (57). This sacrificial embodiment of the people consummated the volatile revolutionary fusion
of "political power and civil society." Thus, according to Furet, the
revolution was over.

Furet's "'story' of the Revolution," his account of it as "a specific
dynamic of collective action," stands in relation to the account of the
"historical process," the "set of causes and effects" in which the Revolution occurs, much as the practice of biography, which focuses on the
contingent life course of an individual agent, stands in relation to a
historiography that "sees the past as a field of possibilities within which
'what actually happened' appears ex post facto as the only future for
that past" (18–19). Furet's brilliant twist is to identify this latter "historical consciousness" as "revolutionary consciousness," a move that
allows him to tell the story of the Revolution as the collective subordination of manifold, contingent individual life courses to the idea of
an inevitable historical event, which is imagined as a massive effect
that answers to a single, overpowering cause. We may conclude, then,
that the biography of the Revolution is the story of the supersession
of biography by typology — which is one way of explaining why it
has always appeared so short-lived. Extending Furet, we might suppose that the end of the Revolution, considered not as a conceptual
break occurring within the terrain of French historiography but as a
moment of change executed by Englishmen whose history had been

bound up with the course of the Revolution, might begin with the renewal of biography.

Furet's claim that the Revolution is over had its harbingers — most famously Napoleon Bonaparte, who repeatedly proclaimed the end of the Revolution. Earlier yet, however, there was Coleridge, writing to William Wordsworth on the eve of the Brumaire coup d'état: "I wish you would write a poem in blank verse, addressed to those who, in consequence of the complete failure of the French Revolution, have thrown up all hopes of the amelioration of mankind, and are sinking into an almost epicurean selfishness."[2] Coleridge's notion of a break with revolutionary discourse has, I argue, as much to do with Words-worth's blank verse as with his elevating theme. For Coleridge, that is, the end of the Revolution will occur not only at the level of the concept but, more immediately, at the level of form — form radicalized to its elemental, sensuous insistence. To explain what he had in mind, Cole-ridge required, as we do, a biographical inventiveness. As we shall see, the vindication of Romantic hope demanded that the spectacular ap-pearance of revolutionary man be answered by the imagination of a new poetical character.

If Coleridge can be said to have anticipated the concerns of Furet, it should be noted that Coleridge's own sense of biographical possibility was formed in response to the fierce precedent of Edmund Burke, who transformed both the English grammar for the formation of political statements and the code for recognizing a "new description of men."[3] Cochin's interpretation of the Revolution is visible in embryonic form in Burke's remarkable observation of September 1789 that "it does not appear to me, that the National assembly have one Jot more power than the King; whilst they lead or follow the popular voice . . . I very much question, whether they are in a condition to exercise any function of decided authority — or even whether they are possessed of any real deliberative capacity. . . as [long as] there is a Mob of their constituents ready to Hang them if They should . . . in the least depart from the Spirit of those they represent."[4] Not only the concepts that drive the Revolu-tion but also its whole life story are immediately visible to Burke's speculative eye. From the outset he sees Rousseau's theory being en-acted: he sees the emptying of the sphere of power; he sees the ignition of the engine of the "popular voice." And, earlier than Robespierre, he foresees the Revolution's destiny. "All these things have happend [sic] out of the ordinary Course of speculations," he writes. "One man may change all. But when and where and how is this man to appear?"

(*CEB*, 6:37). Burke's forecast of the return from the extraordinary to the ordinary through the agency of the coming man who will redeem the time is the first sounding of the *Ecce Homo* theme in English revolutionary discourse.

Burke could visualize the shape of the Revolution because he figured it as theater. August 1789: "As to us here our thoughts of everything at home are suspended, by our astonishment at the wonderful Spectacle which is exhibited in a Neighbouring and rival Country — what Spectators, and what Actors! England gazing with astonishment at a French struggle for Liberty and not knowing whether to blame or to applaud!" (*CEB*, 6:10). The sublime suspension of the English spectators' thought matches the interdiction of deliberation in the revolutionized National Assembly.[5] Each attests to the crucial revolutionary proscription of thinking in favor of speaking. The spectators' astonishment will, of course, soon be followed by "reflections." But reflection is not exactly thinking; it is not the kind of deliberation that goes on among duly elected representatives in Parliament, for example. Reflecting is the strategic equivalent of parliamentary deliberation; it is an imitation of thinking, generated by and answerable to the spectacle of the Revolution. For Burke the reflections of the spectator presuppose his leap across the footlights to become an actor himself.[6] If, as Furet writes, the "logic of revolutionary consciousness . . . by its very nature, tends to promote a Manichean explanation and to personify social phenomena," it is because the revolutionary "illusion of politics" is in truth a theatrical state, where all — actors and spectators — must speak and, speaking, struggle (Furet, 20, 26).

While Rousseau is acclaimed by his ideological children as the father of the Revolution, Burke could legitimately claim authorship of the counterrevolution. Burke countered the Revolution's obliteration of the partition between the political and the social with a project equally totalizing. "The grounds upon which [he] went," Burke affirmed, were "the necessity of which this time imposed upon all men, of putting an end to differences of all sorts" (*CEB*, 7:312). The first step Burke took toward ending "differences of all sorts" was to condense differences into an antithesis of one sort, pro- or anti-Jacobin; the second, to personify difference as a general threat to an individual and national integrity that must be protected at all costs. Burke's strategic ambition entailed both the supersession of party politics in a counterrevolutionary coalition — which Burke engineered — and the dissolution of the partitions between theater and world, the seat of government and seat of retirement — which he fantasized. "Foreign politics," he claimed, "are foreign only in name; for they are not only connected with our domestic politics, but the domestic politics are actually included in them" (*CEB*, 7:305). The coalition that Burke formed with Pitt marks the invention of a new, incipiently totalitarian politics, christened "anti-Jacobin" — but one which, as Coleridge will argue, is anti-Jacobin only in name, for Jacobinism is not only connected with anti-Jacobinism but is actually included in it.

Burke and Robespierre were equally obsessed with the destruction of the "privileged corps of the Ancien Régime" (Furet, 50). Robespierre adopted the guillotine as the executive instrument of an animus against the many bodies of aristocrats, each thinking only of its own interest. Burke just as furiously denounced all challenges to the privileges of ancient corporations. John Brewer has demonstrated, however, that Burke's quasifeudal model had little actual pertinence to Great Britain, where the administrative monarchy that was the future of postrevolutionary France was already in place and progressively undermining privilege by the steady expansion of a fine-grained network of financial and social regulations.[7] The supposed menace to corps and corporations was Burke's own anachronistic reflection of French affairs within the borders of Great Britain, his incorporation of a body politic into British political discourse. In revolutionary iconography, the severed head is that which cannot think but can be made to speak.

The dismemberment of the human body and the severance of a natural life are supplied by a picture and caption that graphically present this type of a revolutionary life as a talking head (fig. 2). The caption "Ecce Custine" satirizes both the man who lived under that name and the Christ, to whom the phrase canonically refers. Yet it poaches on the Christological association to announce a new, amalgamated man — all the more powerful for being the product of a historical rupture and the political construction of the people. The mechanical reproduction and organized dispersion of this biographeme facilitated widespread recognition of the revolutionary subject.[8] In the figure of the talking head, every man sees his own life typed as a life abridged. Under the dispensation of Enlightenment, guillotine and printing press alike perform as instruments of what Lacoue-Labarthe calls "mechanical exemplarity." Every man regards himself characterized as someone subject to the career of the Revolution, cut off from the corps, from the past, and from the possibility of autobiographical remembrance in order that the Revolution can come to speak through him as with his own voice. Burke answers meetly. If the difference between Jacobin Revolution and Burkean counterrevolution is negated by their shared ambition to

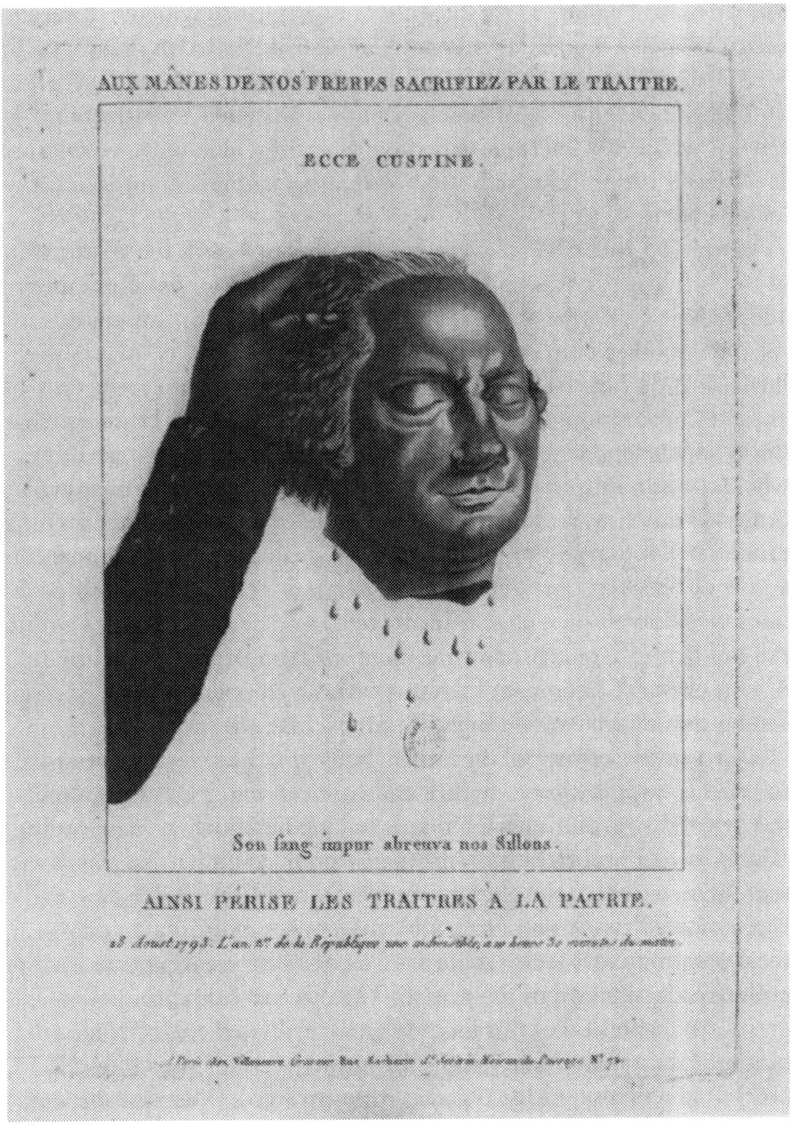

Fig. 2. "Ecce Custine," reproduced from *French Caricature and the French Revolution, 1789–1799* (Los Angeles: Grunewald Center for the Graphic Arts, 1988), 194. Image courtesy Bibliothèque Nationale de France.

abolish all differences, they are also positively leagued by the foresight that this cancellation of differences enables the reconstruction of an exemplary man: "I think Europe is recoverable yet. But it must be by a great and speedy Effort of this Country. This can never be done but by the extinction, or at least by the suspension, of Parties amongst us. Whatever our Sentiments or likings may be in this point we ought to act as if we were but one man" (*CEB*, 7:307). Taking advantage of the emergency he has called into being, Burke promotes the extinction of corporate interests and the deliberative function of the Parliament as the precondition for the sovereignty of the counterrevolution, which speaks "as if" with one voice and acts "as if" one man — a legal fiction militant.

The French Revolution ended with the execution of Robespierre. The British counterrevolution, however, lasted until 1832, terminated only by the passage of the Reform Act, the political sphere's decisive recognition of new social arrangements.[9] The asymmetry can be assigned to a stray contingency. Robespierre's consummation was followed a week later by the consumptive death of Richard Burke. Richard had been his father's mouthpiece to the European princes and French emigres, the successor to his father's Parliamentary seat, and the sole repository of his father's hopes. For Edmund Burke, the proximity of the deaths induced a symbolic connection. For the grief-stricken father, his son's death forever sealed the counterrevolution's incapacity to embody itself fully in a true hero who would redeem a Europe hellbent on chaos. Burke's Thermidor, then, was a period of protracted mourning for Richard — not just for the son but for the ideal of the new, postrevolutionary man he had been meant to embody. Although Burke resorted to a series of surrogates, such as the Earl of Fitzwilliam and William Windham, and even the vague prediction of a "military character" (*CEB*, 8:141), he never found the single figure who could triumphantly answer the galvanic threat of the revolutionary stereotype.

After 1794, under Pitt, the counterrevolution turned inward in a sustained campaign of self-inflicted violence, the so-called repression. The repression was prosecuted under Pitt but after Burke, who had always imagined the revolutionary war "as a war on [his] ideas and principles." The militant contradiction that is Burke's text can only be appreciated if the equivocalness of that "on" is acknowledged: a war according to Burke's principles must be a war against his principles. "It is with nations as with individuals."[10] And it was the crowning consequence of Burke's individuation of the counterrevolution, the fruit of his authorship, that he was able to personalize the moment by projecting the symptomatology (a word first used in 1798) of his own "old and infirm constitution" on the English nation (*CEB*, 8:253). The dynamic of the counterrevolution after 1794 was, as Coleridge saw, a continuing self-contradiction — an infliction of injury on the very body that the anti-Jacobin war had been mounted to protect. Thus, the fierce vision of Burke's "Letter to a Noble Lord": "Why will they not let me remain in obscurity and inaction? Are they apprehensive, that if an atom of me remains the sect has something to fear? Must I be annihilated, lest, like old John Ziska's, my skin might be made into a drum, to animate Europe to eternal battle, against a tyranny that threatens to overwhelm all Europe, and all the human race?"[11] Behold Burke, who, in default of the redemptive hero, imagines himself cut off from thought in order that he might speak with power, who wills that he be flayed so that he might sound and resound the eternal alarm to everlasting battle!

Fathered by Burke, counterrevolutionary self-contradiction propagated itself in the distinctive neurotic form of melancholy. Thus the counterrevolution survived, despite the loss of its ambivalent object in Robespierre/Richard, by blaming itself both for the loss and for surviving the loss of that object that justified existence. After 1794, the "shadow of the object," in Freud's memorable phrase, "falls on the ego"[12]; the one who survives — Burke, England — becomes the homefront and is punished with renewed violence for a dangerous inclination toward foreign manners and "men of theory" (*Reflections*, 128). As Rousseau's theoretical rigor propelled Robespierre to the sacrificial embodiment of the general will, Burke's melancholy authorized Pitt's sorry repression of traditional voices and domestic hands in the name of "the little platoon." Pitt made war on Burke's principles. Defending against a perceived lapse in legitimacy, the government routinized itself as the serial administration of punishment to a subject people who could be said, sadly, to have gotten what they deserved.

Appearing in the glory year of his partnership with Wordsworth, Coleridge's thin quarto volume *Fears in Solitude, Written in April 1798, During the Alarm of an Invasion* separates itself from the collaboration that produced *Lyrical Ballads* materially (it was published by Joseph Johnson, the radical publisher of Godwin and Wollstonecraft, independently of Wordsworth), thematically (as the title announces), and tonally (conversational or meditative style tenses into high-strung declamation).[13] The year 1798 marked not only the *annus mirabilis* but also the thunderous dawn of the Napoleonic invasion threat and the heyday of Pitt's repression.[14] Though the publication of the volume seems to indicate Coleridge's assertion of a distinctive poetic identity, the poems movingly demonstrate that the claim for poetic identity is incoherent except in terms of a triple analogy among poetic, personal, and national identities. For the English poet, responsive to his circumstances, the attempt to go his separate way does not demonstrate autonomy but its illusion; in these times, if the poetic must be personal, the personal is nonetheless fully political.

The title poem begins with the invocation of a place, "A green and silent spot, amid the hills, / A small and silent dell!" A description of the "heathy hills," a "swelling slope" covered by the golden "never-bloomless furze," and the "quiet spirit-healing nook" follows. It is a fluid, feminized, almost maternal landscape where one can peacefully organize a presexual innocence, the kind of place that all would love, "but chiefly he, the humble man, who, in his youthful years, / Knew just so much of folly, as had made / His early manhood more securely wise!" "In a half sleep," this man, too tranquil actually to desire anything, "dreams of better worlds." But the silence and dreams are soon dissipated:

> My God! it is a melancholy thing
> For such a man, who would full fain preserve
> His soul in calmness, yet perforce must feel
> For all his brethren — O my God!
> It weighs upon the heart, that he must think
> What uproar and what strife may now be stirring
> This way or that way o'er these silent hills —
> Invasion, and the thunder and the shout,
> And all the crash of onset; fear and rage,
> And undetermined conflict . . .
> (ll. 29–38)

In light of Burke, the similarity between the imagined invasion and a rape or primal scene fantasy looks less like Coleridge's confusion of the political with the sexual than an accurate rendering of the world as viewed from within the counterrevolution. The historical facts negatively confirm the entanglement of the psychic and the political here: both kinds of invasion — sexual and military — were imaginary. The opening of the poem does not render some real event in terms of poetic fantasy, nor does it project a fantasy onto the political landscape; it represents "England" (place, poetry, and mind) as already invaded and occupied by a sexualized politics, afflicted by the prejudice that all domestic relations are secretly tainted, the suspicion that every touch disguises rape.

A corollary of this occupation is the curiously suppositional biography by which the poet makes his appearance. Unlike in "Frost at Midnight" and "Reflections on Having Left a Place of Retirement," the poet does not here speak autobiographically; instead he supposes "such a man"—a composite of the Romantic type of a poet (recognizable from both Coleridge's and Wordsworth's earlier poetry and a type of Christ (suffering his passion in the garden). The poem imagines a possible life (and that life the merest possible, little more than revery) whose private, blameless conduct is usurped by unwelcome thoughts of "uproar" and "strife" that erupt from the political unconscious. Plainly regressive, suppositional biography symptomatizes an inhibition on autobiographical meditation. The representation of a way that "such a man" could lead a life appears to be the precondition for the appearance of an "I" that can claim personal responsibility for its thoughts. But, as it happens, violation of the quiet tenor of "such a man's" life by a political crisis triggers instead the abandonment of biographical narrative for fierce jeremiad, which turns on the apostrophic fiction that all men form a single man: "We have offended, Oh! my countrymen!" declaims the poet (l. 41). That fiction answers to the metastasis of individual Englishmen into a sensation-hungry, counterrevolutionary public:

> We, this whole people, have been clamorous
> For war and bloodshed; animating sports,
> The which we pay for as a thing to talk of,
> Spectators and not combatants! No guess
> Anticipative of a wrong unfelt,
> No speculation on contingency,
> However dim and vague, too vague and dim
> To yield a justifying cause . . . (ll. 93–100)

The counterrevolution is, first of all, a discourse (the war is a "thing to talk of"). They who talk are "this whole people"—the nation as a paying audience shaped and aroused by the systematically propagated illusion that the eventful pains of others are distantly staged for its pleasure. That pleasure may be designated as political because it is immunized from moral reflection by the justifying postulate of a first cause: the foreign instigator, the conspiratorial plotter. The theatricalism of the counterrevolution elaborates a longstanding governmental strategy for controlling civil society by scripting its speech. In the arena that is Great Britain,

> All individual dignity and power [is]
> Engulfed in Courts, Committees, Institutions, Associations and
>   Societies,
> A vain, speech-mouthing, speech-reporting
> Guild.
> (ll. 54–57)

Here even "the sweet words / Of Christian promise . . . / Are muttered o'er by men, whose tones proclaim / How flat and wearisome they feel their trade" (ll. 63–67). Pursuing his critique of the regime, the poet assails the Test Act:

> Oh! blasphemous! the Book of Life is made
> A superstitious instrument, on which
> We gabble o'er the oaths we mean to break.
> For all must swear — all and in every place,
> All, all make up one scheme of perjury,
> That faith doth reel; the very name of God
> Sounds like a juggler's charm . . .
> (ll. 70–80)

How can the Christian promise be credited if uttered by a perjured cleric, if eternal life is routinely jeopardized for the sake of a cozy living?

"Fears" assigns the suspension of Coleridge's life and living its full political significance. The poet sees that the transformation of the orders of French society into a "people," that voice which answers "yes" or "no" to propositions put to it by its spokesmen, has already been accomplished in England, where civil rights have long depended on a willingness to subscribe to the Thirty-nine Articles — whether or not one believes in them.[15] In Great Britain, where civil rights had not yet been extricated from a confessional submission, citizenship is the reward for paying lip service to a creed, acting *as if* (the fiction is Burkean) one believes in it. Hegemonic maintenance demands the dissociation of words — those that the newspapers report, those that one says — from their meaning: the outrages to which words refer, the beliefs to which they attest.[16] The prophet avows that there is something that escapes the predictable violent antithesis of revolution and counterrevolution, something outside the generic conflicts staged within theater walls, something eventful not to be tagged to a personifiable cause. The "sweet influences of nature" may succumb to invasion by the abstract imperatives of the Revolution, but, the poet trusts, because abstraction is aberrant, it cannot long thwart the divine economy of meaning. The poet brandishes the threat that

> Providence,
> Strong and retributive, should make us know
> The meaning of our words, force us to feel
> The desolation and the agony
> Of our fierce doings.

Meaning involves bringing abstractions back to the body. The apocalyptic embodiment of meaning would destroy a counterrevolutionary polity that sustains its melancholy existence by doing injury to itself as to others. Despite his indignation, the prophet seeks to forestall apocalypse. Relenting, he prays, "Spare us yet awhile, / Father and God! O spare us yet awhile!" (ll. 129–30). Aversion, not punishment, is the goal of the poem. The poet exhorts "Sons, brothers, husbands, all / Who ever gazed with fondness on the forms / Which grew up with you round the same fire-side" (ll. 134–36) to

> Stand forth! be men! repel an impious foe,
> Impious and false, a light yet cruel race,
> Who laugh away all virtue, mingling mirth
> With deeds of murder; and still promising
> Freedom, themselves too sensual to be free,
> Poison life's amities, and cheat the heart
> Of quiet hope, and all that soothes,
> And all that lifts the spirit!
> Stand we forth.
> (ll. 139–46)

That eloquence is not in the manner of Burke. The poet does not imagine a hero who comes to a tragic scene of oedipal conflict, threat, and triumph. His simple aim is to repel. A simple aim achieved by simple means: by stirring his reader (as himself) to a standing forth that will show a "sensual" enemy he is a man. The poet summons up the phallus for an apotropaic display that will ward off the evil of an invasion that was invited by doubts whether Britons, supine before the provocative stimuli of their rulers, are really men.[17] It is not the British female that the sensual French invader desires. In the intense climate of revolutionary conflict, there is no passion to spare for the "form" of the female. The British male dangerously opts for personifications of abstract ideas; the French revolutionist prefers the British male. Standing forth, the British phallus will, however, deter the invader, who, in that most abstract of all personifications, will clearly behold the man. As a signifier of manhood with no body behind it, the juggler's charm of the phallus is the exact counterpart to the Jacobinical severed head and all the more potent for its signal lack of meaning.

Yet we might inquire how Coleridge can hope to get the phallus to stand. If the best defense is a phallic standing forth — a proof that I am a man and therefore must repel your masculine desire — the poet must attempt to provoke a somatic response more primordial than that achieved by the powerful but mediated Burkean scenario of insulted queens, interdictory forefathers, and incestuous sons. Burke authored tragedy. Coleridge writes romance. He aims to distill his provocation to its volatile linguistic essence, a magical word. Written during the alarm of an invasion, the poem was designed as a watchword to alarm British men. The "watch-word," as Coleridge elsewhere writes, is "some un-meaning term" that "acquires almost a mechanical power over [a man's] frame."[18] In the present war, there is reason of state to exploit the unreasoning body. And in "Fears in Solitude," the sexualization of politics refers aesthetic pleasure to its radical intimacy with power. As an antidote to the pictographic force of revolutionary iconography, this "unmeaning" poem aims to refashion the old mechanism of exemplarity in order to gain a pornographic, Geraldinelike power over the frame of the Englishman, to compel it to repel.

It nonetheless remains a question whether the watchword does not, in fact, constitute that evil which it averts. If the revolutionary pictograph renders the revolutionary subject as an instantaneously recognizable biographical sign, Coleridge's "answer meet" is little more than the fabrication of an ideologeme capable of polarizing the world into good and evil, advents and consummations.[19] Despite himself, the poet becomes politicized, an instrument of the ideological apparatus of what, in 1800, Coleridge will call "the Jacobin state":

> Is the nation in danger? Every man is called into play; every man feels his interest as a *citizen* predominating over his individual interests; the high, and the low, and the middle classes become all alike politicians; the majority carry the day; and Jacobinism is the natural consequence. Let us not be deceived by words. Every state, in which all the inhabitants without distinction of property are roused to the exertion of a public spirit, is for the time a Jacobin state.[20]

Although he diagnoses the antithetical illness that afflicts the disembodied polis, the poet cannot fully imagine an authentic alternative; he cannot conceive of a body that is not sexual or of a transition that would conduct him to some new place. Although he wills a break with the counterrevolution, the poet nonetheless avails himself of a heightened counterrevolutionary rhetoric. His dread of rhetorical power fuels the desperate wish for that power, to use it just once. His fear of being abstracted energizes the dangerous wish to be objectified as irresistible charm, not as a man but as that mechanism which mans men by producing a single stiffening that will magically repulse invasion. The (counter)revolutionary poet dreams of things happening on time, pat on what Theodor Adorno calls the "cipher of catastrophe": punctual invasions, instant erections.[21] Such is the dream in which Romantic poetry has always participated. Such is the dream which, by those native cadences that befall verse, Romantic poetry continually falsifies.

So goes this poem's cadenza. Having vented his "filial fears," the poet says farewell to his solitary spot and winds his way "Homeward":

> and lo! Recalled
> From bodings that have well-nigh wearied me,
> I find myself upon the brow, and pause
> Startled! And after lonely sojourning
> In such a quiet and surrounded nook,
> This burst of prospect, here the shadowy main,
> Dim-tinted, there the mighty majesty
> Of that huge amphitheatre of rich
> And elmy fields, seems like society —
> Conversing with the mind, and giving it
> A livelier impulse and a dance of thought!
> And now, beloved Stowey! I behold
> The church-tower, and, methinks the four huge elms
> Clustering, which mark the mansion of my friend;
> And close behind them, hidden from my view,
> Is my own lowly cottage, where my babe
> And my babe's mother dwell in peace! With light
> And quickened footsteps thitherward I tend.
> (ll. 210–27)

Home is the dreamer, home from the dell. Or almost. The poet (call him Coleridge) returns to the first person as he nears his own place. The suspension of biography is ended by a return to autobiography. Yet that appearance of progress is undermined by the failure of the autobiographical account to complete the homecoming it imagines. The narrative halts as the poet stops to overlook a cottage that remains visibly hidden from him. We might suspect that what gives his footsteps their tendency may very well be what gives him pause. Although he stands in Stowey, the poet observes a landscape uncannily Wordsworthian. In Wordsworth, the "four huge elms" spot a ruined cottage, haunted by the ghosts of an abandoned wife and children. Coleridge's prospect is also anticipated in "Adventures on Salisbury Plain," where it is said of the wandering sailor: "Long had he fancied each successive slope / Conceal'd some cottage, whither he might turn / And rest."[22]

In Wordsworth's poem, the price of the sailor's return is his discovery that he is a criminal forbidden entrance to his cottage and debarred from participation in a society proved kind by its exclusion of him.[23] The poem maps a series of uncanny transfers of agency and victimization between narrator and auditor — call them revolutions and counter-revolutions in the exercise of poetic power — a series that is only halted when the sailor, confronted with the wretched form of his abandoned wife, is identified by the assembled populace: "He is the man." That annunciation seals his criminal separation from domestic life and prepares for his suspension in an iron case as an example to all.

No wonder the poet halts. In the intertext through which Coleridge makes his anxious way, he is on the verge of returning to a home configured as the familiar Christological plot. Homecoming bodes the same old ending of recognition, indictment, and sacrifice, rendered meaningless for the modern as for the unitarian by virtue of its mechanical exemplarity. Worse, it is not just the same old plot: it is Wordsworth's plot. On returning home after driving out the French invader, Coleridge finds his domestic space newly invaded and occupied by his brother poet, who has settled in as he stood forth. Later, in Chapter 4 of the *Biographia Literaria*, Coleridge would identify his audition of the *Salisbury Plain* poems in 1795 as the occasion when he became as convinced of Wordsworth's genius as if it were the annunciation of his own destiny. In "Fears in Solitude," the resumption of autobiography is stigmatized as premature; it entails assumption of the biographical plot that Wordsworth has already written. For "such a man" to say "I" means assuming the penalty assigned to another thief of voice as his own. That uncanny effect is justified, however dimly, by this cause: in becoming the man who potently stood forth, he unthinkingly cut himself off from what was his own and became as another (a preternaturally potent figure) to those whom he served with a revolutionary fierceness. In any event, the watchman cannot enter the house or even risk the threshold. Better vagrancy than a homecoming. Another Wordsworthian figure puts it plainly: "Oh! dreadful price of being! to resign / All that is dear in being; better far / In Want's most lonely cave till death to pine / Unseen, unheard, unwatched by any star" ("Adventures," ll. 379–82). For the poet in search of his life, "home" is just another evil he must avert.

The poet's attempt to resolve "undetermined conflict" fails to do more than disclose its dread overdetermination — again. As Coleridge had already observed, the distress of England could not be ascribed to any single cause, except perhaps the ministerial obsession with a single, exclusively political cause. In his 1795 lecture "The Plot Discovered," Coleridge had already mockingly rehearsed Pitt's justification for the Sedition Act: "The outrage offered to his Majesty . . . is ascribed to 'the multitude of seditious pamphlets and speeches daily printed, published, and dispersed with unremitting industry and with a transcendent boldness." 'Coleridge answered that the "dispersion . . . of seditious pamphlets was not the cause: that was the cause which gave to sedition the colouring of truth, and made disaffection the dictate of hunger[—]the present unjust, unnecessary and calamitous War . . . !" (LPR, 287). The cause of seditious writing is hunger, the cause of hunger is "the PRESENT WAR." And of the war? "Its total Causelessness must be proved," Coleridge urges, " — as if the War had been just and necessary, it might be thought disputable whether any Calamities could justify our abandonment of it" (LPR, 54).

Although neither just nor necessary, the war is nonetheless supplied with justification after justification by those who step forward to attest to Jacobinical plotters. The false witness men bear has political uses. Even so they do not lie for a political cause. They who swear do so for money. "POWER CAN PAY PERJURY" (LPR, 291) not because the minions of power are right- or left-wing but because they are hungry. Betrayal, like sedition, follows the "dictate of hunger," which has no author, presents no identifiable face. The "dictate of hunger" is the categorical imperative of self-maintenance. And perjury is the inevitable effect of the bias that the ministry of fear communicates to all professions by its command over the supply of food.

Coleridge adopted similar language to describe his anguish at the prospect of relying on his writing to make a living for himself and his family in a 1796 letter to his friend the gentleman farmer Thomas Poole: "Surely, surely, you do not advise me to lean with the whole weight of my Necessities on the Press? Ghosts indeed! I should be haunted with Ghosts enough — the Ghosts of Otway & Chatterton, & the phantasms of a Wife broken-hearted,· & a hunger-bitten Baby! O Thomas Poole! Thomas Poole! if you did but know what a Father & Husband must feel, who toils with his brain for uncertain bread! I dare not think of it!" (*CL*, 1:275).

But he did more than think of it; in 1797 he accepted Daniel Stuart's tempting offer to write for the *Morning Post*. The decision did nothing to change Coleridge's mind about the debasement associated with writing for hire. He opportunistically adapted the principle of the "dictate of hunger" to his own circumstances as a "hired paragraph-scribbler" in a letter to the industrialist and philanthropist Josiah Wedgwood in January 1798: "Something must be written & written immediately — if any important Truth, any striking beauty, occur to my mind, I feel a repugnance at sending it garbled to a newspaper: and if any idea of ludicrous personality, or apt anti-ministerial joke, crosses me, I feel a repugnance at rejecting it, because something must be written, and nothing else suitable occurs" (*CL*, 1:365). Coleridge convincingly vouches for his familiarity with a mode of social existence wholly subject to necessity and where the rhythm of production dictates the shape of opinion, where the ethical "ought" decisively yields to the economic "must." It would be stretching a point, however, to describe Coleridge as completely degraded to the exigent status of the laboring poor; although he claims to be pressed by the need for "subsistence," he also fastidiously proclaims his desire to "preserve . . . delicacy of moral feeling" — a kind of capital, one assumes, not shared by the vast number of those who slave for wages in the capital.

The letter to Wedgwood is the vehicle for a frank exploration of vocational options — between pulpit and press — as well as a demonstration designed to appeal to a benefactor who aimed to give him "leisure for the improvement of [his] Talents at the same time that [his] mind should be preserved free from any professional Bias which might pervert, or at least hamper, the exertion of them" (*CL*, 1:364). Nonetheless, if "worker" does not accurately designate Coleridge's social identity, neither does "cleric," "poet," "journalist," or even "man of letters." The label "bourgeois" is perhaps the least suitable tag for a man who veers between country and city, between "ministerial office" and journalistic "Trade," between a corporate existence lost and a class solidarity imaginable only as its spectral projection. The best description of this modern, low mimetic Adam (the world is all before him as a congeries of repugnant options) is that, like William Godwin's protean

Caleb Williams, he corresponds to no description of man. And Coleridge will construct himself in that break of correspondence.

There was no necessity for him to do so. He had before his eyes the example — placed on earth as if to lesson him into prudence — of a man who ordered his parts into a machine of regular habits and estimable productivity, his brother-in-law, Robert Southey. Rather than follow Southey's lead, however, Coleridge counseled the former pantisocrat on the perils of his way:

> My dear Southey! it goes grievously against the Grain with me, that you should be editing anthologies. I would to Heaven, that you could afford to write nothing, or at least, to publish nothing till the completion & publication of the Madoc. . . . Whereas Thalaba would gain you (for a time at lest) more ridiculers than admirers — & the Madoc might in consequence be welcomed with an Ecce iterum. (*CL*, 1:546)[24]

The difference between *Ecce iterum* and *Ecce Homo* captures Southey's exemplary accommodation to the endless daily piecework required to breathe a momentary, lackluster life into the old formulas by which hegemony is maintained. To behold the *iterum* rather than to behold the *homo* is to see the same as repetition — and to imagine the prudent author as a composite figure, constituted by a repetition that homogenizes one heroic poem with another as it merges authorship and anthologization.

The career of Southey ("a man who has sacrificed all the energies of his heart and head — a splendid offering on the altar of Liberty" [*LPR*, 15]) exemplifies the routinization of counterrevolutionary melancholy into the specific form of alienation appropriate to a serial mode of cultural reproduction. To break with the counterrevolutionary machine demands the release of a worth of words not determined by the market's preestablished codes of value. It requires writing for a future that cannot be clearly seen and that is not subject to a justifying cause. It requires imagining a biography of a man who has not yet been beheld: suppositional become prefigural biography. The Coleridgean prefigure is troped as transition:

> The death of a young person of high hopes and opening faculties impresses me less gloomily, than the Departure of the Old. To my more natural Reason, the former appears like a transition; there seems an incompleteness in the life of such a person, contrary to the general order of nature; and it makes the heart say, this is not

all. But when an old man sinks into the grave, we have seen the bud, the blossom, and the fruit; and the unassisted mind droops in melancholy, as if the Whole had come and gone. (*CL*, 1:267)

"The good die young" not because they are good — there is no fatality to goodness (or the insufferably decent Southey would have perished in his cradle) — but people are good because they die young. Because they live lives as yet unwritten, they are apparitions of a future as yet unknown. Like old, mad Burke, they die before they learn the meaning of their words. *Ecce Homo* is the caption for a severed head, a pictograph of the revolutionary subject. *Ecce iterum* captions the life of the Southeyean man who kept his head and made his living by trading in the stereotyped repetition of a period style. But what do we behold when transition appears?

Persuaded by Coleridge's diagnosis of his predicament, spellbound by Coleridge's promise, in early 1798 the industrialists Josiah and Thomas Wedgwood offered him a subsidy of 150 pounds a year, no strings attached, thus enabling him to avoid compromising his principles against "preaching for hire" and affording him what, in "Reflections on Having Left a Place of Retirement," he calls the "luxury to be" — the luxury, that is, of having to write nothing. Being gifted by such unexampled bounty did not delude Coleridge into believing that the Revolution was over. "Fears in Solitude" may owe some of its moral conviction to Coleridge's newfound sense of financial well-being, but it also testifies that money cannot stop the rain. Furet has written of the impossibility even for a twentieth-century Frenchman of getting sufficiently outside the Revolution so that he or she could see it for what exactly it was, for "one cannot practice ethnology in so familiar a landscape" (Furet, 10). Coleridge's historical perspective was similarly constrained by the counterrevolutionary genius that had usurped the English place. Staked by the Wedgwoods, however, Coleridge could resort to the terra incognita of Germany on a funded project of research into otherness to practice what we have come to call ethnography.

Germany was not, of course, a savage culture.[25] Nevertheless, the peculiarity of the place is registered by Coleridge's letters and journal entries. There he described the social world through which he moved in painstaking detail: from the shape of hats to the rules of card games. Walter Jackson Bate has astutely suggested that Coleridge, suffering from a "floating anxiety," fled to Germany in search of a "purified self or 'body-image.' "[26] I want to redefine "floating" as a biographical anxiety in order to indicate that the breakdowns, felt and observed, of the partitions between the private and the public, between the psyche and the polity, between the felt and the observed, were the occasion of Coleridge's search for a biographical paradigm purified of revolutionary and counterrevolutionary stereotyping. The synthesis of a "purified self" awaited (not logically, but historically) a new description of "man" on which Coleridge could hope to improvise — he sought, that is, a biography fit for autobiography. As we have seen, Coleridge's anxiety was aggravated by the well-founded sense that biographical embodiment according to any available model would end with the objectification of the self in an image framed, captioned, and suitable for hanging.[27]

Coleridge's ethnographical and biographical impulses were in uneasy harness. On the one hand, he displayed a scrupulous attention to the fine grain of German society. On the other, he attempted to fulfill a promise to the Wedgwoods by preparing the ground for a comprehensive biography of the celebrated Lessing. Compounded of a desire to meet the conventional expectations of his patrons and a need to satisfy his own craving for a companionable form, Coleridge's biographical impulse expressed itself in a hunt for observable correspondences. He sought resemblances between the physiognomies of renowned writers and his own; he remarked on the possible parallels between pictures of the famous and their countenances, between their countenances and their characters. Here is Coleridge at the house of the younger brother of the poet Friedrich Gottlieb Klopstock: "We saw at his house a fine Bust of his Brother — there was a solemn and heavy Greatness in the Countenance which corresponded with my preconceptions of his style & genius. — I saw likewise there a very, very fine picture of Lessing. His eyes were uncommonly like mine — if any thing, rather larger & more prominent — But the lower part of his face & his nose — O what an exquisite expression of elegance and sensibility!" (CL, 1:437). The bust not only presupposes an encoding of the inside by the outside but, because it is a portrait of a living man, is also a promise of a correspondence between representation and a reality, a kind of foresight of the future. The bust's promise proved unreliable, as Coleridge makes clear in his artful account of his later meeting with the poet: "The Poet entered. — I was much disappointed in his countenance. I saw no likeness to the Bust. — There was no comprehension in the Forehead — no weight over the eyebrows — no expression of peculiarity, either moral or intellectual, in the eyes; — there was no massiveness in the general Countenance."

The biographical aim ends in negation. But the ethnographer's hand continues writing: "He is not quite so tall as I am — his upper jaw is toothless, his under jaw all black Teeth; and he wore very large half-boots, which his legs completely filled. They were enormously swelled. — He was lively, kind and courteous. He talked in French with Wordsworth — &, with difficulty, spoke a few sentences to me in English." Coleridge notes Klopstock's "rapture" at the surrender of the French in Ireland and his presentation of himself as a "vehement Anti-Gallican." But then,

> The Subject changed to Poetry — & I enquired, in Latin, concerning the history of German Poetry, & of the elder German Poets. — To my great astonishment he confessed, he knew very little on the subject — he had indeed read occasionally one or two of their elder writers — but not as to be able to speak of their merits. . . . He talked of Milton & Glover; & thought, Glover's blank Verse superior to Milton's! — Wordsworth & myself expressed our surprize — & Wordsworth explained his definition & ideas of harmonious Verse, that it consisted in the arrangement of pauses & cadences, & not in the even flow of single Lines — Klopstock assented, & said that he meant only in single Lines that Glover was the Superior. . . . He spoke with great Indignation of the English Prose Translation of his Messiah. . . . Wordsworth told him that I intended to translate a few of his Odes as specimens of German Lyrics — "I wish, you would render into English some select Passages of the Messiah, & revenge me of your Countryman." . . . I looked at him with much emotion — I considered him as the venerable Father of German Poetry; as a good man; as a Christian; with legs enormously swelled; seventy four years old; yet active and lively in his motions, as a boy; active, lively, chearful and kind and communicative — and the Tears swelled into my eyes; and could I have made myself invisible and inaudible I should have wept outright. (*CL*, 1:442–43)

The ethnographic character of this moment is identified by the interview format, by Coleridge's scribal posture, and by the prevailing sense of Klopstock as a "specimen" — a specimen father, as vengeful as venerable; a specimen body image, albeit bathetic rather than exemplary.

Ethnography requires a nontheatrical distance. Because Coleridge and Wordsworth did not have the advantage of either the invisibility or the inaudibility of the audience in a darkened theater, they could not weep outright. The Englishmen could pay their respects without submitting to the Burkean prescription of acting as if in the presence of a canonized forefather.[28] Klopstock's gouty legs are not Priam's wounded heart. Tragedy tears unshed are ethnographic disappointments transcribed.[29] This specimen poet, complete to the point of overripeness, is, as Coleridge says of his poetry, "sad stuff" — surprisingly out of touch with that national past which could grace him with authenticity. All of Europe has gone into the making of a poet already invaded by revolutionary discourse, already suffering from the anxiety of influence.

Yet if the cosmopolitanized Klopstock is degraded from the Teutonic purity that would make his life worth writing and his poetry worth reading, there remains a significant difference between him and his interviewers. Unlike the self-conscious and mobile English ethnographer, the German poet does not seem able to take strategic advantage of his alienation; for him, to change his mind means simply shifting from one position to another (French to English, Homer to Milton, Glover to Homer) according to what, in the "Advertisement" to *Lyrical Ballads*, Wordsworth calls "pre-established codes of decision." Even so, Klopstock performs his shifts clumsily, Germanically. There is, in James Clifford's terms, something tellingly "off-center" about this encounter, which is registered in Klopstock's blunder about Glover and in his failed adaptation of Homeric hexameters to German heroic verse.[30] The off-centeredness advantageously turns a potential standoff between Self and Other or between anxious sons and "venerable" father into a blessedly oblique communication between brother English poets: Wordsworth gets to lay out his theory, and Coleridge gets to overhear, record, and transmit it. Poetry, Wordsworth instructs, is not the iterum of a flowing line, what anyone can see, but cadences and pauses, those contrivances that are off the center of translatable meaning but that articulate the historical authenticity of English verse — of Milton and beyond.

Coleridge goes on to catch Klopstock in a lie about the date of his exposure to Milton. The facts prove that Klopstock's majesty is altogether derived, his *Messiah* the offspring of an English divinity. Thus Klopstock's life story differs in no fundamental regard from the biography of anxiety and repression by which every post-Miltonic poet is presupposed. Nonetheless, although meeting Klopstock is no encounter with the new, Coleridge's disappointment crystallizes the conditions for its appearance. In wedding a mechanical anti-Gallicism to a paralyzed anti-Miltonism, the Klopstockian crux suggests a possible means of getting beyond both. By determining the radical character that gives

English, and therefore Miltonic, verse its identity and its allegorical strength, Coleridge can hope to transform the condition for past majesty into the occasion of future glory.

Having detected Klopstock's untruth, Coleridge evenhandedly goes on to admit to a lie of his own about his knowledge of German hexameters. Only Coleridge's falsehood was remediable. And he diligently applied himself to the remedy in Ratzeburg, where he dug in alone, William and his sister Dorothy having departed for Goslar, to an isolation deeper far. The above letter to Poole remarks on Coleridge's receipt, after six weeks, of the first words from William, whose "violent hatred of letter-writing had caused his ominous silence [and] for which he accuses himself in severe terms" (*CL*, 1:445). What, exactly, Wordsworth had been doing at Goslar is not clear. "Dorothy says — 'William works hard, but not very much at the German.' — This is strange — I work at nothing else, from morning to night — / — It is very difficult to combine & arrange the German Sentences" (*CL*, 1:445). If Wordsworth had turned strange, Coleridge's labors became increasingly, even acutely, definite. Absent from family and friends, disappointed with the countenance of German poetry, anxious to discover a lifeline that would be something other than a "joyless form," Coleridge took a decisively linguistic turn. His notebooks record his intense application to the combination and arrangement of German sentences and to his classification of German vocabulary. But the pages are also crowded with notations of a staggering array of poetic meters, clouds of diacritical marks combined and arranged into the phantom of verse.[31]

As if clinging to the formalites of their erstwhile collaboration strangely disparted, Coleridge labored in strict accord with Wordsworth's supervisory mandate. For if writing "harmonious verse" consists in "the arrangement of pauses & cadences," the solitary Coleridge concentrated on the cadence, the modulation or fall of voice that accents poetic language. In his analysis of the German hexameter, the preferred vehicle of Klopstock's epic aspirations, he specifically identified its characteristic failing as a falling: "Is the German, in truth, adapted to these metres? I grievously suspect that it is all pedantry. Some advantages there, doubtless are, for we cannot fall foul of any thing without advantages" (*CL*, 1:450). In theme and tenor that observation epitomizes what I mean by Coleridgean.[32] Here he notices that in falling afoul of the heroic hexameter, the peculiar cadence of the German appears. Thus begins the breakthrough.

Soon Coleridge Englishes the effect in a remarkable prosodic exercise sent to the Wordsworths. His demonstration hexameters begin with the representation of a technique for marking the regularity of the beat:

> William, my teacher, my friend! dear William and dear Dorothea!
> Smooth out the folds of my letter, and place it on desk or on table;
> Place it on table or desk; and your right hands loosely half-closing,
> Gently sustain them in air, and extending the digit didactic,
> Rest it a moment on each of the forks of the five-forked left hand,
> Twice on the breadth of the thumb, and once on the tip of each
>   finger;
> Read with a nod of the head in a humouring recitativo;
> And, as I live, you will see my hexameters hopping before you.

Beat on yourself as do I. As we (he, they, you, and I) read with body English, beating out the time, so Coleridge lives, sensuously at hand.

It is a milder fate than Burke's vision of being flayed, stretched, and drummed. Not yet subject to a figure, he lives according to a characteristically tactful rhythm. But though materialized physically before us by the handreading of his handwriting, it is at the cost of self:

> I would full fain pull in my hard-mouthed runaway hunter;
> But our English Spondeans are clumsy yet impotent curb-reins;
> And so to make him go slowly, no way have I left but to lame him.

No centaur the English hexameter, but an idiot man on a runaway horse.

Although the English is no more suitable for the heroic pace of the classical mount than the German, each language falls afoul of the Homeric antecedent in its own way. Here the meter runs because of a lack of fit between the quantities of the Greek and the quality of the English. Only the dead weight of lumpen monosyllables finally lames the hunter's legs and brings the race to a dead stop. Coleridge has not learned — will never learn — to arrange pauses, which invariably come upon him as momentous separations, violent breaks, guilt-ridden betrayals — overdetermined, melodramatic. This laming, as is so often the case with Coleridge's verse, has the force of a self-infliction — oedipal damage done to the legs of his own poetry — even as it hints at a castrative aggressivity against Wordsworth, whose "digit didactic," extended and animated in response to Coleridge's beat, is momentarily blocked.

Yet Wordsworth is not a father; verse is not a man; a finger is not the body. Nor is collaboration identity. The "laming" of the verse is the occasion of an apostrophe that turns away from the heroic strain, that unhands Wordsworth and brings the note of English pathos in: "William, my head and my heart!" The exercise plunges into ten lines of physical complaint — the same old pitiable Coleridge — and then a textual break, and then a startling turn:

> . . . my eyes are a burthen,
> Now unwillingly closed, now open and aching with darkness.
> O! what a life is the eye! what a strange and inscrutable essence!
> Him that is utterly blind, nor glimpses the fire that warms him;
> Him that never beheld the swelling breast of his mother;
> Him that smiled in his gladness as a babe that smiles in its
>   slumber;
> Even for him it exists, it moves and stirs in its prison;
> Lives with a separate life, and 'Is it a Spirit?' he murmurs:
> Sure it has thoughts of its own, and to see is only a language.

It is as if the laming of the hunter has blankened Coleridge's sight, allowing him to imagine the life of the eye as the story of what it does before it sees. He imagines a pre-Homeric, pre-Miltonic, pre-oedipal, and, most importantly, prefigural "separate life" that "stirs" the murmurous supposition that the self and all it sees are contingent codes, a "language."

This "separate life," then, is the suppositional biography of the "eye" (that it could be deciphered as equally plausibly Wordsworth's or Coleridge's is just the point), logically precedent to the integrated, insightful "I" on which autobiography will mount its vexed and vexatious mountings. Although a prisoner that sees not, the "eye" is not sequestered in a noumenal isolation, for somehow it befalls that the prisoner makes its absence felt; somehow it befalls that, though blind to the schemata by which sight grammaticizes the world into sense, the "eye" nonetheless stirs a murmur, which affects to respond in kind. Hear it:

> William, my head and my heart! dear William and dear Dorothea!
> You have all in each other; but I am lonely, and want you!
> (CL, 1:451–52)

The closing cadence is not visible but audible, and then only to the ear of an English speaker. Indeed, hearing here we learn now (as, after so much labor, Coleridge heard and learned there and then) that the real self-contradiction of Klopstock was not that he lied about the age at which he read Milton, but that he could have imagined he read Milton at all, when his only access was to a prose translation.[33] Without English, Klopstock could easily prefer Glover to Milton, since without English Klopstock could not hear the Miltonic voice. His foreign eye was not alive to its parochial stirring, to the way the modulation of verse falls on an English ear; hence like the untutored child of Coleridge's "Nightingale," Klopstock "mars all things with his imitative lisp."

Klopstock's self-contradiction is merely a German version of the deafness that disabled the response of the eighteenth century to Milton, which read his blank verse as prose because it could only read with its bodily eye. Coleridge's trip to Germany allowed him to imagine a transition to the future — a new century and a new poetry — in terms of his acquired understanding of the past as a foreign country. And the Augustans' prosaical insensitivity to the cadenced music of blank verse was remedied in large part by Coleridge, the poet with the nicest ear for cadences, those falls dying or desiring that are the accidents and the peculiar distinction of English verse.[34] We hear that remedy in this renegotiation of the relations between the classical model and the English instance, no longer considered in terms of revival or correspondence but as a lapse into a personal speech whose historicity is exactly the note of a pathos previously unheard.[35] The pain of absence has been articulated as the slight slippage between the manly beats of the heroic spondee, steadfast in the assertion of its timeless objectivity, and the soulful falling off of the final, ever-diminishing trochee ("want you"). Coleridge makes audible what the physical eye cannot see. Without trope or figure he hopes to move one with whom he no longer corresponds.[36] Having escaped apocalyptic consummation on the altar of (counter)revolutionary spectacle, the abstracted "I" returns to the body in the sensuous detail of its breathings.

It is in its cadences that English escapes polarization with the French or appropriation by the German. It is by the English tongue's delicate fallings off from brute symmetry that the "loss of national character" (LPR, 60), hastened by the murderous tradeoffs between revolution and counterrevolution, is obstinately questioned. It is in its falling off that the advantage of English as a language for pathos, and thus its genius for poetry, appears. Having fallen off from Wordsworth, the decadent Coleridge has acquired the singular advantage of hearing the vital music in the blankest of verse.[37]

As Coleridge refined the cadence, so his collaborator mastered the pause. It was Wordsworth who insisted on the separation; and Wordsworth gave that space its own slow time by protracting the interval between his departure and his first letter, thereby suspending the responsive exchange of collaborators each to each with an "ominous silence" that mocked his correspondent's best skill. Coleridge has thought and will think again and again of "a man who should lose his companion in a desart of sand where his weary Halloos drop down in the air without an echo" (*CL*, 1:471). But this time, his voice drops down to find not its echo but something else. It is Wordsworth, on whose heart Coleridge's cadence has gently fallen, who arranges cadences and pauses into a responsive passage that both answers and incorporates the moving call. To Coleridge, for whom every interval is an absence and every absence a pain, Wordsworth replies with a letter of instruction in the management of pauses.

We know it only from Coleridge's response:

> The blank lines gave me as much direct pleasure as was possible in the general bustle of pleasure with which I received and read your letter. I observed, I remember, that the fingers woven, &c., only puzzled me; and though I liked the twelve or fourteen first lines very well, yet I like the remainder much better. Well, now I have read them again, they are very beautiful, and leave an affecting impression. That
>
>> Uncertain heaven received
>> Into the bosom of the steady lake,
>
> I should have recognised any where; and had I met these lines running wild in the deserts of Arabia, I should have instantly screamed out "Wordsworth!" (*CL*, 1:452–53)

That is what the silence, the suspension of all correspondence, has omened.

Transition appears. Something completely unforeseen and providentially incomplete falls to him who has hung listening. Neither a body nor a joyless form but living lines — lines that have a peculiar music and give a peculiar, unidentifiable pleasure. This then, retrieved from the dinning revolution of hoots and counterhoots, is the figure of biography: the impression of a transient affect that continues, transiently, to be affecting; a life written as the cadenced suspension of the identity we know it "must" become. And we may take for our own the moral or "theoretical consequence" that Philippe Lacoue-Labarthe points out: "The figure is never one. Not only is it the Other, but there is no unity or stability of the figural; the imago has no fixity or proper being. There is no 'proper image' with which to identify totally, no essence of the imaginary."[38] What has fallen by chance is received across a pause that suspends, that uncertains, all past determinations of who or what "I" must be. These lines about a boy coming to be as one-who-was render poetry's cadence and pause as a transition to a future as yet unseen. It is given to Coleridge to name that future. His Arabia is not the world historical desert where, in the fall of 1798, fearlessly prowls the solitary Bonaparte. It is a Romantic, textual wilderness where, after the Revolution, language invisibly changes into something new and strange, with a glory that Coleridge says he immediately apprehended. But then after the instantaneous moment of recognition, Coleridge freely acknowledges what appeared to him by the name of "Wordsworth."

We do not know what in fact Coleridge perceived it *as*, if anything. No doubt Coleridge — separated from his friend's physical presence, with ample time to read and analyze — could have shouted some other name: "Behold Milton!" (thinking of "Lycidas") or even "Behold Coleridge" (thinking of "The Nightingale") — but it might as well be "Wordsworth," that name which capitally allegorizes the surplus value that language acquires by the fiction of authorial attribution. Wordsworth, to be sure, will repay this gift as if Coleridge's acknowledgment were nothing but his echoic due, hollowly resounding the sublime note of Wordsworth's own noble soul. He will close the biography of "a boy" with a death, as if it were the story of a person, say a rival poet, who has generously departed the world in order that another, more gifted one might stage his life in all the glory of its dialectical progress toward dominion. But there is nothing personal about the essential music of this cadenced pause, nor is there anything personal in Coleridge's acknowledgment of Wordsworth as the hybrid figure of this consubstantial labor, this radical meter of transition.

And in truth Wordsworth's autobiography will, despite itself, unfold as the allegorical understanding of this image of meter's destabilization of the imaginary: it will be a poem beginning with the pure cadences of his native stream, which will measure its progress beat by beat, foot by foot, extricating its grand theme from the soil of native English meter. Coleridge's greeting heralds that "philosophical poem" which meditates the cadences with which the mind steadies its footing in the suspenseful world. It is a text that Coleridge names and can in good faith profess. After the Revolution, Coleridge does not in fact die; but he does fall off from poetry. And that falling becomes his calling: criticism. In one of his early and enthusiastic letters home from Germany, Coleridge mentioned a visit to "Professor Ebeling." He added, "Now what a Professor is, I know not," and promised to "enquire & inform" his wife in a subsequent "account of the German Universities & the condition of their Literary Men" (*CL*, 1:436). Once again, Coleridge's aim answers to an act of counterrevolutionary closure, brutally voiced by Burke:

"Here the Magistrate must stand in the place of the Professor. They who cannot or will not be taught must be coerced" (22 July 1791, in *CLB*, 6:304). Like so many of Coleridge's promises, this one was only partially fulfilled.[39] Yet the demonstration of "what a Professor is" occurs in the letter we have been reviewing, where, outside of the coercive kingdom, professing Wordsworth supersedes confessing Coleridge. We might be inclined to describe this moment as an epochal transfer of powers: that moment when Wordsworth, who has since ruled the modern poetic imagination, finally impressed his dominion on the subjected Coleridge. But Coleridge's acknowledgment of the Wordsworthian text presupposes that power is lodged in the kind of affective transfer that disables mastery's dialectic.[40] The personal may be the political, but this transitive arrangement of cadences and pauses suspends persons as it renews the vitality of English verse in order to frame new social bodies, based not on a mythic contract (only adults can engage in those) but on a continued metrical contact: "I am sure I need not say how you are incorporated into the better part of my being," Coleridge writes to his friend, "whenever I spring forward into the future with noble affections, I always alight by your side" (*CL*, 1:453).

Chapter Four

The Dark Romanticism of
the *Edinburgh Review*

No mere bogeyman, dark Romanticism is a phenomenon in which we should believe, but only in order to shape it to our own good use. Dark Romanticism is neither the negation nor the antithesis of some hypothetical Romantic idealism, which was in fact only cobbled together as an officializing strategy at the end of the Napoleonic wars. Dark Romanticism is the name for a design unseen — unseen because closeted, conspiratorial, eclipsed. In this case, the dark design belongs to that nineteenth-century standard bearer of the Scottish enlightenment, the *Edinburgh Review*, by far the most conspicuous, influential, and durable among those discursive bodies that emerged along the faultline of the Treaty of Amiens. In its inaugural issue of October 1802, the *Edinburgh* published three review essays worthy of note: a sympathetic review of M. Mounier's *On the Influence Attributed to the Philosophes, to the Freemasons, and to the Illuminati, on the Revolution in France*, which debunks "conspiratorial theories of revolutionary agency"; a scathing review of Robert Southey's *Thalaba*, which attributes conspiratorial agency to a "sect" of poets derisively called "the Lake School"; and an ostensibly hardheaded review of Henry Thornton's *An Inquiry into the Nature and Effects of the Paper Credit of Great Britain*, which mentions no conspiracy at all but nonetheless produces one. It is not only the acutely felt incapacity of the *Edinburgh Review* to do without conspiratorial explanations of social and economic movements but also the pathos of its inadvertently becoming the accomplice to those sects it must, as the precondition for securing cultural autonomy, stigmatize that constitute the review's exemplary history and its dark Romanticism.

The *Edinburgh Review* opened its first issue with a review of Mounier's book, written to combat the pernicious effect of the conspiratorial theories of the French Revolution given currency by Abbe Barruel's *Memoirs Illustrating the History of Jacobinism* and James Robison's *Proofs of a Conspiracy against All the Religions and Governments of*

Europe. The stake of "moderates" in this debate was clear: Robison's redaction of Barruel's charges, published in London in 1797, had provoked reactionary thunder from pulpit and Parliament.[1] Mounier counters Barruel's paranoid insistence on deriving deplorable general consequences from the insidious individual intentions of intellectuals by explaining the Revolution as the effect of what he calls the "ordinary causes of political change" (*ER*, 2). His book offers what might be called a liberal rejoinder to the reactionary scenario, according to the broad definition of liberalism offered by Immanuel Wallerstein, who, as we have seen, identifies it as "the emergence of the ideology of normal change." Mounier thereby initiates a historiographic line that would eventually include Alexis de Tocqueville and, more recently, François Furet.[2] The predominant trait of this liberal descent is the identification of the emergence of the *ideology* of normal change: for Mounier, as for the editors of the *Edinburgh Review*, normal change is, by definition, nothing new; it had been proceeding all along — it became necessary to shift from a revolutionary ideology that misconstrued beneficial social change as necessarily violent and discontinuous to a political economy that redescribed change as continuous, systematic, and, therefore, predictable.

Although the review generally approves of Mounier's puncturing of reactionary horror stories, it balks at his depreciation of the philosophes' contribution to the revolutionary impulse.[3] The *Review* mildly notes that Mounier has an interest in soft-pedaling the philosophers' contribution: he feels for the "philosophers some of the partialities of a brother." Impartial, the review can offer a more accurate diagnosis of the philosophers' role: it judges them "responsible for the French Revolution" while exonerating them from "guilt." The review elaborates that distinction as it outlines Mounier's conjunctural theory of the outbreak of the Revolution, which explains it as a response to a unique set of circumstances "to which no parallel could be found in the history of the world" (*ER*, 5). The review endorses Mounier's theory but with the reservation that those circumstances were "symptoms of disorder and not the efficient and ultimate causes. To produce the effects that we have witnessed," it insists (with a realism that the suspension of hostilities afforded to writers on the left and the right), "there must have been a revolutionary spirit fermenting in the minds of the people, which took advantage of those occurrences, and converted them into engines for its own diffusion and increase" (6). That revolutionary spirit, it adds, arose from "the change that had taken place in the condition and sentiments of the people; from the progress of commercial opulence; from the diffusion of information, and the prevalence of political discussion." And it is undeniable that "the philosophers were instrumental in bringing about this change; that they had attracted the public attention to the abuses of government, and spread very widely among the people the sentiment of their grievances and their rights" (7–8) — thus effectively readying public opinion for a revolutionary spark, which, however, they could in no way have foreseen. Although "their writings may have begun that motion, which terminated in ungovernable violence," that indirect consequence in no way impeaches the philosophers' motives or their project of enlightenment. "Their designs . . . were pure and honourable; and the natural tendency and promise of their labours was exalted and fair. They failed, by a fatality which they were not bound to foresee; and a concurrence of events, against which it was impossible for them to provide, turned that to mischief, which was planned out by wisdom for good" (11).

The review nicely splits the difference between Mounier and Barruel: imputing social agency to the philosophers while exonerating them from *revolutionary* agency, from executing a conspiratorial design to subvert the established order. "The idea, in short, of a conspiracy, regularly concerted, and successfully carried on by men calling themselves philosophers, for the establishment of a republic, appears to us to be most visionary and extravagant. Such a supposition has, no doubt, a fine dramatic effect, and gives an air of theatrical interest to the history; but in the great tragedy of real life, there are no such fantastic plots or simple catastrophes" (*ER*, 13). Not only Barruel but also Burke seems to have been the target of this effort at detheatricalizing and de-Gothicizing the history of the Revolution. The *Edinburgh Review* applies to foreign events the transactional model of normal change that Scottish philosophy had long found apt for the Great Britain that emerged in the Glorious Revolution of 1688 and that was formally enacted by the Act of Union in 1707. The generic tag of *tragedy* seems to have been invoked to patch over the gaps in what is an embryonically functionalist account of the role of the philosophers, who are instrumental in readying public opinion for a change. *Tragedy* confers a normative tone and tendency on real life and, like Scottish historiography and English novels, wards off the conspiratorial and the prophetic by embedding the "concurrence of events" within the elastic precincts of the probable.

Considered from the perspective of the history of political theory,

Mounier's book is a document of liberalism. Considered from the perspective of the history of regimes, it is clearly a consular document, intent on legitimizing the Bonaparte regime's revolutionary antecedents. The *Edinburgh*'s briefs for circumstantial fatality and for the preponderant importance of commerce in goods and ideas announce its liberal commitments. Considered as a social act, the appearance of the review would seem to signal the reemergence of a civil sphere in which views could be exchanged, claims made and disputed, without danger of state intervention. The review thus appears as an exemplary document of the Addington administration—the ministry patched together in 1801 out of those pacific Tories favored by the king subsequent to Pitt's resignation from power following his bad gamble on Catholic emancipation. From its inception, Addington's ministry had been wholly identified with the tense suspension of hostilities between the British and French effected by the ill-fated treaty signed at Amiens in May of 1802. Sheridan probably captured the national mood best when he famously called it "a peace at which every man rejoiced, and of which every man was ashamed."[4] The general opinion seems to have been that Britain had conceded more to France in Europe and the West Indies than France had yielded elsewhere; yet news of the peace was greeted with popular jubilation, and public opinion seems to have accepted that the concessions were worth the respite from a long war.[5]

"Respite" is the key. Few were persuaded that the treaty would resolve the longstanding quarrel between Britain and France, whether by guaranteeing the former's security or satisfying the latter's appetite. Addington found some support in the peace party of the Whigs, but it could not long balance the objections leveled against the Treaty by those such as Grenville, who, stiff in his distrust of France and the man who led her, expressed his confidence "that there is no hope of peace for Europe, or for England, but by raising up some sufficient barrier against Bonaparte's ambition, which aims at universal empire, not in the figurative, but in the most literal acceptation of those terms."[6] Grenville put the issue severely but accurately: the Treaty of Amiens did not so much establish peace as set the conventions for an epoch defined by the continued *hope* for peace.

The *Edinburgh Review* had good reason to be hopeful. Mounier's formulation of a "conjuncture" theory of Revolution encouraged the opportune belief that the incendiary set of circumstances was unlikely to be repeated—especially not in Great Britain, where contemporary philosophers (i.e., *Edinburgh* reviewers) had the example of the French behind them and the truths of political economy before them. The Tory-engineered treaty justified a dismissal of conspiracies abroad and legitimated Whiggish complacency about the kind, intensity, and extent of popular disturbances at home.

In that light, the stridency of the review of Robert Southey's *Thalaba, the Destroyer*, which keeps company with Mounier in the first issue of the *Review*, seems bizarre. The *Edinburgh Review* adopts the strikingly unphilosophical perspective of the "catholic poetical church" and zealously sets about discharging what it calls "its inquisitorial office." "The author who is now before us," proclaims the review,

> belongs to a *sect* of poets, that has established itself in this country within these ten or twelve years, and is looked upon, we believe, as one of its chief champions and apostles. The peculiar doctrines of this sect, it would not, perhaps, be very easy to explain; but, that they are *dissenters*, from the established systems in poetry and criticism is admitted, and proved, indeed, by the whole tenor of their compositions. Though they claim, we believe, to a creed and a revelation of their own, there can be little doubt, that their doctrines are of *German* origin, and have been derived from some of the great modern reformers in that country. Some of their leading principles, indeed, are probably of an earlier date, and seem to have been borrowed from the great apostle of Geneva. (*ER*, 63)

Although the characterization of Southey and the "sect" of poets sounds like a paranoid version of M. H. Abrams's *Natural Supernaturalism* — secularism's repressed — we are not, I suppose, meant to take it altogether seriously. The passage flagrantly indulges in the kind of hyperbolic sarcasm that speedily made the *Edinburgh Review* notorious. Even so, it is surprising to find the students of Dugald Stewart aping the hysterical diatribes that resounded from English pulpits following the publication of Barruel and Robison in 1797, such as that of Charles Dauben, who decried "a wild sectarian spirit growing up in this country, which, if not properly counteracted, will work to the utter subversion of its constitution."[7] To find such a sentiment erupting in 1802 during the "hope of peace" and penned by the epigones of the Scottish enlightenment suggests something both out of character and out of time.

The *Edinburgh Review* proceeds to unpack its references, which play on parallels between protestant reformers Luther and Calvin and poets Schiller and Rousseau, respectively. Deciphering the allegory only intensifies the affect, however. The reviewer warns that

the authors of whom we are now speaking have, among them, un-
questionably, a very considerable portion of poetical talent, and
have, consequently, been enabled to seduce many into an admiration of the false taste . . . in which most of these productions are
composed. They constitute, at present, the most formidable conspiracy that has lately been formed against sound judgment in
matters poetical; and are entitled to a larger share of our censorial
notice, than could be spared for an individual delinquent. (*ER*, 64)

This just pages away from the praise bestowed on Mounier for scorning
"the supposition of an actual conspiracy of philosophers and speculative men" in France. Indeed, when the reviewer goes on to reveal that
the conspiracy's "most distinguishing symbol is undoubtedly an affec-
tation of great simplicity and familiarity of language" (64), his insinua-
tion that the poets' provocatively demotic diction doubles as a sectarian
sign or password invokes a third context for the "German" origins of
this conspiratorial sect: not merely Lutheran reformers or Schillerian
Sturm und Drang, but the secret protomasonic rituals of the Illuminati,
supposedly founded by Dr. Adam Weishaupt at the University of In-
golstadt in Bavaria in 1775, and the stuff of Barruel's nightmares. The
first formal identification of a Romantic movement in English letters —
what would become known as the Lake School — coincides with the
detection of a dark design that motivates that movement and colors
even its most apparently innocent productions. And that, as they say, is
no accident.

The inconsistency between the Mounier and the Southey pieces is
clear enough. But what to make of it? Do we want to call it a contradiction? And if so, is it a self-contradiction? What does it mean to think of
a periodical review in terms of a "self"? Almost no readers of the review
knew whether or not the two anonymous essays were written by the
same person. Does self-contradiction apply when two reviews in the
same journal come to antithetically different conclusions about similar
phenomena? Does anonymity excuse contradictory articles, or should
it operate as a severer constraint against them? Do we attribute the
contradiction to the failure of editorial oversight or to a deeper, perhaps
conspiratorial design?

The *Edinburgh Review*'s sarcasm, I suggest, symptomatizes a will to
construct a "self" immune to the consequences of contradiction, a self
something very like a nation-state. Benedict Anderson has addressed
the vital function that this overcoming of self-contradiction serves for
the modern nation: The nation is "imagined as a *community* because,

regardless of the actual inequality and exploitation that may prevail in each, the nation is always conceived as a deep, horizontal comradeship. Ultimately it is this fraternity that makes it possible, over the past two centuries, for so many millions of people, not so much to kill, as willingly to die for such limited imaginings."[8] In her recent study of the progressive consolidation of rivalrous regions and suspicious classes into the British nation at the turn of the nineteenth century, Linda Colley has similarly argued that the unstable legitimacy of that imaginary community came to rest on precisely the question of the populace's willingness to die for it. The overriding question for the British government, facing a fully mobilized and aggressive enemy across the Channel during the last decade of the eighteenth century and the first decade of the nineteenth, was "How many Britons could be got to fight?"[9]

During the early years of the war the British government had been as afraid of its own people as the enemy. The dramatic change came in 1797, "when Napoleon's Army of England encamped along the French coastline" (Colley, 289) and threatened imminent invasion. The problem of getting Britons to fight was solved by making Yorkshiremen, Highlanders, and Welshmen, men and women, who might have differing or conflicting commitments, to think of themselves as Britons, members of a single Protestant nation threatened by an inveterate foe, whose novel atheism was only an outgrowth of their superstitious Catholicism. Colley gives a good, circumstantial account of the mobilization of a British people during 1797 and 1798, when the Defense of the Realm Act was published, and vividly describes the agitation in 1803, when, as she says, "panic about an imminent French invasion was at its height" and a rush of volunteering occurred, especially in the Southern counties (283). But Colley omits from her narrative the period when the Treaty of Amiens officially suspended the specular configuration of British Self and French Other, on which the fraught ideological project of forcibly constructing the national imaginary rested. In its review of *Thalaba* the *Edinburgh* provides a rhetorical justification for an Amiens-type respite in its criticism of the Lake poets' monotonous attempts at sublimity: "The effect even of genuine sublimity, therefore, is impaired by the injudicious frequency of its exhibition, and the omission of those intervals and breathing-places, at which the mind should be permitted to recover from its perturbation or astonishment" (*ER*, 70). As for rhetoric, so for statecraft: for the ministers of the British state as well as for the poets, preservation of the sublime force of threats of annihilation demanded occasional respite.[10] The need to economize on stimulation seems reasonable enough (Pitt's shocking fall from power was widely attributed to his exhaustion after so many years at the helm), yet neither the *Edinburgh Review* nor Colley offers an explanation of what, during this breathing-place, continued to make Britain Britain. How did men imagine that the nation could be held together when fear was no longer a prod? Why didn't things fall apart?

That question would not have occurred to the previous generation of Scottish social philosophers, who had read their Hobbes and historicized him in terms of a civil war that was the one unrepeatable event in English history (as opposed to the Glorious Revolution, which guaranteed that all other apparently unique events had already been rehearsed). If all had gone according to theory, the cessation of hostilities in 1802 should have made possible the restitution of what Adam Ferguson had identified as civil society, a zone of secure property rights, voluntary associations, unfettered commercial transactions, and tranquil domesticity, where citizens could freely exercise "moral sentiments and natural affections."[11] But during the war years the cause of aggrandizing Great Britain had demanded the strenuous production of natural affections in Parliament, pulpit, and print; under the instigation and after the example of Edmund Burke, the nation had consolidated its identity by means of an intense political antagonism in which the very notion of civil society had become a conception ideologically polarized against the totalized state of Jacobin or Napoleonic France. As we have seen, from the perspective of agonized dissent — starkly represented by Coleridge's 1798 "Fears in Solitude" — there could be no true civil society where civil rights were still subject to the Test Act. And though the Sedition Acts had expired when Addington came to power, the condition of his accession was compliance with the monarchic insistence that Great Britain remain a Protestant nation and a confessional state.

In short, Ferguson's theory was no longer practical. In *The Idea of Civil Society*, Adam Seligman identifies this deficiency with the rise of liberalism during the Napoleonic era and indirectly addresses the conundrum of British society at this conjuncture, arguing that "it is only in the devolution or disintegration of the civil society tradition that we can understand the growth of liberalism or, rather, liberal-individualism, with all its attendant problems in the 'representation of society'" (Seligman, 36). For Seligman, the "devolution" fulfills Ferguson's vision that "the separation of professions . . . serves in some measure, to break the bands of society, to substitute mere forms and rules of art in place of ingenuity, and to withdraw individuals from the common scene of occupation" (39). Ferguson predicted bad consequences for that fraternity so necessary to the maintenance of a national spirit, for

> if nations pursue the plan of enlargement and pacification, till their members can no longer apprehend the common ties of society, nor be engaged by affection in the cause of their country, they must err on the opposite side, and by leaving too little to agitate the spirits of men, bring on ages of languor, if not of decay. The members of a community may, in this manner . . . lose the sense of every connection, but that of kindred or neighborhood, and have no common affairs to transact, but those of trade: Connection, indeed, or transactions, in which probity and friendship may still take place; but in which the national spirit . . . cannot be exerted. (39)

The cheerful exponent of the anomie that Ferguson feared was David Hume, who approvingly conceived of a man whose social being reduces to the self-regulating "passion of self-interest." The scene where that man associates with others constitutes a social composition that is nothing but a vast network of serial transactions:

> Your corn is ripe today; mine will be so to-morrow. 'Tis profitable for us both, that I shou'd labour with you today, and that you shou'd aid me to-morrow. I have no kindness for you, and know you have as little for me. . . . Hence I learn to do a service to another, without bearing him any real kindness; because I foresee that he will return my service, in expectation of another of the same kind, and in order to maintain the same correspondence of good offices with me or with others. (quoted in Seligman, 40–41)

Hume's example illustrates the three fundamental rules governing market transactions: the stability of property (I know that my green corn will be my ripe corn tomorrow), transfer by consent (I am happy to give you my labor today), and the performance of promises (if you promise to give me your labor in exchange tomorrow). Seligman joins the long line of those who have observed that Hume's naturalistic view of human association allows only a description of its workings, not a prescription of how it ought to work. Any prescription that could pretend to philosophical standing (any one, that is, that does not reduce to proverbs or fables) would require a representation of society, which would ipso facto subordinate the natural behavior of individual men to an arbitrarily rationalized model of the whole and thus impede the fluidity of those exchanges that come as natural to men as their avidity.

Civil society was civil in Ferguson's view because society *could* be adequately represented. The emergence of the militant nation-state entailed the breakdown of civil society. The wartime nation-state is the failure of representations of society and the paranoiac substitution of the imaginary bipolarity of totalized Self and hostile Other. Given that conjectural history, the inability of the *Edinburgh* to represent society is no doubt symptomatic. But it is also programmatic. The *Edinburgh*'s pacific commitment to political economy, the theory that "separates" this particular "profession" of men in the line of Hume, Smith, and Stewart from all other men of letters who appear before the reading public, is also a theory that fully justifies the *Edinburgh Review*'s lack of a representation of society. The format of the *Edinburgh*, which allows the writers to appear periodically in essays that are individual transactions between anonymous reviewers and their anonymous readers, neatly epitomizes market principles. The *Edinburgh* aims to be the medium of an exchange carried out in a philosophical spirit indistinguishable from the commercial spirit, as Francis Horner (one of the founding editors) attests when he records in his journal: "an idea which broke in upon me during the course of my argument, and which I fancy might admit of a successful prosecution; viz. that with respect to diffusion among the community at large, knowledge may be considered in the light of a commodity, prepared by a separate profession, and consumed or enjoyed by the community as a luxury."[12] The *Edinburgh Review* commodified Horner's epiphany, thereby communicating to its enterprise a certain transparency and a kind of objectivity; for, as the *Edinburgh* affirms, "even in theory, no definite boundary can be marked between the circulating medium, whether paper or metallic, and the commodities of which it facilitates the exchange" (*ER*, 176).

From such a perspective, ardent speculations about better and worse political systems are dangerous; they breed divisive factions. According to the cautious Horner, "the general principles of internal economy and regulation are far more worthy of the interest and attention of the political philosopher, because more immediately connected with the public happiness, than discussions with regard to the comparative advantages of different constitutions." He worries about

> the share which the contagious spirit of party disputation almost insensibly leads most people to take in the parties of the day; a subject on which I ought soon to bring myself to a decision. The plan of sentiment and conduct can scarcely be difficult to form in my situation, and with my views; at too great a distance from the

scene of public action for a man of liberal ambition to entertain
any desire of political eminence, it can be no arduous task for me
to fix myself in uncontrollable independence, and, by the intrench-
ments of liberal opinion and candid judgment of character, to
insulate myself altogether from all forms of faction. (Horner,
1:131–32)

If the supercilious review of *Thalaba* is in part motivated by the
Edinburgh's desire to differentiate its editorial board from a faction,
perhaps its hyperbole obeys the same impulse that pressed Horner to
insist on insulating himself "altogether." For Lowland Scottish intellectuals, factionalism had long been a stigma, less for the classical republican reasons than out of allegiance to a cosmopolitan ethos which,
transformed into nationalist ideology, had become an effective vehicle for the professional advancement of those canny Scots who had
adopted that ethos and formulated that ideology. The "separate profession" of those Scottish men of letters was that being Scottish is no
profession at all — merely an accident of birth. Like Hume and so many
others who traveled the high road from Edinburgh to London, whether
by coach or by moral essay, Francis Horner labored to eradicate what
he called "the old leaven of Scottish corruption" from his speech and
writing (Horner, 1:26). In part, this purgation of telltale marks of
the peculiar Scottish character reflected that tropism for the center,
whether for London or Paris, that distinguished Scottish intellectuals in
the late eighteenth century. In part, it was also a defense against the
Wilkesite attacks on the interlopers from the North during the administration of the Scottish Lord Bute. Wilkes succeeded in stigmatizing the
Scots as a faction whose extraordinary success in finding places under
George II suggested favoritism and the kind of clandestine influence
that had been traditionally associated with the conspiratorial plottings
of the Jesuits (Colley, 120–32).

Anxiety about avoiding the appearance of such partiality surfaces in
the review of *Thalaba*, which vigorously ferrets out and harshly indicts
suspected provincialisms. Apparent simplicity degenerates into "slov-
enliness and vulgarity": a single word or misplaced accent is enough
to make poet, speaker, or tragic hero ridiculous: "We are apt enough to
laugh at the mock-majesty of those whom we know to be but common
mortals in private; and cannot permit Hamlet to make use of a single
provincial intonation, although it should only be in his conversation
with the grave-diggers" (*ER*, 65). The same anxiety speaks in a journal
entry made by Horner near the end of his first foray into London in

1802, when he was trying to make up his mind whether or not to relocate from Edinburgh and only a month or two before he began working on his own contributions to the first issue of the *Edinburgh*. Horner compared his "idea of a perfect conversation," which involves a "candid, liberal and easy discussion of opinions" with the manner of his countrymen: "I shall only remark farther in this place, that between Sharp and Mackintosh, for example, there seems to me too much of an assentation with respect to canons of criticisms, &c.; as if they lived too much together; as if they belonged to a kind of sect; or as if there was something of compromise between them" (Horner, 1:185). "Compromise" suggests a sectarian collusion, an excessive intimacy between men that suppresses candor and restrains liberal discussion. There is more than a suggestion of homosocial anxiety in this description of men who live too much together and compromise, as if there is no stopping point between a public exchange of opinions that are attached to no particular bodies and an "assentation" so private that it is inarticulate, bodily intimacy.

What Horner calls "intrenchment in liberal opinion" insulates one from the lure of sectarian truth claims and the contagious consequences of excessive assentation just as trading insulates men from closeness that could be misprized as collusive or sexual. Hume's three principles of social exchange — stability, promise, and consent — are abstract, serially articulated, and reciprocally presupposed. They do not entail a contract theory. A transaction is not an event that wins its identity from the observance of outward forms. The promise need not be overtly performed to be made, for the promise, like the act of consent and like stability of property, is presupposed by the transaction. Although it does not require the formality of a contract, a promise is nonetheless different from the tacit understanding that Horner calls "compromise," which requires a moment of mutual presence, breathing together. No one need be present to intimate or to sense a promise, which is impersonal and nonconspiratorial — that is, conventional. No one need be present for an exchange to occur.[13] Liberal opinion insulates itself in a kind of transcendental empiricism: no formal promise or act of consent need be locatable, no promise need have been kept, yet exchange will prosper as long it is still theoretically possible for a promise to be kept. By "theoretically possible" I mean that a participant in the transaction can be brought or can bring himself to believe that the promise presupposed by an act of exchange will, despite any and all appearances to the contrary, eventually be kept.

The *Edinburgh* reviewers aspire to be for their place and time what the philosophes of Paris were for theirs, instruments of change. But if the Enlightenment ethos of the philosophes put the emphasis on bringing about change, the professionalist ethos of the *Edinburgh* reviewers lays the stress on the instrumental cultivation of belief—which is only prudent, since change will occur anyway. Or so things have been opportunely disposed in Great Britain. And in Great Britain, as the review of Henry Thornton's *An Inquiry into the Nature and Effects of the Paper Credit of Great Britain* (1802) argues, that "national establishment" which most effectively regulates change and combats sectarianism— and with greater force than either the Church or government of England—is the Bank of England, the "mainspring of that complicated mechanism, by which the commercial payments of this country are transacted" (*ER*, 187). The review of Thornton strongly foregrounds those themes of political economy which reflect on the *Edinburgh Review*'s own ambitions: the concept of the division of labor is applied to the distinction between author as particularizing informant and reviewer as generalizing theorist; the regulation of the distribution of commodities is given priority over their production; and, most importantly, the responsibility for controlling the fluctuation of credit is annexed to the general project of exerting influence over the nation.

The pause in hostilities brought about by the Treaty of Amiens was the occasion for Thornton's sustained reflection on the suspension of payments in specie, which had been imposed during the first serious invasion scare in 1797 to prevent a likely run on gold and thus inexorable ruin for the central bank, the government, and the war effort. The political importance accorded to the suspension of specie payments demands that a major subplot be added to the story of nation-building told by Colley. If, as she argues, the British nation was consolidated in response to the threat of an invasion in 1797, whether real, perceived, or invented, that selfsame act of self-defense also entailed the suspension of the central promise that until that time had been assumed to guarantee the regular operations of the British economy: the promise that every bill of exchange and bank note could be exchanged for gold at the central Bank of England. Preferring to risk a drastic devaluation of money rather than countenance the possibility of a panic-stricken run on the central bank (country banks had already suffered ominous catastrophes), Pitt opted to intervene in the financial system on a scale rivaled only by the Jacobin innovators denounced by Burke in 1791. By suspending payment in gold, the Prime Minister struck directly at the "mainspring of that complicated mechanism," as if, reckless theorist, he was determined to prove that in the last instance political emergency trumps political economy.

The emergency suspension had lasted for five long years by the time Thornton, confident that the treaty would mean a return to normal conditions, assessed its results. The review summarized those results in wholly positive terms:

> That the immediate convertibility of paper into gold is an indispensable condition of its credit, as we are taught by the language of system, has been disproved by the recent history of the Bank of England; which has happily quieted the apprehensions, to which our best informed politicians yielded, on account of the event of 1797. The maintenance of credit during a short interval of suspended payments, was a case, indeed, which might have been foreseen from theory, and was not wholly unknown to our previous experience. But that a restriction of this kind should have been continued for more than five years, without any depreciation of the paper from a failure of confidence, is a fact which has falsified all reasonable prediction, and forms an exception to the most confident maxims of all former economists. (ER, 177)

By the time that summary appeared in the *Edinburgh Review* in October 1802, Addington, in the quietest revolution in British financial history, had extended the term of the restriction indefinitely. The suspension of specie conversion would now prove to be the norm, and the exception to the maxims of economists would prove the following nongolden rule: "The necessity of immediate access to gold, for the credit of paper, may be superseded, it appears, by *a full persuasion on the part of the public*, that the paper is secured by ample funds" (ER, 177; emphasis added). In other words, the government officially replaced the gold standard with a rhetorical standard.

Consequences follow: First, once immediate access has been superseded, eventual access becomes indefinitely elastic, and the guarantee of value, physical contact with gold, becomes drastically attenuated. A system based on the virtual possibility of immediate conversion of paper into gold has become a system sustained by the actuality of the continual transfer of credit from trader to trader. Second, the episode proves the economic importance of the rhetorical ideal of "full persuasion," which funds the transfer of credit and which is the psychological precondition for the national realization of Horner's ideal of the perfect conversation. Third, if full persuasion is crucial to the prosperity of the nation, so is the discursive instrument for inducing it and shaping it to appropriate ends. Fourth, although sectarianism jeopardizes full persuasion by splintering the totality, nevertheless the ardor that welds the sect is the quality of affect that political economy will have to exploit in order that full persuasion in the supersect called the nation might be sustained.

The conviction that the economy does rule defines political economy, and if the *Edinburgh* has an overriding mission, it is to convince the reading public that what defines political economy should rule "England, which is the native country of political economy" (*ER*, 173). Thanks to Amiens's lifting the heavy hand of political interference, it has become possible in 1802 to determine the sovereign reason why the usual business persisted through the turbulence of a perilous war and despite the spasmodic interventions of the king's ministers.

> If the Bank of England must now be considered as a national establishment, not merely influencing, by the superior magnitude of its capital, the state of commercial circulation, but guiding its movements according to views of public policy, an important revolution has taken place since the first erection of that corporation to a banking establishment. That power of issuing the medium of exchange, with the opportunities it implies of varying its quantity and value, which, while precious coin was in use, was exercised under the immediate prerogatives of the Crown, is now virtually invested in the Governor and Directors of the Bank of England. In the official character of the Board, some of the functions of sovereignty are united to those of a trader; and the opportunities of banking profits are blended with a trust and charge of the public interest. It will be pleasing, if these shall prove more happily compatible, than they have been found in other instances. The organization of this establishment, possessed of such means to controul the operations of commerce, as well as to facilitate the advance of financial supplies, may, into our political constitution already so complicated, introduce a new principle of action, the effect of which cannot be clearly discerned. Perhaps, an unbounded field will be opened for the extension of ministerial influence. Perhaps, an unexpected controul may be gained to the people, over the views and measures of the executive. (*ER*, 196)

Pitt's radical surgery had the unintended consequence of establishing a bank possessing something like Horner's "uncontrollable independence." No longer slave to the requirement of immediate conversion of paper into gold, and protected from the mindless "contagion" that breeds panic among the uninformed, the bank — monolithic, disinterested, and irresistible — has become a new establishment that guides the movement of money and presides over the network of concurring transactions which compose the financial system. The *Edinburgh Review*'s apt annunciation of this as "an important revolution" anticipates and crucially supplements P. G. M. Dickson's twentieth-century identification of the seventeenth-century "financial revolution" by naming the epochal British answer to the world-shaking of the French. In historiographic time Dickson's revolution must drop to third place, after the articulated event of 1797/1802 — a joint venture attributable to Pitt's act, Thornton's study, and the *Edinburgh*'s review.[14] As in 1688, a new establishment has emerged in a glorious revolution that, however bloodless and protracted, is nonetheless truly revolutionary, for it introduces an altogether new principle of action and a new locus of sovereignty.

The review of Thornton's investigations disclosed a truth that Thornton could not himself deduce: the capital of banks is not gold but confidence. As Thornton provides detailed information for the review's systematic generalizations, so do local banks gather information on individual traders, which enables them "to measure out confidence very nearly in a just proportion" and to communicate that information vertically, up the scale of banking, to the Bank of England, where the intelligence of the system is lodged and where individual confidences are profitably generalized into the capital of credit, which the bank can then reallocate down the chain to its subordinate banks throughout the system. Its discernment of that new principle of action qualifies the *Edinburgh Review* as the coequal of those philosophes who sparked the revolutionary spirit during the *ancien régime* — with the signal difference that the reviewer's ex post facto generalizations satisfy the man of letters' ambition to participate in the revolutionary spirit while remaining immunized from any blame that might attach to those who spin out theories and promote agendas.

The *Edinburgh*'s vision of a revolution accompli does not tempt the future by hope; it pacifies the future for prediction. Henceforth there will be nothing to fear from any conjuncture of events; no change will bring great change. And if the peculiar blend of sovereignty and finance opens a potentially boundless field for a ministerial influence that may be well or ill considered, the possibility of increased "control" by "the people" opens an exciting prospect for the fulfillment of the *Edinburgh*'s ambition to be that "instrument of change" for Great Britain that Quesnay, Turgot, and Necker had been for France. In Great Britain, who the people are, as well as what the people want, are matters of opinion, and what opinion matters will, if the future works out as planned, be subject to the judgment of the *Edinburgh Review*.

If the social function of the *Edinburgh* as influential instrument of normal change seems generally clear, its qualifications to fill this niche are not. Determining the rules by which editors combine opinions and the protocol by which that group or board settles on views, commits to them, and propagates them to produce a self-regulated economy of public opinion is a matter of public importance, a matter as important as understanding how money actually circulates in the bank-regulated financial system. Deep in his research into the financial system of Great Britain in 1801, Horner had confided in his journal, "I find the circulation of money a very dark subject, though a few gleams of light have struck me" (*ER*, 109). Although Thornton's book demonstrates that the Bank of England's board of directors moves the economy, the actual circulation of money remains obscure. It is not clear how the board itself is moved, how accounts are finally and decisively settled. What is the practical consequence of installing sovereignty within a commercial system and distributing authority among a board of governors? Just as the bipolar model of national identity cannot explain social cohesion during the suspension of hostilities, so political economy lacks a theory to explain how the banking establishment exercises its authority in practice.

To fill in the gap the *Edinburgh Review* renders a scene of accounting designed to exemplify the way the banking system reaches a decision. The scene appears at the end of a long description of the way the

> establishment of such a system of [vertically integrated] banks, and the transference of ultimate payments to one particular place, are in the natural course of that progressive subdivision of labour, which extends itself over an opulent and industrious country. The receipt and payment of money, instead of being conducted at home, are transferred, by every trader, to his banker, who devises means both of abridging his labour, and of economizing the use of money, especially of that costly part of it which consists of specie.

The reviewer goes on to supply his readers with a glimpse of that "particular place" where "ultimate payments" are made:

> The ingenuity of these money-dealers, in sparing the circulating medium, is aptly illustrated by a custom which prevails among the

city bankers. Each of them sends a clerk at an appointed hour in the afternoon, to a room provided for their use. Each clerk there exchanges the drafts on other bankers received at his own house, for the drafts on his own house received at the houses of other bankers. The balances of the several bankers are transferred from one to another, in manner which it is unnecessary to explain in detail, and the several balances are finally wound up by each clerk into one balance. The difference between the whole sum which each banker has to pay to all other city bankers, and the whole sum which he has to receive from all other city bankers, is, therefore, all that is discharged in bank notes or money; a difference, evidently, much less in its amount than that to which the several differences would be equal. (*ER*, 189)

The national bank weighs in at the end of a series of transfers occurring in a "system of banks, connected in subordination to each other." Just as traders transfer receipt and payment from their home to their metropolitan bankers, so do these city bankers send their clerks from their home offices to convene in a room reserved for their exclusive transactions, where, in Ferguson's words, they "withdraw from the common scene of occupation." There the clerks tote up debits and credits, tick after tick, until just one difference remains between the whole sum owed and the whole sum to be received. It is the economizing genius of the system, its marvelous reversal of entropy, that the whole difference thus synthesized is less than the sum of its parts. But how could this be? The *Edinburgh* can produce no general answer. The difference of this particular difference cannot be explained from a position outside the particular room where it appears to the eyes of the exclusive company; the secret of the difference is embedded in the canny and intimate practice of this sect of clerks who combine together to make the economy work. The clerks may enter the room as representatives of the bankers, but the duties they perform answer to no sovereign prescription or rule. The *Edinburgh* does discover why things did and do not fall apart; but it does not isolate the mechanics by which self-regulation occurs — it discovers no self at all. Instead, with a kind of fraternal intuition, the reviewer unveils a clerkly cult at the heart of the machine, impelled by a radically social passion and darkly devoted to performing the vital discharge of difference.

What do we learn about this difference? It is, the *Edinburgh Review* informs its readers, "discharged in bank notes or money" — an equivocation, for the review has already defined *money* as including bank notes, and, as we know, since 1797 the difference could not legally be converted into gold. By holding onto a distinction between bank notes and money, the *Edinburgh* flinches in the face of the appearance of the new principle of action, which requires no gold at all. For if, prior to 1797, paper money was a "formal representation of value," subject to immediate conversion, the difference at the center of this goldless system might be called form itself: the form of a promise is transferred, but without the content; the form of money discharges difference without a representational office. What could a promise mean in a place where the full persuasion *in* the system and the full persuasion *of* the system are all but identical? Absolutely singular and immediate, the formulation and discharge of this difference is nonetheless an everyday occurrence, banking's *culture*. Although completely conventional, the clerks' cultic transaction could only result from what, in his disapproving comments on Mackintosh and Sharp, Horner called "assentation," the kind of conspiratorial agreement or "compromise" reached by men of the same full persuasion, who are in the habit of intimacy, whose agreement on the canons of banking go unspoken, that is, a compromise reached by clerks who trust one another more than gold itself. Compromise occurs by the synthesis of a difference that does not represent value but is the formal device by which members of the sect at once acknowledge the "partialities of a brother" and discharge their obligations — a formality of the same kind as the masonic hieroglyph or the handshake of the Illuminati. The Bank of England's sovereign principle of action ultimately depends on a clerkly coalition's discharge of difference, an improvisation impenetrably dark to the empirical eye and ungraspable by "pre-established codes of decision." That sectarian discharge of difference is a Romantic movement, insofar as that unprincipled act, like the affect induced by the poet's shifts of meter or diction, is, first, before it can be designated anything at all, an elementary form of social feeling.

Common to the reviews of Mounier, Southey, and Thornton are two not completely harmonious themes: (1) There is no need to fear the activity of sects or conspiracies; and (2) there now exist influential groups of men who are organized on new principles of action and who operate secretly. The first theme serves two fundamental aims of the *Edinburgh*: first, it makes a positive claim that insurrectionary activity does not threaten the peace — the only conspiracies abroad are the burlesque conspiracies of visionary poets; second, it fends off potential characterizations of the *Edinburgh Review* as a faction or clique that threatens established power. To criticize is not to dissent. Yet, critical analysis does matter; it influences. The problem is imagining how influence works without having recourse to a paranoid hypothesis, how to describe agency that is simultaneously effective and social without being revolutionary and collective. We have seen this aim expressed in the qualifications that the *Edinburgh* makes to the Mounier thesis. It also accounts for the intensity of the affect that the *Edinburgh* lathers on the Lake poets, for although they are mocked as a sect, the *Edinburgh* invests in the notion that these men of letters have some kind of appeal, that their doctrinaire abuse of poetic language strongly affects their readers, however few.

If the *Edinburgh Review*'s assertion of its own influence does imply possession of what Horner called "uncontrollable independence," it looks like a claim to something like sovereignty. No wonder the claim is so guarded. In a nation where sovereignty still flows from the monarch, as value flows from gold, it is difficult to conceive how sovereignty might be distributed and easy to imagine that a claim to sovereignty would inevitably be tainted by Jacobinism or Rousseauism and construed as a challenge to the legitimacy of the regime and what F. H. Hinsley has called the "absolute sovereignty of the Crown-in-Parliament," which received its finished form in the Glorious Revolution of 1688.[15] Part of what it means to be "intrenched in liberal opinion" is to avoid making claims of or about sovereignty — to restrict oneself to descriptions that lead to generalizations and entail judgments by virtue of their ineluctable reasonableness. Yet though political economy — the school of Hume, Smith, and Stewart — concerned itself with the allocation of credit rather than the distribution of sovereignty, that discursive orientation originally presupposed the effective transfer of sovereignty from the state to the economy. If Hume's earlier adherence to gold answered to a fear that the credit economy would be subject to the whims of greedy speculators and needy monarchs, it was also true that an economy that lodged full and final authority in gold could not, finally, escape the tropology of the monarch and subjection to the temperamental state. In the epochal clearing of Amiens, with civil society defunct and with the engine of the national imaginary idling, the darkling editorial board of the *Edinburgh Review* completes a quiet coup by discharging the difference between the sovereign bank and the sovereign king.

The *Edinburgh Review* completes a coup on behalf of the economy and the Bank of England as that establishment best placed to guide it. Sovereignty for the bank is not sovereignty for the *Edinburgh*, however, which lays claim only to influence — and then, only indirectly, as if it were a guilty secret. That guilt is of intellectual, not psychological, origin; it is just the embarrassment of having no theory to justify its own social standing and political assertion. Earlier I introduced the metaphor of the faultline to characterize the peculiar opening that occurred during the transitory peace concocted by the Treaty of Amiens. It is the metaphor deployed by Ernesto Laclau and Chantal Mouffe in their inaugural definition of hegemony, which, they declare, alludes

> to an absent totality, and to the diverse attempts at recomposition and rearticulation which, in overcoming this original absence, made it possible for struggles to be given a meaning and for historical forces to be endowed with full positivity. The contexts in which the concept appear will be those of a *fault* (in the geological sense), of a fissure that had to be filled up, of a contingency that had to be overcome. "Hegemony" will be not the majestic unfolding of an identity but the response to a crisis.[16]

Any description of the 1802 crisis of suspension that scrupulously attempts to sort out the struggle between poetry, reviews, and clerks to provide the language that will discharge the difference between English civil society as it was and postwar Britain as it will be would soon devolve into an indefinite inventory of overdeterminations (much as the Preface to *Lyrical Ballads* does in its attempt to account for the value of poetry). In the absence of a general theory of society (or in advance of Mill's espousal of the label "utilitarian" and Bentham's founding of the *Westminster Review*) which could hope to account for the interaction of the conflicting sovereignties of bank and crown, it was *a fortiori* impossible to derive, let alone apply, one law that would register and control hegemonic competition. Into the clearing carved out by the temporary suspension of the imaginary community of the nation which succeeded on the Treaty of Amiens, emerged not civil society but miscellaneous sectarian societies, each a conspiracy of persuasive imaginings.

In that clearing the *Edinburgh Review*, self-consciously progressing according to enlightenment principles, meets a kind of poetry, regressing according to sectarian delusions. But in that clearing the *Edinburgh* crosses with what it contemns, darkly acknowledging the necessity of Romantic movements among men who would venture to discharge the difference between a social and political system and its absent cause; only its sarcasm prevents the *Edinburgh* from the recognition that it has become the conspiracy it beholds. The *Edinburgh*'s wild sarcasm marks political economy's bafflement by the darkness at the core of those coalitions: the mysterious formalities by which poets group to write poems with indubitable if elusive social consequences, by which clerks efficiently concoct a banking culture, and by which an editorial board put its stamp on the yammering of contemporary discourses. Its sarcasm marks the felt incapacity of the *Edinburgh Review* to comprehend its own social being and force, its inability to face its own occulted Romanticism.

Chapter Five

Romantic Hope
The Maid of Buttermere,
the Right to Write,
and the Future of Liberalism

An idea has taken place among the poor that they should pay no Taxes,
That a better Order of things will ere Long be Brought about. Thousands
Carry about with them Secret Conviction & Indulge a Hope that matters
are growing Ripe.
— William Cookson, Mayor of Leeds, to Lord Fitzwilliam, July 1802

Thy letters have transported me beyond
This ignorant present, and I feel now
The future in the instant.
— *Macbeth*, 1.5.57–59

In September and October of 1802, during the lull in the Continental
War named the Peace of Amiens and roughly when the first issue of the
Edinburgh Review was being readied for the press, Samuel Taylor Coleridge devoted three articles in the *Morning Post* to mining the Bona-
partist analogy between contemporary France and ancient Rome. The
parallel has been given the veneer of plausibility, he indicates, by "a
coincidence of names [that] has been adopted by design and for political
purposes."[1] The question of motive — design and purpose — is crucial to
Coleridge's critique. He approves in principle of historical analogy as a
vehicle of historical truth. Later in the year he would instruct Charles
James Fox that, "as we anticipate the future only by the analogies of the
past, so can we truly and vividly apprehend the past, only by a close
observation of whatever is apparently [analogous] to it in the present"
(*EOT*, 1:392). But imposed correspondences do not constitute true
analogy. However much the French Government aims "to represent
their country as a new Roman Republic" the "exact analogy with consular France," Coleridge argues, "is not the republican period," but "that
when Rome ceased to be a Republic, and the Government was organized into a masked and military despotism." (*EOT*, 1:312–14). Like
the first emperors, the First Consul has strategically preserved the re-

public "in name" only, by mechanically repeating outmoded stereotypes in order to prevent a counterrevolution that would seize on "a mass of old names which had been violently suppressed." Although in its salient features the current regime offers an exact analogy for imperial Rome, French despotism, Coleridge reassures his readers, is unlikely to have the same durability, for "in a great majority of the circumstances, external and internal, it is wholly unlike those of Rome" — whether Julian, Augustan, or even (to compare vile things with vile) Tiberian (*EOT*, 1:333–34). Coleridge lays down the principle that

> fear, hope, and memory are the three great agents, both in the binding of a people to a government, and in the rousing them to a revolution. All three worked together in favour of Tiberius; but it should appear that the First Consul must rely chiefly upon the first. His power is an isthmus of Darien, beat upon by the two oceans of Royalism and Republicanism: of Royalism, aided by a powerful superstition; of Republicanism, aided by the detestation of that superstition (*EOT*, 1:337).

Agents seems an odd word for what might be better called "stimulants," "instruments" or even "agencies." *Agents* hearkens back to the sensational personifications that paraded through Coleridge's frenzied poems of the nineties, such as "The Destiny of Nations," where "From his obscure haunt / Shrieked Fear, of Cruelty the ghastly Dam," or the aggressively allegorical poetic drama "Fire, Famine, and Slaughter," published in the same *Morning Post* in 1798. Coleridge's chronic reliance on hyperbolic agents to dramatize political conflict illustrates David Erdman's distinction that Coleridge was a "political enthusiast" rather than a "political thinker" (*EOT*, 1:lxi). But very few who thought about politics in Great Britain during the revolutionary era did not think enthusiastically. Consider the treatment of Mounier by the self-styled political economic thinkers of the *Edinburgh Review*. Despite criticizing Mounier for his enthusiastic rationalism, the reviewer nonetheless has trouble identifying agency as either individual or collective or precisely locating its source on the imaginary map of the nation. Similarly, in the absence of a coherent theory of how people could be bound together by anything other than the countervailing drives of self-interest or an imperative reason of state, the reviewer of Thornton's *An Inquiry into the Nature and Effects of the Paper Credit of Great Britain* has recourse to the Burkean notion that formal representations with no real referent — banknotes severed from the backing of gold — could galvanize men's bodies into forming bodies of men. Enthusiasm acts before thinking reacts. Coleridge's real limits as a political thinker do not change the fact that others more influential than he (ministers of state, editors) were equally perplexed as to the actual ways in which individual men were roused to depart their homes, amalgamate, and die. They could not explain how commanders as well as cannon fodder were ready to stake their careers, lives, and the fortunes of their nation on the summons of agents such as "King and Country" or "the Ancient Constitution," which are only one step removed from the demonic ground of bardic verse.[2]

If we can credit Coleridge's enthusiastic thinking so far, it seems logical to find sense in his confident prediction that, unlike the Caesars, Bonaparte could not succeed in binding the future to his plans because he relies only on fear to weld the people to his government.[3] Given the options of "fear," "hope," and "memory," the reader of Burke or Wordsworth might conclude that, failing a Tiberian grasp of the entire triad, the greatest of these is memory. Our best reader of both Burke and Wordsworth, Coleridge self-consciously endeavors to appeal to the educated memory of his readers and put recollection of the past to work anticipating, even determining, the future. Indeed, in the contemporary article "On the Circumstances, That Appear Especially to Favour the Bourbons at This Present Time" Coleridge turns historiographic principles directly to the service of reactionary ideology. He assures his readers that a future disciplined by analogical reasoning will be nothing more than the controlled repetition of the past: its legitimate return will coincide with the return of legitimacy. Whether or not Coleridge's legitimist analogizing is any less a "figure dance" than the designed coincidences of the French usurper may be doubted, however — as it was by one resistant reader, Charles Lamb, who stubbornly remained unmoved by Coleridge's elaborate analogies. Lamb observed, "I certainly recognize that your comparisons are acute and witty; but what has this to do with truth?" (*EOT*, 1:339 n. 8). By "truth" Lamb includes truth present and truth future. Another way to express Lamb's skepticism would be to note the omission of "the more sublime and humane excitement of hope" (*EOT*, 1:215) from Coleridge's repertoire of agents. During a suspension of hostilities, when fear of the enemy has lapsed and the "hope of peace" is presumably shared by all Englishmen, it is surely pertinent to ask how reliable an agent hope might be. To what end does hope rouse? Ought hope to be indulged? Can hope be trusted?

"On the 2d instant a Gentleman, calling himself Alexander Augustus Hope, Member for Linlithgowshire, and brother to the Earl of Hopetown, was married at the church of Lorten, near Keswick, to a young woman, celebrated by the tourists under the name of *The Beauty of Buttermere*" — so begins the first of what was to become a series of five articles by Coleridge in the *Morning Post* that appeared from October to the end of December in 1802 under a sequence of heads which epitomize the fatal career of Hope: "A Romantic Marriage (I and II)," "The Fraudulent Marriage," and, finally, "The Keswick Imposter (I and II)." Those articles, interwoven with Coleridge's most provocative political journalism of the Amiens period, serially take advantage of the suspense generated by the unfolding of distant events. The series proceeds as a deliciously suspenseful unpacking of a chest of conjectures. The first article describes Mary "the daughter of an old couple, named Robinson, who keep a poor little pothouse at the foot of the small lake of Buttermere, with the sign of the Char," where Mary "has been all her life the attendant and waiter, for they have no servant." Mary is "now about thirty, and has long attracted the notice of every visitor by her exquisite elegance, and the becoming manner in which she is used to fillet her beautiful long hair; likewise by the uncommonly fine Italian hand-writing in which the little bill was drawn out." Coleridge adds that "she has ever maintained an irreproachable character, is a good daughter, and a modest, sensible, and observant woman" (*EOT*, 1:357–58). Coleridge, who had just visited the scene in August, combines personal knowledge of the woman with an awareness of her celebrity; he was undoubtedly familiar with the body of tourist literature in which she prominently figured.

The so-called Mr. Hope had arrived in Buttermere in July. Although discursive intelligence is a gift the journalist presumes to offer his intimate readers, there is no reason to believe that Hope was not himself conversant with the tourist literature designed to attract the visitor to the locale. He claimed, however, to be on a "fishing expedition," drawn to Buttermere by nothing more than the report that the deep, chill lake was well stocked with char. While in residence, he nonetheless found the opportunity to court simultaneously Mary under the name of Alexander Hope and "a lady of youth, beauty, and good fortune" to whom he was known as Charles Hope. The reporter concludes his first article on an equivocal note:

> The mistake in the name, the want of an establishment suited to his rank, and the circumstance of his attaching himself to a young lady of fortune, had excited much suspicion, and many began to consider him an imposter. His marriage, however, with a poor girl

without money, family, or expectations, has weakened the suspicions entertained to his disadvantage, but the interest which the
good people of Keswick take in the welfare of the beauty of Buttermere, has not yet suffered them to entirely subside, and they await
with anxiety the moment when they shall receive decisive proofs
that the bridegroom is the real person whom he describes himself
to be. The circumstances of his marriage are sufficient to satisfy us
that he is no imposter. (*EOT*, 1:358)

Despite the propitious circumstances, the continuation of what
Coleridge calls "the novel of real life" proved unhappy. Although the
ingratiating stranger boldly franked mail and signed for loans with a
Liverpool merchant in the name of Hope, those locals who knew the
family denounced him as an imposter. It was soon revealed that he had
made three other marriage proposals at the time he had been courting
Mary. Luckily, after their marriage Mary resisted his entreaties to sign
over her mite of property and join him in a Scottish honeymoon.
"Hope" was swiftly apprehended and charged with fraud. But the re-
sourceful scoundrel managed a daring escape across the lake with the
aid of "his old friend the fisherman." "No intelligence," the journalist
comments "has since been received of him." He adds:

> I cannot express the sincere concern, which every inhabitant of the
> country takes in the misfortune of poor Mary, of Buttermere. I
> knew her well; and I can truly say, that she would have been an or-
> nament to any rank of life. She was intelligent, and well-informed,
> and uniformly maintained her dignity, as a woman, never forget-
> ting, or suffering others to forget, that she was the Maid of the Inn,
> the *attendant* of those who stopped at the ale-house, and not the
> *familiar*. (*EOT*, 1:375)

They knew her well, the men and women of Buttermere. And so the
lurid revelations following the Maid's ill-fated marriage proved all the
more shocking. Among the possessions Hope abandoned in his flight,
Coleridge later reports, was a "costly dressing box," which had a double bottom; and in the interspace were a number of letters addressed to
him *from his wife and children,* under the name of "Headfield." Suspected of being the member of some Irish gang, arraigned for felonious
fraud, the Maid of Buttermere's double-dealing husband had now been
exposed as a bigamist. "The Fraudulent Marriage" concludes with the
sigh that "Poor Mary is the object of universal concern."
Coleridge's last two articles actually exhibit less concern for Mary's

plight than for the plunder of information brought to light about the itinerant and promiscuous villain, since recaptured and remanded to Carlisle for trial under the name of Hatfield on the capital charge of forging a parliamentary frank. Coleridge minutely details Hatfield's physical features, including the peculiar "hitch" in his gait, mentions his suspicious Irish connections, and reconstructs his "double game" — observing that it seems to have been Hatfield's maxim "to leave as few white interspaces as possible in the crowded map of his villainy" (*EOT*, 1:408). The final article inventories the adventurer's trunk, which, besides expensive silver toilet trinkets, contains "one letter, a cash book, and the list of several cities in Italy, with a couple of names attached to each." Coleridge reports that from

> the letter, aided by the list of towns, a marvellous story was extracted. The letter was said to be from an Irish banditti, urging this Col. Hope to escape with all possible speed, informing him that a price had been set upon his head, and stating the writer's eagerness to assist him, but that his wounds confined him to his bed. It was concluded, therefore, that this pretended Colonel Hope was a great leader in the Irish rebellion; and the only doubt that remained was, whether the names of the Italian towns in the list were meant for Italian towns at which different agents from the United Irishmen were residents, or whether they were only marks of conspiracy; *names by convention* for different towns and cities in Ireland. [emphasis added]

Coleridge debunks the marvels: on perusing the letter that supposedly records Hope's crowded map of villainy, he learned that it was not from an Irish bandit but "a simple, honest, pious, Scotchman, and an exceedingly loyal subject. That such a story should have been deducted from such a letter, and that too by four or five intelligent men, proves no more, than that they thoroughly expected to find something very wonderful; and what people thoroughly expect they are very apt to create." "I venture to guess," Coleridge adds, with an eye to Pitt's notorious excesses of the nineties, "that blunders, as gross as this, have been made from the same cause, by other secret committees and of higher functions, and of infinitely greater importance" (*EOT* 1:415). And that's about it. No "mark of conspiracy" except to those inclined to find conspiracies everywhere. After pointing the moral, Coleridge devotes a couple of perfunctory paragraphs to an account of the transmission of the "mass of papers" from Mary to a Mr. Moore and then concludes.

Romantic fantasies dissipated, the novel of real life has taken shape: Hope lured Mary forth. And Hope proved false. As it had to French and English Jacobins, to Margaret enisled in her ruining cottage, and to Annette Vallon abandoned on the darkling continent. As hope will for all it rouses. And for those who indulge it. Or so the allegory might run. Hope, the story lessons, whether offered by a military savior or a negotiated peace, is a misnomer or an alias for something that should in fact be feared. Hope is a name only by convention and is allegorical in the most impoverished sense — an arbitrary darkening of the real. Considered as an agent, Hope is nothing but a counterfeiter of false credit. Under the cover of a frank demeanor, Hope bore false witness to a future in which the harsh constraints of "real life" would be suspended, a future in which wishes could be fulfilled and debts forgotten. As events proved, however, Hope's romantic promises were not founded on sound principle or a firm establishment but on a double-bottom. Hatfield's letters are the material evidence of an inescapable biographical past, tokens of memory that curtail Hope by binding him to those he has abandoned.

For Mary, the story ends as Coleridge's literate readers might have expected. Like many heroines before her and since, she mistook fantasy for reality, the romance that she dreamed for the novel that she lived. It is no doubt disturbing that the all too plausible Hope held such appeal for her that she willfully ignored the circumstantial evidence that her suitor was an imposter. Sadly, but on the whole reassuringly, circumstances exert their gravity; the category "novel of real life" describes the generic possibilities that fund the construction of Mary's field of dreams and the generic constraints that delimit her field of action.

Once Mary has completed the Richardsonian progression from someone whose welfare was the interest of her neighbors, to an exemplary beauty who would be an "ornament to any rank," into a "universal object of concern," her novelistic destiny has been fulfilled; and the journalist shifts his attention from bride to groom — apparently attracted by the opportunity to speculate on "the crowded map" of his villainies. Let us follow the reporter's lead. Given that hope had lured Mary forth, suppose we ask what had lured forth Hatfield? The motives for the French government's adoption of names wrested from the fabric of republican Rome are clear enough. But why should a "shaper" undertake this pilgrimage to one of the most remote areas of the kingdom to tie the knot with the waitress in a country inn? Coleridge addresses the question of motive by ventriloquizing the puzzlement of the community:

"What motive could he have to marry poor Mary? Would a shaper marry a poor girl without fortune or connections? If he had married the Irish young Lady, there would be something to say for it;" &c. It was no doubt delightful to the people of the Vales, that so great a man, that a man so generous, so condescending, so affable, so *very* good, should have married one of their own class, and that too a young woman who had been so long their pride, and so much and so deservedly beloved by them. Their reasonings in the imposter's favour were, to be sure, very insufficient to counteract the evidence against him; yet of themselves they were not unplausible. (*EOT*, 1:414)

Debunking the political superstitions of the credulous, who fancy a sect of subversives behind every bush and crag, is one thing. Determining a credible motive is another. And once he has gone on to mock those who misread Hatfield's abandoned documents as evidence of political conspiracy, Coleridge is not left with much to hang a theory on. The likeliest step after sects would be sex. Both sentimental and Gothic novels exploit the possibilities of such a slippage in signification, as Coleridge, aggressively moralistic reader of Richardson, Radcliffe, and Lewis, knew full well. In one light, of course, Hatfield's desire for Mary goes without saying: before her rash marriage turned her into an "object of universal concern" she had been promoted in the tourist literature as an object of general esteem and had "long attracted the notice of every visitor." But a double-bind looms here. The claim that Mary attracted notice gives at least some prima facie support to Hatfield's claim, reported in the *Morning Post*, that "he was *seduced* in the affair!" And the responsibility for such seduction would then have to be lodged either with the comely Mary or with those organs of publicity such as the *Morning Post* which had fetched her into prominence. However superficially plausible, Hatfield's defense cannot finally be credited. Apostate in politics, Coleridge will not turn on the newspaper business that butters his bread. And Mary, proverbially innocent, must be immunized from any suspicion of solicitation.[4] Coleridge must prove that Mary's attractions are not physical—the kind that might excite sexual desire—but aesthetic, a figure that arouses contemplative admiration from a respectful distance. Indeed, he goes far in depreciating her physical features (her face is "pock-fretten," Coleridge notes with a novelist's sense of detail) in order to confer on her a beauty of "figure," or what he prefers to call a "grace."

The capacity of Mary eventually to be transformed into a universal

object of concern (rather than, say, a disputed topic of morals) dictates
that the original apprehension of Mary had to be an affect without sects
or sex, like the "fondness" with which "sons, brothers, husbands" are
imagined to have once gazed on the female "forms / Which grew up
with [them] round the same fire-side" in Coleridge's "Fears in Solitude"
(1798). Mary is in Coleridge's account the kind of formal object about
which there is nothing sexual. But that status cannot be subject to the
definitional attachment of a name alone, for Coleridge wants to insist
that this aestheticized beauty or grace is without motive or design, that
it is natural rather than merely conventional, like the republican vocabulary in Bonaparte's France. For Coleridge's plot to work, it must be as
natural to be drawn to Mary as it is to be drawn to the lakes and their
beauteous environs. Coleridge claims that "there is a larger proportion
of fine forms, or pleasing countenances . . . among the women and
children of this vale, than [he has] ever noticed elsewhere" (EOT,
1:406). And Mary graces that by which she has been graced.

In order to negotiate the double-bind between the aesthetic and the
natural Coleridge constructs a double-plot, the narrative equivalent
of the double-bottomed portmanteau that Hatfield carries along with
him. Although he eventually dismisses the vulgar's reduction of motive
to the options of power and money, Coleridge initially entertains the
possibility of mercenary motives. What alternative is there? The "pock-
fretten" Beauty of Buttermere is not really physically attractive. And
despite the mood of suspicion that prevails in places high and low, there
is no Jacobinical conspiracy afoot against the public peace. Under the
circumstances the only reasonable interest is economic self-interest;
and the only crime economic crime: counterfeiting. That Hatfield coun-
terfeited is undisputed; but, as the narrative of disclosure unfolds, that
he did so from financial motives becomes increasingly dubious, for it is
hard to say how the counterfeiting profited him. The very reasoning
that the reporter had used in the first article to argue for the suitor's
disinterest undermines his subsequent imputation of mercenary motives. What calculation of interest could justify committing the capital
crime of forgery on speculation that a woman would, after her marriage, persuade her parents to sign over a "little pothouse" to a bridegroom in a document that would have no standing in any court of law,
and to do so when he had already obtained the consent of a "lady of
youth, beauty, and good fortune"?[5]

If counterfeiting is the crime, the crime has something other than
financial implications: Hatfield forfeits his life to pay for unilaterally
taking a name by convention, for allegorizing himself in the way that

Napoleon has done. He dies, as Fergus MacIvor would later die (and at the same place, Carlisle), for having understood himself as a character in a romance rather than a novel. His interest? Perhaps celebrity. By attaching himself to Mary's name he may have aspired to attract notice to his own. But, true or not, the attribution of such a motive is merely the shadow cast by the eclipse of biographical knowledge. Indeed, one of the curiosities of this "novel" is that the more details about Hatfield that accumulate, the more he recedes as a biographical subject and the more his inexplicability becomes a kind of literariness. Eventually, in a letter to John Rickman, Coleridge goes so far as to portray Hatfield as a type of Iago (later to be described as a character of "motiveless malignancy"), who exemplifies the ability of vice to counterfeit "whatever shape Virtue can assume" — a characterization that flirts with redundancy.[6] In Hatfield's case (and under British law), the counterfeit of virtue (that which is universally recognized as having value) is a vice itself; it doesn't matter whether or not Hatfield has evil intentions. Motiveless malignancy follows the abandonment of economic interest, which, as the political economists teach, is the horizon of motive. By the same token, crediting Hatfield with a motiveless malignancy reciprocally implies that Mary makes a motiveless marriage — social climbing on a ladder to nowhere, she avidly acquires the counterfeit signs of rank. It is not that she creates what she expects that is disturbing, but that she expects, hopes for, what, according to the rules of the game, she cannot have.

De Quincey, who held no truck with hope, would later solve the question of motive to his own satisfaction by blaming Mary's "vanity." A similar social shorthand is applied to Hatfield in a filler from the *Morning Post*, which Donald Reiman attributes to Charles Lamb: "Hatfield is to be tried at Carlisle for forging franks. As *Skirmish* says in *The Deserter*, 'this comes of your learning *to write*.'" Reiman notes that the "bitterness of the humor . . . seems appropriate to the way that Charles Lamb . . . would have regarded any London gentry and bourgeoisie who accepted John Hatfield as a mode."[7] It is not the least interesting aspect of Hatfield as celebrity villain that he was such a plastic model, shaping and being shaped by the imagination of Britons both near and far. As Coleridge interprets the buoyant hopes of the villagers: "If he was not this great man, they were sure that he would prove to be some other great man" (*EOT*, 1:413). And, indeed, Hatfield both recalls and anticipates numerous great men who will strut their hour on the front page of the *Morning Post*. He is a figure for Napoleon Bonaparte, whose fickle alliances were a scandal to the decorum of international affairs and whose career, despite the lull of Amiens, seemed designed "to leave as few white interspaces as possible in the crowded map of his villainy." He calls to mind the weak-willed Charles James Fox, whose seduction by Bonaparte at his levee in Paris had provoked a remarkably abusive pair of open letters by Coleridge to the Whig leader contemporaneous with the "Maid of Buttermere" episode. Hope/Hatfield was also a prototype for later engines of compulsive emulation: Beau Brummell and especially that roving philander and Whig, Lord Byron, who is shaped right down to the hitch in his gait.

More immediately, the villain works as an unintended model for Coleridge as well. He is a man without an establishment whose overdetermined mobility parallels Coleridge's own shifting movements and preoccupations during the so-called breathing space engineered by the convention of Amiens. That mobility can be tracked in the transformation of the villain's names. "Hope" and "Hatfield" are circumstantially motivated labels — the former assumed for purposes of creditworthiness, the latter presumably given. But the third name, "Headfield," is interjected by Coleridge with little justification: dropped quickly, it is not clear whether Headfield was an alias that was in circulation or a mistaken attribution on the part of the journalist. Nonetheless, the slip, if slip it is, contributes to the allegorical implications of the account for Coleridge. The move from Hope to Headfield echoes the transition from the Jacobin politics of the dawning revolutionary period to its dark aftermath in the Reign of Terror. In France, as Wordsworth bleakly recalls in Book 10 of *The Prelude*, the headfield was literal on the Place du Carrousel in Paris. In Britain the correlative is quasiprofessional: Headfield is a kind of verbal acrostic for a newspaper and the place of the journalist who composes it. Headfield is simultaneously a metaphor for the death of a social class (or in Benedict Anderson's terms, of the expiration of a language caste) and for the emergence of a new kind of journalistic intelligence — a quiet revolution not only indicated by but (it is Coleridge's wish) achieved by metaphor. Legible in Coleridge's slip is an attribution of an uncanny intelligential energy to the journalistic occupation that makes slips meaningful — which has the power to denominate and to shape incidental facts into novels of real life.

"Headfield" names an imagined community that is, as Benedict Anderson has argued, the historically advantaged preserve of the novel and the newspaper, which link strange people in unprecedented ways. In a newspaper, Anderson argues, "this imagined linkage derives from two obliquely related sources. The first is simply calendrical coincidence. . . . The novelistic format of the newspaper assures them that somewhere out there the 'character' Mali moves along quietly, awaiting its next appearance in the plot. The second source of imaginary linkage lies in the relationship between the newspaper, as a form of book, and the market"[8] which induces the "mass ceremony" of newspaper reading performed in what Anderson calls the "lair of the skull," an apposite correspondent to "Headfield." Anderson imagines that

> each communicant is well aware that the ceremony he performs is being replicated simultaneously by thousands (or millions) of others of whose existence he is confident, yet of whose identity he has not the slightest notion. Furthermore, this ceremony is incessantly repeated at daily or half-daily intervals throughout the calendar. At the same time, the newspaper reader, observing exact replicas of his own paper being consumed by his subway, barbershop, or residential neighbours, is continually reassured that the imagined world is visibly rooted in everyday life. (Anderson, 35)

The imagined community of the readers of the *Morning Post* may be a community without hope, but it is a community of indefinite reassurance. The flip side of the visible rooting in everyday life is the claim, implicit in most journalism and fiction but hyperbolically explicit in Coleridge's "Romantic Marriage" series, that everyday life is completely visible. The same claim will be made by realistic novels (most famously by Henry Tilney in *Northanger Abbey*), by quarterly reviews (it is the prevailing theme of the various essays of the first issue of the *Edinburgh Review*), and even by the poetry of the Lake School. These claims will be made by the newspaper, the novel, the review, and poetry on behalf of the newspaper, novel, review, or poetry as the privileged vehicles of intelligence into an everyday life which is legible to the reader's relaxed gaze but which is dramatically different depending upon the particular discursive instrument by which it is accessed.[9] Although the lost everydayness of a prerevolutionary world would not be fully restored until the final defeat of Bonaparte and Britain's triumph over the threat to her commercial hegemony, the Peace of Amiens offered a glimpse of a different world and provided the occasion for competition among managers of discourse to become that organization which could most authoritatively provide intelligence of that world and prove most creditworthy for the general reader. Hope's success franking letters and obtaining money in the Lakes reads as a parable of the paradox of creditworthiness: it represents both the necessary ease of obtaining credit and the inherent fragility of credit so easily achieved.

If the interjection of Headfield suggests that Coleridge's interest is of the same order as Mary's, allowing him to indulge in the hope of realizing possibilities that exceed his menial circumstances as hireling, the correction to Hatfield returns from the realm of romantic metaphor to the novelistic metonymy of commercial society, where supposed political conflicts and social differences can be sublimed into the trivial codes of fashion. Such is the "tonish" world in which the self-consciously urbane Coleridge, separated from his wife and children, has become an object of desire. In a letter to his wife early in 1802, Coleridge makes much, however mockingly, of his gilding:

> I assure you, I am quite a man of *fashion* — so many titled acquaintances — & handsome Carriages stopping at my door — & fine *Cards* — and then I am such an exquisite Judge of Music, & Painting — & pass criticisms on furniture & chandeliers — & pay such very handsome Compliments to all Women of Fashion / that I do verily believe, that if I were to stay 3 months in town & have tolerable health & spirits, I should be a Thing in Vogue — the very *ton*ish Poet & Jemmy Jessamy fine Talker in Town. (CL, 1:789)

Coleridge has become a man about town because he has entered the discursive life of the period as a kind of literary landmark. In a letter to his "other wife," Sara Hutchinson, he quotes descriptions of himself from "WARNER'S 'Tour thro' the northern counties':" "In the walks of Literature &c &c Bristol has made & still makes a figure, &c &c. The gigantic Intellect & sublime Genius of COLERIDGE, which were here first publicly developed, &c &c' . . . Vol. 2. p. 100. 'The animated, enthusiastic, & accomplished COLERIDGE, whose residence at Keswick gives additional charm to its impressive Scenery.'" (CL, 1:826–27). He goes on to pray, as the Maid of Buttermere might have prayed, had she known better: "From foolish men, that write Books, Lord deliver me! — It has been my Lot to be made a Fool of by Madmen, & represented as a Madman by Fools!" A slightly more skeptical take on Coleridge's status as at once a grace of the Lake District and a fashionable journalist in London would produce the suggestion that he has, not without some anxious pleasure, discovered himself to be *binomial* — made a Mary for the Hatfields and represented as a Hatfield by the Marys.

Such analogizing is, I believe, legitimate. Perhaps too legitimate. It is not clear where it gets us except to reinscribe the familiar quicksilvery chiasmic mobility of Coleridge as a serviceable template for the novel of real life. Coleridge was ever ready to reduce the everyday to a dyadic encounter between victim and persecutor, reader and writer, critic and poet, or patient and agent. In this case he gets the decided advantage of doubling victimage: Mary as the innocent, seduced beauty, and Hope as the philandering man of fashion who is justly punished by the state for his apostasy from fidelity. This chiasmic figure, which we can configure through a collation of articles and letters, will later be formalized in the pages of *The Friend* as the figure of the friend and will be made an object of universal concern in the biographical deduction of the mutual indefinite implication (not collaboration) of philosophical critic and poet in the first four chapters of the *Biographia Literaria*.[10] But to project that figure here has the effect of prematurely closing off the question of motive by detaching it from the historical actors and relocating it in Coleridge's style, as type of a relatively unchanging psychological disposition and set of social habits. That is, Coleridge's tropology becomes a kind of psychology — and willy-nilly invokes a novelistic mode of explanation that wards off historicity, the uncertain notice of change.

More importantly to assign motive to the structured, social ambivalence of the quasiprofessionalized writer, lured and luring in the unstable formation of early-nineteenth-century print culture, is to divert attention from another motive that Coleridge rules out, "power." Coleridge surely knows but does not directly avow what the government certainly knew but attempted to disavow, that there *was* significant insurrectionary activity in the North of England during the Peace of Amiens, conspiracies initiated by the United Irishmen (themselves responsive to French instigation) and aimed at forging fighting alliances with those British artisans whose discontent had become a matter of alarm to the government. In *Insurrection: The British Experience, 1795–1803*, Roger Wells gives a detailed account of these fugitive combinations, especially the revival of the United Britons in the North, the revolutionary conspiracy of Colonel Despard, and the government's successful attempt to contain working-class insurrection.[11] Worth noting here is the remarkable coincidence between the analysis of the Home Secretary charged with preempting insurrection in his private memoranda and Coleridge's analytical survey of the ideological map in the 1802 article "Once a Jacobin Always a Jacobin." Pittite propaganda may have veered between claims of rampant Jacobin sedition and of absolute domestic tranquility, but, according to Coleridge, it was programmatically committed to applying the term *Jacobin* to "all, who from whatever cause opposed the late war, and the late Ministry" (*EOT*, 1:368).

Coleridge proposes a more nuanced distinction among those who, critical of the government, had a "*shade* of Jacobinism," those "Semi-Jacobins," who accepted the principle of popular sovereignty, and those who were committed to the full "Jacobin's creed," which necessarily includes the commitment to the revolutionary overthrow of constitutional governments. That spirit of discrimination, if not the exact classificatory scheme, was echoed by Sir William Fitzwilliam, the West Riding's Lord Lieutenant, in his confidential response to the alarm raised by William Cookson, the Mayor of Leeds. Cookson was convinced that the Combinations of workmen for higher wages had been motivated by Jacobin conspirators, who had cultivated the ground for insurrection by planting "an idea . . . among the poor that they should pay no Taxes, That a better Order of things will ere Long be Brought about" (Wells, 228). In his reply, Fitzwilliam disentangles the economic discontent, which he liberally regards as a private matter between workers and masters, from the radical political aims of the true Jacobins, who were no doubt ready to take advantage of workers' discontent but who were readier still to exploit government repression as a means to cement a political alliance with those whose grievances were fundamentally and traditionally economic. Fitzwilliam discounts alarm because "the whole character of the Language held out by the Principal Actors was moderate, & such the Terms used that the ignorant multitude might easily consider them as referable to the price of Provisions, Stagnation of Trade & matters of that description: Subjects that alone probably collected the Numbers together" (224). Cautioning against precipitate action, the Lord Lieutenant observes, "I am not sure that we should not afford them the ground of complaint against the Constitution, that we should not drive them into the service of the true Jacobin, and by our own acts, furnish a justification for theirs; for if the Legislature does not deal out equal justice and equal protection, much is to be said in justification of the subjects who attempt to withdraw from it" (228). In light of Fitzwilliam's observation, Coleridge's complacency looks not only reasonable but strategic: contain discontent by refusing to make linkages between the economic and the political that, one hopes, do not exist.

We know that Coleridge, who will imminently be tarred by the same Scottish brush that blackened Southey as a sectarian poet in the *Edinburgh*'s 1802 review of *Thalaba*, had an interest in disproving the existence of conspiracies in the Lakes and in confirming that there could be nothing politically subversive in the adventurer's maneuvers. His wry mention of the mistakes made by "secret committees" not only refers to those responsible for sending out nosy spies to track him and Words-worth during their poetic intelligence-gathering expeditions in the 1790s (Coleridge was crowding out the white interspaces on the map with his jottings for the proposed pastoral epic "The Brook") but also anticipates the hostile tack that the anonymous panel of *Edinburgh* reviewers will take as it ferrets out sects in the Lakes and apprises its readers of conspiratorial poetic seducers slavishly obedient to a foreign dictate. However interested he was, Coleridge's skepticism about politi-cal conspiracies nonetheless seems sensible enough. After all, if Hatfield did have political motives, what could he possibly want with Mary?

To approach an answer to that question we need to adopt a paranoid hermeneutics along the lines suggested by Norman Bryson, who argues that "paranoia is a representational crisis in which nothing can exist for itself or innocently, for everything is perceived as sign. To the paranoid, all existence is plot, not only as conspiracy but as narrative: paranoid reality is entirely discursive."[12] Our justification for a paranoid reading of Coleridge's reportage must be that the story he tells is in truth not a novel of real life but an allegory of discursive life. Consider the plot. No one disputes that Hatfield likes to fish or that he visited Buttermere, famous for its char, on a fishing expedition. But how was he to know where to drop his line? He read a sign. According to Joseph Budworth, who published the first account of the setting in 1792, the pothouse at the foot of the lake had the generic name "Fish Inn." Generic, but not entirely prosaic, for the name exploits the ambiguity characteristic of the names of inns of this sort between the nominative and the impera-tive (my favorites are the Dew Drop Inn and the Stumble Inn). Is Hope being informed that the Inn is *near* fish or is Hope being exhorted to *fish in*? And if the latter, is he being summoned to fish in the lake or fish in the inn? Perhaps to avoid such dangerous ambiguity Coleridge does not mention the name *Fish Inn* but only "the sign of Char," a simple, osten-sive reference. As Thomas Love Peacock's Dr. Opimian will later ob-serve in *Gryll Grange*, *char* names a simple fish. "There is much to be said about fish," he opines; "but not in the way of misnomers. Their names are single and simple. Perch, sole, cod, eel, carp, char, skate, tench, trout, brill, bream, pike, and many other, plain monosylla-bles."[13] Plain monosyllables, plain fish — it is, as Socrates first com-plained, the fisherman who has all the angles.[14] Whatever his profes-sional distinction, it was well for the security of the British state that Dr. Opimian was not charged with the responsibility of preventing stirrings of discontent from developing into uprisings, a duty that required one to read reports such as this from government informant Wickham in

April 1798: "they were found sitting in consultation at a House in Clerkenwell on the question of what was the most proper sort of Pike to be used by their friends in case of necessity, and they had the models of four Pike Heads laid before them on the table" (Wells, 122).

Given potential French infiltration of every gathering of the working or the idle poor (of every gathering, that is, that could possibly be infiltrated by a government spy) — pike could no longer be considered "single and simple." Mistaking pike heads for fish heads might mean that one's own head would eventually ornament the revolutionaries' table.[15] And if *pike* and *Hope* are misnomers, so, potentially, is *char*. Under the sign of the char, Hope meets a young woman who waits, attends, and, we may assume, in the stipulated absence of a servant, must do those odd household jobs that are the province of a charwoman. To what does the sign refer, the fish in the lake or the woman by the lake? We might want to say that this equivocation is a mere coincidence, that it has nothing to do with the woman herself. What then are we, what then was Hope, to make of Coleridge pointing to "the becoming manner in which she is used to *fillet* her beautiful long hair" (*EOT*, 1:357; emphasis added)? This is Coleridge's association. And surely he is implying, however mildly, that there is something fishy about this char filleting her hair. Perhaps Mary gets the fisherman she deserves.

Such misogynistic innuendo is hard to counter; at times like this it seems to be built into the language, the irrepressible demotic joke (women are fishy) beneath the vernacular's double-bottom. I'm not interested in refuting that demotic misogyny so much as answering it. Let's try a little dialectic. If making the woman natural is making her fishy, we might suppose that making the fish a woman is making it something more than an object to be angled for. (If the woman is something other than a fish, the char is something other than a mere servant — but what is she?) Mary's fishiness suggests not so much an available sexuality as an enigmatic quality distinct from the objecthood to which woman is socially assigned — a quality that makes her rightly suspicious, as if she claims a political position distinct from mere subjugation. And if it is true, as I believe it is, that to introduce sex is to introduce politics (that is, the simple word *sex* is always a misnomer for *sects*, subject to the same condescension or contempt by the custodians of the dominant culture), it may be that the politics of this woman, whose sexuality is enigmatically distinct from objecthood, is neither the politics of economics nor the politics of domination.

What kind of politics could that be? We want a historical category far more fluid than Toryism, Whiggism, or Republicanism. We want a label given to be taken as a misnomer. Perhaps liberalism. But Mary could only be a liberal by the strangest of associations. It was perfectly possible to be a political economist in Britain in 1802, but to be a liberal in the accepted sense would be an anachronism, literally impossible until after 1815. Even then, liberalism as a reformist program of individual freedom, consent-based government, and religious toleration is integumented with a Benthamite social calculus, which predicates individual desires as subject to statistical analysis and constrained by the horizon of probability, assuring that reform is merely the relegitimation of the status quo. What, after Claude Lefort, we have come to call political liberalism, best exemplified by the emancipatory movements of the *liberales* in Spain and the insurgents in Italy and Greece, which erupted in the second and third decades of the nineteenth century and which were supported spiritually and materially by Shelley, Byron, Hazlitt, and Hunt, never does disembark in Britain.[16] When finally translated into England, the emancipatory drive of liberalism will be channeled into the service of a property-owning class whose discourse of liberty is a kind of doubletalk, what, in the English Cantos of *Don Juan*, Byron contemptuously calls *cant*. The British jargon of liberty presupposes that for some to be free others must serve.

To tag someone a liberal in the Lake District in 1802 would be a misnomer. But misnomers did and do riddle the language and, under cover of anachronism, did and do roam the land. For that reason (and this is to move from dialectic to paradox) it may be that just because Mary cannot confess to being a liberal, cannot give an autobiographical account of how she might be an agent of that cause, it is all the more important to suppose a biography of her (which would not be hers and hers alone) that would plot her as a liberal plotter. It is a Romantic tenet that the only politics worth having is the politics that one cannot in fact have: a politics of the future. And it is as a politics of the future, a Romantic politics, that liberalism is important.

Coleridge adumbrates this future in his essay "Once a Jacobin Always a Jacobin," which interrupts the series on the "Romantic Marriage." There, as we have seen, he sets out to discredit Pitt's notorious adage by separating the term *Jacobin* from its propagandistic usage as the "watchword of a faction" and by analytically discriminating it into its varieties. Although Coleridge finds that the distinct historical and ideological meanings of *Jacobin* have been confused by the abusive and paranoid simplification of the ministry, he nonetheless aims to rehabilitate the term to describe a new and permanent political orientation: "Whoever builds a Government on personal and natural rights, is so far a Jacobin. Whoever builds on social rights, that is, hereditary rank, property, and long prescription, is an Anti-Jacobin, even though he should nevertheless be a Republican, or even a Democrat" (*EOT*, 1:370). Jacobinism so defined is scarcely different from a definition of Mill's liberalism, had the phenomenon been available for Coleridge to define it. Coleridge's rejection of "personal and natural rights" identifies his principled illiberalism within the emergent commercial society of nineteenth-century Britain. Yet his endorsement of "social rights," which looks conservative and Burkean is, when followed by the qualifiers of "hereditary rank, property, and long prescription," at a critical distance from the Burkean conception of bedrock social obligations. The affirmation of a rights-based politics anchored in the social aligns Coleridge's critique of Jacobinism with later communitarian movements of the left, which will similarly revisit the past to discover antidotes for the toxin of political economy. If we are looking for a sign of the politics of the future rather than of the defunct nineteenth century, however, it may lie in the uncharted interspace that connects the politics of personal and social rights. Such a politics is not, in 1802, theorizable by Coleridge or by anyone else, but, it is the burden of this reading to argue, such a politics is figurable in the period of eventful suspension named the Peace of Amiens. Political liberalism is figured by the foregrounding of an ambiguous alliance between a man and a woman, one that makes no sense according to "pre-established codes of decision" — that is, those traditional motives of passion or interest for a man and woman to cleave together.

That the personal is the political for Coleridge goes without saying. But to intimate that the personal is the social and the social is the personal is an unspoken assertion that acquires political force by virtue of its anomalism, or, to give that virtue a teleological impulse, its necessary anachronism. By necessary anachronism I do not mean what Lukacs (after Goethe) meant by the term, an authorial strategy of projecting on an incident or agent the causative power to have produced the present, but rather the necessity that the most timely event in the present must appear anachronistic because it is the sign of an unforeseeable future. To imagine a welding of the personal and the social may, at this time, require the figure of a wedding, just as later it will attract the figure of the chiasmus, but the uncanny underdetermination of this particular wedding suggests that the event is less a reenactment of that social rite by which the personal is subordinated to the social than it is a tactical alliance of agents. The wedding is not a union sanctified by church and state but a particularly intimate *analogy*, "a coincidence of

names [that] has been adopted by design and for political purposes."
The result of adopting this convention is not a marriage but a secret
combination, a liberal sect, or (let us name it for what it does) a Romantic movement — an affectional rather than a logical connection, which is
to say that a Romantic movement looks more like the incarnate unrea-
son of sex than the suave casuistry of common sense. It is a principle of
the natural history of politics that before there can be class consciousness there must be sect consciousness. To reformulate that principle in
the vocabulary of the unnatural or the uncanny history of modern
politics: where class consciousness is, sect consciousness has been and
may yet be.

What is sect consciousness? Recall that Lamb did not simply object
to Hatfield's modishness when he mocked, "Hatfield is to be tried at
Carlisle for forging franks. As *Skirmish* says in *The Deserter*, 'this
comes of your learning *to write*.'" He gloats over Hatfield's conviction
as apt punishment for the man having learned to write. It is surely
reasonable to condemn someone who knows how to write and who has
been taught the rules which govern the way writing is to be used for
violating the rules of composition and copyright, for writing in the
wrong place, for stenographic abbreviation, for usurping the proper-
tied name and signature that belong to another. Hatfield's story turns
out the way one would expect because it is a novel of real life, the kind
of story about which we have heard regarding economic man, whose
politics and economics come to the same thing: exploitation of the body
of the woman as of a commodity and usurpation of the authority that
belongs to the father or the state. He's the kind of man from whom laws
are designed to protect people. But if it makes all the sense in the
kingdom to blame a man for using his writing ability to frank (or, in the
case of Coleridge, to plagiarize), it is quite another to blame someone
for *learning* to write, for breaking rules that cannot be known until
after they are learned. Blame ought to be put on the teacher — if there
were one.

Central to the rebuke administered by the *Edinburgh Review* to the
Lake poets for their licentious use of the real language of men was the
social a priori that "the different classes of society have each of them
a distinct character, as well as a separate idiom" (*ER*, 68). The duplicitous idiom of Hope crosses those classes of society — but it does not
merely cross: it acts to produce unprecedented combinations. Under the
circumstances, *writing* means producing language by radical convention, not traditional prescription. Behind Lamb's status anxiety, we

hear the preposterous and even more anxious supposition of a biography of someone who might have taught himself to write, without what Coleridge calls "the purifying alchemy of Education."[17] It is as if learning had some agency of its own, as if the student had a capacity that was somehow foreign to his objecthood, an allegorical gift that communicated to him things he could not know and that individualized him in ways that elude the metaphorical discipline of church and state and school. It is as if the student had a motive to learn, prior to memory, prior to fear — call that motive hope. And it as if that hopeful motive to learn bound him to another, who was ready to indulge it and help it ripen into action.

If we take Lamb's bitterness to be the sign of an emotion in excess of its ostensible object, perhaps it's because he's suppressing the actual object. Does it help to suppose misogyny? Suppose we substitute maid for man and rewrite Lamb's comment this way: "Mary Robinson is to be delivered of a child conceived by Hatfield; as Coleridge might have said in the Post, 'this comes of your *filleting your hair.*'" Blaming Hope for learning to write is a lot like blaming a Mary for attracting a seducer. Seduction begins to look much less objectively, *naturally* sexual when linked with writing by the logic of these suppositions — especially so when we consider that Coleridge calls attention not only to Mary's filleting of her beautiful hair but also to "the uncommonly fine Italian hand-writing in which the bill was drawn out." How did this woman, who, we are informed, has spent "all her life" as attendant and waiter, learn this fine Italian hand? At whose hand? What, we may ask, does this talent have to do with the writings in Italian found in the bottom of Hatfield's chest? At the very least they are connected as writings — we will say that there is, as it were, a native connection between her hand-writing and his letters as mutually elegant, conventions that have no natural support.

By saying those writings are connected at the level of the signifier I mean only to assert that there is linkage that is not reducible to an objectifiable lure and also that the signified lies in a future that is truly the future and not another version of the present. The motive to write, to hope, is social; the right to write is personal, as personal as that will, which, in the *Biographia Literaria*, Coleridge will denominate the "principium commune essendi et cognoscendi, . . . [the] primary ACT of self-duplication."[18] That the will is the common principle of being and knowing means that before the charters of governments and the discipline of the school, the primary act of self-duplication enfranchises a radically democratic right to write. In a capitalizing Britain, where the demos is either denied access to any means of reproduction except the biological or (as in the case of Coleridge, who wrote to feed the hungry mouths at home) has its access to the mechanical means of reproduction routinized into a necessity for life maintenance, the exercise of the right to write must appear as counterfeiting, which is the primary political act of self-duplication. Writing without need is inherently willful, as writing without fear or memory is intrinsically hopeful. Circumstanced by a world in which hope, as much as access to the mint and the printing press, is ruled out for the demos, the handwriting, as Coleridge fears and remembers, is a political act of personal will and social hope for the Irish, the Northern weavers, and for women everywhere.

Having invoked this somewhat abstract language of rights, it may be useful to tether my unprecedented claims for political conspiracy in the Lakes with some circumstantial evidence. Despite the government's attempt to play down popular discontent, the signs of insurrection in the fall of 1802 were widespread and ominous. Wells reports that

> In October 1802 the Home Office reported increased activity between the UI [United Irishmen] in Dublin and their contacts in London to the Irish authorities, but although the Home Office was originally satisfied that the plot of Colonel Despard to execute a *coup d'état* in London in September had no 'connexion with Treason in Ireland,' letters intercepted later proved that Dowdall knew Despard's plans very well. Thus the evidence strongly suggests that the revolt in London was to be the signal for a supportive effort in Ireland, as well as elsewhere in England [including West Riding and Lancashire]. (Wells, 242).

Wells informs us of the real-world background for the novel of real life serially published by Coleridge, who was himself a middleman between activities in the Lakes and London during the fall of 1802. Wells thoroughly canvasses all the pertinent documentary evidence of the period — all, that is, except Coleridge's Maid of Buttermere articles.

The fundamental question is, What does Coleridge's text tell us about insurrectionary activity that Wells does not? Answering that question is relatively easy. Among all the various agents who troop through the secret correspondence of spies and ministers, one figure briefly appears, to be mentioned only once — a figure so shady that he does not earn a mention in Wells's exhaustive index. During Wells's account of the interrogation of the arrested Despard conspirators, he mentions that "the conspirator J. S. Wratten, when under interrogation by Ford [Richard Ford, Superintendent of Aliens] admitted that he had been at the Bleeding Heart tavern on 5 September, and agreed that he was there with a man named Hatfield. On being asked where Hatfield was in November, Wratten replied, 'Hatfield is now in Yorkshire.' If Ford took the matter up, Wratten refused to answer. No more is heard of Hatfield, but a man named Heron was arrested." (Wells, 245)

Although we may be sure that the Hope who arrived in Keswick was not the notorious James Hope, weaver and United Irishman,[19] with Coleridge's help we now know that something more was heard of Hatfield, or at least a man by the name of Hatfield, who was traveling incognito in the northwest of England in the days preceding the September 5 meeting at the Bleeding Heart, and whose explicit message to the rural populace was an offer of hope.

Although it is reassuring to find the empirical clue in Coleridge which suggests the occult transmission of political intelligence of subversion in the Lake District — intelligence that has eluded the gaze of the most thorough investigators — my aim is not to legitimate Coleridge's journalism in light of its capacity to flesh out the historical narrative of aborted insurrection. On the contrary, my claim is that Coleridge's journalism demands continuing interest as a piece of Romantic intelligence that, within the catastrophe of radical hopes, neither annunciates what E. P. Thompson called "Acquisitive Man" nor completely succumbs to the nostalgic dream of clerical man, but actively if inadvertently traces out as yet unrealized possibilities that project an unforeseeable future.[20]

By reducing Hatfield's criminal writing to franking, Coleridge suppresses the other writing that trips up Hatfield, the letters he has exchanged with foreign correspondents, and particularly the inexplicable map of Italy found beneath the double-bottom of Hatfield's chest. Why would a man with a map of Italian cities be fishing for an italicizing char in the Lakes? What romance does this affection materialize? The link between Italian and char has a significant albeit obscure political history in the conspiratorial sect of the Carbonari, or charcoal burners, who organized in the early nineteenth century in Southern Italy to resist French rule and who are forerunners of those groups of emancipatory liberals that would rise across Europe in the second decade of the century. The origins of the Carbonari remain occulted — some connect them to the Freemasons, some to the Illuminati. Coleridge finds early evidence of their conspiratorial activity in a place we would not expect: the Lake Country of England, where two agents who are using their plausibility as characters from a novel of real life — as man and woman, subject and object, seducer and abandoned — to furnish cover for a personal and political affiliation that cannot be understood in terms of those oppositions.

That occult, international affiliation is, of course, preposterous. We have no other evidence of the Carbonari in England, unless you count the Romantic intelligence of charcoal burners that, thanks to Marjorie Levinson, we now know Wordsworth buried in "Tintern Abbey."[21] The action is as preposterous as a countrywoman teaching herself a fine Italian hand or, for that matter, an illiterate proletarian audience reading *Invisible* on the chest of Jack the Giant Killer at Sadlers Wells. The affiliation is preposterous because its possibility was not yet discursively constructed in the certifiably approved manner. But it is just because the connection is preposterous that the conspiracy binding hope and the char prefigures the emancipatory politics that will galvanize Spain, Portugal, and Italy during the brief time before liberalism had been disciplined into the acceptance of its economic determination. As a political liberalism, Romanticism, like feminism, requires a conspiracy view of history in order to do justice to its keen sense of the intimate analogy of the person with the political. Coleridge's Romantic intelligence invites us to suppose that the future life of an individualized collectivity might be read in the conspiratorial writing linking Hope and maid.

Chapter Six

Clerical Liberalism
Walter Scott's World Picture

The fundamental event of the modern age is the conquest of the world as picture. The world picture now means the structured image [Gebild] that is the creature of man's producing which represents and sets before. In such producing, man contends for the position in which he can be that particular being who gives the measure and draws up the guidelines for everything that is.
— Martin Heidegger, "The Age of the World Picture"

Putting himself in the character of a herald, he says —
— Thomas Paine, *The Rights of Man*

What gave *Waverley*, the first historical novel, its historical significance was its production of a world picture. In Heidegger's influential account of modernity the production of the world picture is the art of the strong hand, an act of conquest by a particular being who imposes a picture that fundamentally restructures the given world. By subscribing to the metaphor of conquest — a metaphor discredited in British commercial society since the defeat of Napoleon at Waterloo — Heidegger forecloses an intimate understanding of the world historical practice of liberalism, which is motivated by its abjuration of conquest as method. The world picture that Walter Scott presents could not exert the definitive power of one of Heidegger's contenders for position because in Scott's worldview no particular being can accomplish the conquest of which Martin Heidegger dreams. Scott moots the monarchic problematic of sovereign cause and subject effect in favor of the liberal idiom of presupposition and belief. His persuasive depiction of the world at the beginning of the nineteenth century was neither a revolutionary nor a metaphysical act but a bureaucratic maneuver by a conscientious official whose self-authorizing task under the post-Napoleonic dispensation was to teach the British people new things as if those things were common knowledge.

Before engaging *Waverley* directly, I want to return to an occasion from an earlier era in order to construct a context that will frame the special charge that Scott takes up in his first published novel. On his tour of Wiltshire in 1724, Daniel Defoe paused to lavish his attention on the "glorious sight" of Wilton House, which he recommends to his readers as

> a princely palace, constantly filled with its noble and proper inhabitants; viz. the lord and proprietor, who is indeed a true patriarchal monarch, reign here with an authority agreeable to all his subjects (family); and his reign is made agreeable, by his first practicing the most exquisite government of himself, and then guiding all under him by the rules of honour and vertue; being also himself perfectly master of all the needful arts of family government; I mean needful to make that government, both easy, and pleasant to those who are under it, and who therefore willingly, and by choice conform to it.
>
> Here an exalted genius is the instructor, a glorious example the guide, and a gentle well directed hand the governour and law-giver to the whole; and the family like a well govern'd city appears happy, flourishing and regular, groaning under no grievance, pleas'd with what they enjoy, and enjoying every thing which they ought to be pleased with.[1]

Sounds good. Looks good. Or it would look good if we could see the picture evoked here rather than merely read about it. Defoe's description involves a peculiar kind of ekphrasis, for the visual representation he suggests does not itself exist.[2] The absence of that picture signifies because Defoe promotes the present Earl of Pembroke as an avid collector of fine art. As Defoe proceeds to catalog the paintings that cover the walls of the house, his discourse shifts from patriarchal and panegyric to a breathless, homes-of-the-rich-and-famous reportage. Here's a sample:

> You ascend the great stair case, at the upper end of the hall, which is very large; at the foot of the stair-case you have a Bacchus large as the life, done in the fine Peloponesian marble. . . . One ought to stop every two steps of this stair-case, as we go up, to contemplate the vast variety of pictures, that cover the walls. . . .
>
> When you are enter'd the appartments, such variety seizes you every way, that you scarce know to which hand to turn your self.
> (Defoe, 194–95)

Having evoked this copia of images, Defoe takes his readers up the front stairs and down the back stairs and through all the rooms in between. He "shows" them that all the walls are jammed with paintings: either family portraits or pictures of mythological subjects that extend the Pembroke family into Olympian realms. The house was designed as a home for this vast collection: indeed, "the largest, and the finest pieces that can be imagin'd extant in the world, might have found a place here capable to receive them: I say, they might have found, as if they could not now, which is in part true; for at present the whole house is so compleatly fill'd, that I see no room for any new piece to crowd in, without displacing some other fine piece that hung there before." Lest we miss the point, Defoe makes it again at the end of his tour: "Nothing can be finer than the pictures themselves, nothing more surprising than the number of them; at length you descend the back-stairs, which are in themselves large, tho' not like the other: However, not a hands breadth is left to crowd a picture in of the smallest size" (Defoe, 195–96).

Defoe's inventory invites a turn from the admiration of patriarchal genius to more practical considerations: Which venerable forefather will be removed to make room for the next painting of the next Pembroke? What deduction from the mythic past will be required for the dynastic record to be extended? By seeing the family through its pictures, Defoe executes a shift from the dynasty considered as a process of ineluctable elaboration to the dynasty as that which *necessarily* represents itself through a process of indefinite accumulation (nobles will breed, sitters will sit, and painters will paint) and which thereby becomes subject to an economy not of its own making. The picture of Wilton House remains virtual, then, not for complicated epistemological reasons but for downright physical ones: if realized on canvas, the picture of the perfection of Hanoverian ideology that Defoe renders could not be hung within the exemplary house that it eulogizes. Because the contemporary readers of Defoe cannot view the picture of Wilton House, they can discern, if not quite depict, the intelligible horizon of the worldview it perfects. By imagining the arrival of the next painting, without regard to what is depicted within its frame, they can virtually visualize the unexampled end of the worldview that Wilton House holds, inhabits, and represents.

Forty-four years later, in his saga of mortifications entitled *The Vicar of Wakefield*, Oliver Goldsmith renders a version of Defoe's imagined displacement as it occurs not among the ruling aristocracy but among emulous members of the middling class. The Vicar's family unanimously resolves "to be drawn together, in one large historical family piece. . . . As we did not immediately recollect an historical subject to hit us, we were contented each with being drawn as independent historical figures."

> The piece was large, and it must be owned he did not spare his colours. . . . We were all perfectly satisfied with his performance; but an unfortunate circumstance had not occurred till the picture was finished, which now struck us with dismay. It was so very large that we had no place in the house to fix it. How we all came to disregard so material a point is inconceivable; but certain it is, we were this time all greatly overseen. Instead, therefore, of gratifying our vanity, as we hoped, there it leaned, in a most mortifying manner, against the kitchen wall where the canvas was stretched and painted, much too large to be got through any of the doors, and the jest of all our neighbours.[3]

Goldsmith satirizes a lapse of prudence and the failure of design. Labor has foolishly been expended on the cosmetic appeal of the painting; no thought has been given to appraising the relations of figures to each other and the frame or to sizing the frame to the site. Uniformity of manner paradoxically spawns a hodgepodge of characteristics. The elephantine size of the painting, which "occurs," like an accident, makes a spectacle of the family's sorry lack of proportion. More generally, by accurately representing the absence of a normative pictorial standard, the painting registers the vanishing of a common world. By bringing the indecorous and contrary aspirations of the family members into the public light, the portrait proves a decidedly inglorious example of domestic harmony — that is, no example at all.

The vanishing of the common world and the accompanying crisis in exemplarity, side effects of the pell-mell consolidation of a commercial society, challenged the generation of writers following Goldsmith. Every literary historian of the period has his or her own story to tell. Mine will be brief. I want to leapfrog to Scott on the observation that the gallery at Wilton House instantiates a series of propositions in an ideally indefinite and unanswerable argument — an extended ethical proof of the House of Pembroke's right to rule. But, as Goldsmith imagines, the unsettlement of the social classes and the proliferation of commodities trumped that ethical argument. Under the pressure of social instability, ethical maxims increasingly came to be perceived as ideological stratagems and were thus less effective *as* ideological stratagems. Whatever their political affiliation or social status, among writers there occurred a rhetorical shift in the age of revolution and empire. Laboring under threat of invasion from abroad or of incarceration at home, enlisted willy-nilly into anxious defense or desperate aggression, those writers veered from styles of argument employing ethical proofs to those exploiting pathos.

Scott endeavored to restore the balance. The charge he undertook as a novelist at the end of the Napoleonic era was to end ideological contention by establishing a new ethos of artistic representation. His brief: design a picture that would represent a house that could contain it and its designer, a house that could contain every new picture that might appear: whether a copperplate of Milton or Shakespeare or an engraving by Stothard or Blake; whether delivered by Armytage from his peddler's pack or by Mr. Elton fresh from the London coach. Scott's brief was to design a kind of picture by which everyone could orient himself and that would thereby renew the guise of the common world.

As it makes its way from romance to history, *Waverley* travels between two sets of paintings. The first, a pair that might have hung in Wilton house, represents exemplary personages in the history of Waverley Honour. They have been designed to assist in the instruction of the heir in the legend of the house and induce him to acquiesce in the legitimacy of the house's right to rule. The viewing of the first painting is inseparable from the narrative commentary by Mrs. Rachel to her nephew Edward Waverley:

> Nor was he less affected, when his aunt, Mrs. Rachel, narrated the sufferings and fortitude of Lady Alice Waverley during the Great Civil War. The benevolent features of the venerable spinster kindled into more majestic expression, as she told how Charles had, after the field of Worcester, found a day's refuge at Waverley-Honour, and how, when a troop of Cavalry were approaching to search the mansion, Lady Alice dismissed her youngest son with a handful of domestics, charging them to make good with their lives an hour's diversion, that the king might have that space for escape. "And God help her" would Mrs. Rachel continue, fixing her eyes upon the heroine's portrait as she spoke, "full dearly did she purchase the safety of her prince with the life of her darling child. They brought him here a prisoner, mortally wounded; and you may trace the drops of his blood from the great hall door along the little gallery, and up to the saloon, where they laid him down to die at his mother's feet. But there was comfort exchanged between

them; for he knew, for the glance of his mother's eye, that the purpose of his desperate defence was attained.[4]

This is a moment in which authority instructs its young into the authoritarian ethos, but both the way authority speaks — through the pathetic speech of an old woman — as well as the effects of that speaking — Waverley's dreamy abstraction from the world — attest to the fragility of authority and of the culture into which it aims to induct. Scott, of course, writes from a later time, one that self-consciously suffered the kind of "crisis of authority" that Hannah Arendt would later identify as a distinguishing and lingering trait of modernity. Arendt writes that the crisis

> has spread to such prepolitical areas as child-rearing and education, where authority in the widest sense has always been accepted as [both a natural and a political necessity]. . . . The continuity of an established civilization . . . can be assured only if those who are newcomers by birth are guided through a pre-established world into which they are born as strangers. Because of its simple and elementary character, this form of authority has, throughout the history of political thought, served as a model for a great variety of authoritarian forms of government, so that the fact that even this prepolitical authority which ruled the relations between adults and children, teachers and pupils, is no longer secure signifies all the old time-honored metaphors and models for authoritarian relations have lost their plausibility. Practically as well as theoretically, we are no longer in a position to know what authority really *is*.[5]

No crisis is without windfall profits. It is Scott's speculative enterprise to *affirm* that doubt about what authority really is. And one way he can discredit an earlier form of "natural" authority is to attach the natural to the female, the biological, and the path of blood.

Although Mrs. Rachel's commentary plots Waverley's romance, the narrative actively undermines paintings as reliable tools of instruction. The ideal world into which Mrs. Rachel inducts Waverley is the land of the picturesque. But the instruction is doubly anachronistic: Mrs. Rachel, who whets Waverley's appetite to pass beyond what Kim Ian Michasiw portentously calls "the portal through which the Other enters," could know nothing of Gilpin's rules by which that otherness would be constructed.[6] Scott, conversely, narrates Waverley's tour into the picture, but from a position that historically succeeds to the pictur-

esque, which is thus framed as a potent yet historically delimited, ideologically marked system of visual representation. Scott programmatically redescribes Mrs. Rachel's lessons in terms suitable for a new age.
Like her, the novelist attaches supreme importance to providing an
hour's diversion, but unlike her he appreciates that it is no longer necessary to earn that hour at the expense of one's life. After history has
cured the ground, diversion can be entertaining. Once endangered
kings have been removed from the picture, the goal remains an exchange of comfort with a feminine figure, but that exchange, no longer
the consummatory reward for an act of political heroism, will be so-
cialized into the daily routine of domestic reciprocity: Rose and Edward
conversing, writing and editing, collecting and transcribing, reading
novels and looking at pictures.

Thus the last of *Waverley*'s paintings: "the large and spirited painting
representing Fergus Mac-Ivor and Waverley in their Highland dress,
the scene a wild, rocky, and mountainous pass, down which the clan
were descending in the background. It was taken," the novelist adds,
"from a spirited sketch, drawn while they were in Edinburgh by a
young man of high genius, and had been painted on a full-length scale
by an eminent London artist" (473). "The whole piece," we are told,
"was beheld with admiration, and deeper feelings" (474). Those private
feelings are left to our imagination as the contemplation of this memento of the "unfortunate civil war" is interrupted by the normative
call of appetite: "Men must, however, eat, in spite of sentiment and
vertu," the novelist moralizes as he calls his characters to the table. The
moral does not undercut the painting's value. For Scott, the aesthetic
moment is one diversion among many with which it tastefully mingles.
With the hanging of this picture, *Waverley* has completed a major portion of its charge: the novel has represented the house of Bradwardine
as demolished and restored — remodeled — in order to make room for a
painting that is a synthetic historical whole rather than a piecemeal
assemblage. Part genre, part history; part Scottish, part English; part
untaught genius, part labored craft — this fitting memento of tense fraternity invites a mode of attention that is admiring, sentimental, and,
above all, fleeting. If, as Wendy Steiner has argued, "Paintings in romance . . . symbolize the endangered self — removed from the vicissitudes and contingencies of life, raised to higher purity of being," then
the passage from the painting of Lady Alice to this final historical genre
painting reflects the romance quest as a "progression from the enthrall-
ment of pictorial aesthetics to an engagement with life"[7] — if, that is, we
amend "pictorial aesthetics" to "picturesque aesthetics" and under-

stand life as a scene of reciprocal exchange, which includes fleeting aesthetic experience of the pictorial as one diversion among others. Scott produces the aesthetic as a synthetic residue of past antagonisms and as fully subject to social rule.

Waverley, we know, represents the shift from an authoritarian regime of didacts and tracts, princes and edicts, to a bourgeois milieu of contracts and conversation.[8] But how does that change occur? Scott is entitled to be called the first historical novelist because he composed a single, justly famous sentence:

> These reveries he was permitted to enjoy, undisturbed by queries or interruption; and it was in many a winter walk by the shores of Ulswater, that he acquired a more complete mastery of a spirit tamed by adversity, than his former experience had given him; and that he felt himself entitled to say firmly, though perhaps with a sigh, that the romance of his life was ended, and that its real history had now commenced. (406)

Edward Waverley is the protagonist of the first historical novel because things change for him as they do not for Charles Edward, the Stuart Pretender, or his adherents. What principally changes is that Waverley comes to recognize that an irreversible change has occurred. For Scott, to count that change as historical does not entail validation of its truth but persuasion that Waverley is "entitled" to make that recognition.

The author seeks to produce that conviction early on. He tells of the day when the child was traveling abroad with his maid:

> It chanced that the infant with his maid had strayed one morning to a mile's distance from the avenue of Brere-wood Lodge, his father's seat. Their attention was attracted by a carriage drawn by six stately long-tailed black horses, and with as much carving and gilding as would have done honour to my lord mayor's. It was waiting for the owner, who was at a little distance inspecting the progress of a half-built farm-house. I know not whether the boy's had been a Welsh or a Scotch-woman, or in what manner he associated a shield emblazoned with three ermines with the idea of personal property, but he no sooner beheld this family emblem, than he stoutly determined on vindicating his right to the splendid vehicle on which it was displayed. The Baronet arrived while the boy's maid was in vain endeavouring to make him desist from his determination to appropriate the gilded coach and six. . . . In the round-faced rosy cherub before him, bearing his eye and name, and vin-

dicating a hereditary title to his family, affection, and patronage, by means of a tie which Sir Everhard held as sacred as either Garter or Blue-mantle, Providence seemed to have granted him the very object best calculated to fill up the void in his hopes and affections. (73)

The young Waverley's heart leaps up when he beholds a crest upon a coach. Indeed, it leaps twice: once in recognition of the family emblem, then in a determination to appropriate all those things appertaining to it. The pacific Everhard regards such appropriation as redundant: the child's recognition of the crest is vindication enough — convincing evidence of a "sacred tie" invisible to the empirical eye but from which property right inexorably follows. What makes the sacred tie seem providential is that despite the apparent contingency of the connection (we are given no account of Edward having *learned* to associate this design with his family), it is felt by actor and observer to be necessary and inevitable. Although the novelist leaves room to believe that Waverley had been instructed by father, mother, or nurse, he has no good reason to override the uncle's providential hypothesis; for the absolute contingency and the absolute necessity of such a fit between the subjectivity of a concrete individual and the objectivity of a precedent design constitute its historicity. The novelist equivocates between nature and nurture on principle, for although this moment entitles Waverley to his recognition of history's commencement later in the novel, the moment is itself ungrounded except by Waverley's eventful fit of recognition. That recognition is not (or at least is no longer) something that fathers can or need teach — Richard Waverley is out of the picture — for the crest is the pattern of paternity itself, which transcends biological connection and preempts the arbitrary intervention of pedagogues.[9]

The incidental quality of this event marks Scott's complicity in what Carl Schmitt calls the "romantic attitude," which "is most clearly characterized by means of a singular concept, that of the *occasio.* . . [which] acquires its real significance . . . by means of an opposition. It negates the concept of a *causa,* in other words, the force of a calculable causality, and thus also every binding norm."[10] In *Waverley* the cause is a "gallant" one that sometimes is called "Prince" and sometimes "Pretender." Considered as inerrant and true cause, Charles Edward Stuart is the prime mover of Fergus's deep but ultimately futile calculations; from him issue those immemorial prescriptions that compel in the Baron Bradwardine an allegiance past all reason. From the perspective of sixty years hence, the very embodiment of cause in a historical figure is itself the negation of cause in favor of occasion and opportunity, but not in favor of mere chance. Although he cops a romantic attitude, Scott's exploitation of the occasion projects its own normative trajectory. By triggering what Edmund Burke called "a liberal descent" with "its bearings and its ensigns armorial,"[11] the moment of recognition both legitimates and regulates Waverley's role as protagonist. In Heidegger's terms, the recognition of entitlement "gives the measure" and "draws up the guidelines" for a civil conduct that is itself a series of occasions for recognition, made possible by a precedent design fashioned by a canny hand and fabricated into a stereotype awaiting application by the ready spirit.

The novel meanders for three hundred pages or so between Waverley's first recognition and the central recognition of "real history" to which it entitles him. That diversion is *Waverley*'s reason for being, the occasion for the kind of Romantic philosophizing endorsed by Richard Rorty. Such "interesting philosophy," Rorty claims, is "rarely an examination of the pros and cons of a thesis. Usually it is, implicitly or explicitly, a contest between an entrenched vocabulary which has become a nuisance and a new vocabulary which vaguely promises great things." This discourse has its own immethodical method, which is to redescribe "lots and lots of things in new ways, until you have created a pattern of linguistic behavior which will tempt the rising generation to adopt it, thereby causing them to look for appropriate new forms of nonlinguistic behavior."[12]

John Dewey, Rorty's precursor, describes such redescription as "an experimental social method," which breaks with those ordinary processes of education which assume "that there must be a mental picture of some desired end, personal and social, which is to be attained, and that this conception of a fixed determinate end ought to control educative processes."[13] If such experimental philosophizing may be described as pedagogical, it is not on the model of the dialectical instruction of Socrates but of the sophistical seduction of Gorgias.[14] Such an undertaking must be speculative because, as Rorty and Scott before him know, there can be no guarantee that a pattern will appear or, if it does, that the pattern will be persuasive rather than, say, merely pretty: no guarantee that it will appear as an unsuspected map or undetected constellation or even an intriguing fractal rather than a kaleidoscopic accident. Although he puts his faith in history as an ongoing narrative of probabilities, what Coleridge calls the "novel of real life,"[15] the sophist, who dangles his lures in the hope that the young will leap to the bait, does so in the knowledge that his sportive labor may yield no more than the fruitless exertion of Everhard Waverley or the barren, onanistic reveries of the young Edward. No doubt one can provide occasions for recognition, but what exactly does an occasion look like? Given the antiquarian commitments of our novelist, the lure will be something retrieved from the past, but if devised to tempt present and future readers, it must not be something, like the Pretender, that is merely *of* the past. The lure must be something that has persuaded before but that has done so because it is intrinsically persuasive, that is, charming.[16]

Comparing realist tendencies in literature and painting, Norman Bryson identifies perspective as one such lure:

> Inbuilt into realist approaches to art is an idea of resistance and mistrust: truth cannot reside in the obvious, the central, the stressed, but only in the hidden, the peripheral, the unemphasized. When a work of prose contains a huge corpus of information which seems trivial, lifelikeness becomes an available criterion: realist prose begins with a refusal to go beyond the surface of the text, into significant patterning. . . . The system of perspective is . . . a [useful] vehicle for the expansion [of the peripheral]: perspective persuades because it creates a particular sign-format which is intrinsically persuasive; persuasive rather than true: not one of the details that a realist fiction or image supplies need correspond to actual events; it need only distribute its data in a certain proportion to have us convinced, and perspective always ensures that proportion simply because there are so few ways in which the data concerning spatial location of bodies can be semantically important.[17]

The ardent pursuit of the intrinsically persuasive sign format preoccupies writers of the period—whether as a weapon in a desperate defense against the dissolvent forces of commercial society or as a talisman against the more pointed coercions of the state, or whether, as in *Waverley*, that impulse responds to the urge to design a picture that will virtually represent a common social world in the aftermath of a quarter century of turmoil that had broken down the old boundaries between the domains of public and private, home and abroad.

Bryson's example is especially apt because in *Waverley* Scott features perspective as part of his narrative strategy. The reality of Jacobitism entirely depends on the changing perspectives applied to the phenomenon: for Waverley himself, Jacobitism made picturesque, whether framed by the artful commentary of Mrs. Rachel or Flora, is Jacobitism made intrinsically persuasive, that is, enchanting. In the Highlands,

Scott insistently renders the artifice by which picturesque effects are produced and clearly dramatizes the psychic regressiveness of Waverley's romantic phase in the key moment of his transformation into the Knight of the Mirror at the court of Charles Edward. Scott's use of the crest thus puts perspective in perspective — and not merely because the heraldic code antedates the Renaissance painters' code. The crest is intrinsically persuasive to Waverley because it has been effectively designed to *constitute* the intrinsic, a picture invested with what Michael Baxendall has called "intentionality," a "pattern posited in behaviour, and . . . used to give circumstantial facts and descriptive concepts a basic structure."[18] The crest gives to events their ordonnance. The adept herald need only distribute the variables of devices and blazons, of ruling line and affecting color, in a certain proportion to convince. The crest theoretically ensures the effectiveness of that proportion both because there are so few ways in which the data concerning the social location of bodies can be semantically important and because there are so few ways in which the social movement of bodies can be motivated, which is why the coat of arms is the appropriate device for that engine of full persuasion, the world picture.

If it is true, as Bryson argues, that "an image can persuade us that it reflects the real only for as long as it effaces the traces of its own production and conceals the independent material existence of the signifier" (Bryson, 27), Scott's historicist practice breaks with realism not only by baring the device but also by disassembling it into its signifying elements of line and color. In Burkean terminology, the analogues would be law, the line that has been laid down from time immemorial, and circumstances, which "give in reality to every political principle its distinguishing colour, and discriminating effect" (Burke, 90). Law is to circumstances as succession is to deviation, as the bloodline of the British monarchy is to Hanoverian hegemony. For Scott as well as Burke, realism has no independent authority; it is merely one tool of the world pictorialist, whose aim is to engineer the viewer's full persuasion not in any particular fiction but in the good faith of the system by which effective fictions are generated. By undertaking the project of constructing a reality that has been historically constructed Scott can have his cake and eat it too.

In his essay "On Taste," Dugald Stewart makes a relevant distinction: "in viewing a complicated machine, the experienced engineer finds himself *at home* (if I may use a familiar, but very significant phrase): while, on the same occasion, a person of different pursuits, feels as if transported into a new world."[19] Stewart's observation resonates powerfully during the post-Napoleonic era. Transport to an "ideal world" is the explicit effect of Waverley's picturesque tutelage by Mrs. Rachel. It is also identified as the numinous achievement of Wordsworth's poetry by Coleridge in the contemporary *Biographia Literaria*. In Chapter 4 Coleridge recalls his audition of that marvelous machine of uncanniness, Wordsworth's "Salisbury Plain" poems—in which the positions of auditor and narrator, agent and victim, the social and the individual, become vertiginously interinvolved—as irresistible evidence of Wordsworth's genius. Coleridge uses that recollection of transport not only to authenticate Wordsworth's poetic genius but also to certify his own quite different pursuits as auditor, reader, and critic. In the *Biographia* Coleridge undertakes a categorical criticism of Wordsworth's poetics, but that critique does not violate the terms of the experience that Wordsworth established as normative for *Lyrical Ballads*, the romance of reading: "They who have been accustomed to the gaudiness and inane phraseology of many modern writers, if they persist in reading this book to its conclusion, will, no doubt, frequently have to struggle with feelings of strangeness and aukwardness [sic]: they will look round for poetry, and will be induced to inquire by what species of courtesy these attempts can be permitted to assume that title."[20]

The passage knowingly evokes the uncanny state of mind experienced by the protagonist of the "Salisbury Plain" poems and registered by Coleridge, their canonical auditor. Although the remainder of the preface endeavors to explain, even justify this feeling of strangeness, any evidence we have from contemporary readers and reviewers indicates it did little to mitigate that feeling. Indeed, anyone who, following Coleridge, has pursued a careful reading of the preface knows that its tortuous complications are less a corrective to than mimetic of the "feelings of strangeness and aukwardness" induced by the poems.

Coleridge's criticism of Wordsworth's poetry in the *Biographia Literaria* takes as its premise the breaking of the metrical contract and adopts as its goal the discovery of a fundamental propriety that unifies the poetry, even if the propriety be the implicit contract of the poet with his own genius. As I have argued, however, that investigation fails; indeed, it has the effect of reproducing in a philosophical register the incommensurability of Wordsworth's language with any conception of propriety that Coleridge can devise. By means of Coleridge's philosophical criticism, Wordsworthian incommensurability develops a genealogy through which the experience is propagated and varied. It is Thomas De Quincey who identifies that propagation as genealogy and holds up literary genealogy as a kind of pleasure, even if it entails forswearing the possibility of being at home in poetry or prose. De Quincey canonically lays claim to his place in a genealogy of incommensurability when, in the *Confessions of an English Opium Eater*, he recalls Coleridge's casual reference to Piranesi's *Carceri* in order to envelope himself in a labyrinthine architecture of inscrutable machines, indeterminate labor, and inexhaustible pathos: "Again elevate your eye, and a still more aerial flight of stairs is beheld: and again is poor Piranesi busy on his aspiring labours: and so on, until the unfinished stairs and Piranesi both are lost in the upper gloom of the hall. With the same power of endless growth and self-reproduction did my architecture proceed in my dreams."[21] De Quincey's exercise is Romanticism for the orthodox: a blissfully ignorant plunge into a new world, a strenuous pursuit without the bother of a portfolio, an elaborate reiteration of difference without notable distinction, an indulgence in the incommensurable as the only terrain where the homeless belongs.

A note of pathos akin to De Quincey's is struck by fellow *Blackwood's* contributor J. G. Lockhart in his *Memoirs of Scott*, where he recalls an 1814 dinner engagement with William Menzies in Edinburgh:

> When my companion's worthy father and uncle, after seeing two or three bottles go round, left the juveniles to themselves, the weather being hot, we adjourned to a library which had one large window looking northwards. After carousing here for an hour or more, I observed that a shade had come over the aspect of my friend, who happened to be placed immediately opposite to myself, and said something that intimated a fear of his being unwell. "No," said he, "I shall be well enough presently, if you will only let me sit where you are, and take my chair; for there is a confounded hand in sight of me here, which has often bothered me before, and now it won't let me fill my glass with a good will." I rose to change places with him accordingly, and he pointed out to me this hand which, like the writing on Belshazzer's wall, disturbed his hour of hilarity. "Since we sat down," he said, "I have been watching it — it fascinates my eye — it never stops — page after page is finished and thrown on that heap of MS., and still it goes on unwearied — and so it will be till candles are brought in, and God knows how long after that. It is the same every night — I can't stand a sight of it when I am not at my books." — "Some stupid, dogged, engrossing clerk, probably," exclaimed myself, or some other giddy youth in our society. "No, boys," said our host, "I well know what hand it is — 'tis Walter Scott's." This was the hand that, in the evenings of

three summer weeks, wrote the last two volumes of *Waverley*.
would that all who that night watched it had profited by its example of diligence as largely as William Menzies![22]

As Lockhart paints the picture, any impulse to profit by the example of
this ethos of diligence is countered by the fascinating display of the
uncanny hand, composing page after page with the speed of an indif-
ferently educated, ill-paid clerk mechanically copying documents.

The effect of reading *Waverley* is not the same as that of watching
Waverley being written. Unlike Coleridge, Scott could imagine himself
as both reader and writer. Unlike De Quincey, Scott had both charge
and brief. Unlike Lockhart, he could play both the old hand and the
dreaming juvenile—as he proved when, no longer anonymous, he
added a preface and an introduction to narrate the occasion of *Waverley*'s appearance. But the added context was redundant, for from the
outset Scott had engineered a narrative machine that would make
the reader at home in its mechanism. By systematically contrasting the
idealizing and uncanny picturesque with the iconic format of heraldry,
he encourages the reader to remain attentive to what Goldsmith called
"the material point." When Scott employs the arcana of heraldry, he
literally bares the device. Recall Baron Bradwardine's indignant objec-
tion to the inference that

> our coat-armour had not been achieved by honourable actions in
> war, but bestowed by way of *paronomasia*, or pun, upon our fam-
> ily appellation, — a sort of bearing which the French call *armoires
> parlantes*; the Latins *arma cantantia*, and your English authorities,
> canting heraldry; being indeed a species of emblazoning more be-
> fitting canters, gaberlunzies, and such like mendicants, whose gib-
> berish is formed upon playing upon the word, than the noble,
> honourable, and useful science of heraldry, which assigns armorial
> bearings, as the reward of noble and generous actions (137).

The antiquarian novelist resorts to a footnote to defend canting heraldry: "Although canting heraldry is generally reprobated, it seems nevertheless to have been adopted in the arms and mottos of many honourable families." He gives the examples of the Vernons, the Onslows, and
the Anstruthers. What Scott surely knows is that paronomasia was the
chief trope for inventing crests for ecclesiastics, who, hungry for signs
of nobility, never performed on the field of battle and were never supposed to breed on the field of satin.[23] Paronomasia covered for a deed
that did not, could not, and need not actually occur. It was the routine

equivocation by which heralds officially assisted ecclesiastics in divesting themselves of their institutional insularity and assuming the tincture of the world.

The paronomastic paradigm underwrites the dramatic, black-letter emphasis accorded to the Bradwardine motto, 𝕭𝖊𝖜𝖆𝖗 𝖙𝖍𝖊 𝖇𝖆𝖗. The novel elaborates a series of allegorical encounters between a protagonist named "Waverley" and "bar" after "bar" in paronomastic exfoliation: there are the "barrier" of the Highlands, "bears, small and large, demi- and full proportion," which were carved "over the windows, upon the ends of the gables, terminated the spouts, and supported the turrets" (103), the "blessed bear of Bradwardine" or *Ursa Major*, from which Waverley drinks the intoxicating brandy, and the baron himself; there are the bars of song that David Gellately sings at the end of the volume and the "fatal bar" that Waverley fears prepossesses Flora against him; and, of course, there is the bar, as always in Scott, that refers to the law and the legal profession, the profession of the Baillie MacWheeble, whose canny hand provides for the critical transfer of property that re-creates what had been dissolved and dissipated, as well as the profession of Scott's own father, from which the romancing son was diverted. Most tellingly, the heraldic "Bewar the bar" is a self-referential injunction that admonishes one to beware the line that separates one blazon from another. In heraldry the bar is not only a formal line of distinction but also a rhetorical line of interdiction, a legitimate bearing and the mark of illegitimate trespass. In the logic of romance and dreams, as in the logic of families, bars must at once be observed and yet crossed, crossed and yet uncrossed.

Within the novel the bar, as an element of the armigerous schema, has a totemic significance. Aunt Rachel presciently warns that "every desertion of the line of loyalty becomes its own punishment." Colonel Gardiner's ideal of military rectitude is to follow "the line of my duty." The bar delineates the discourse of the crest; within the area that the line describes and rules, tinctures have their figurative way: contingent, painterly, affecting.[24] Nonetheless, that affect only has value because it is codified. The device is a paradigmatic form across which transient tinctures play in manners that change minds and behavior. Consult the case of Everhard, whose determination to alter the terms of his will alteration finds at the sudden burst of sunlight through the gules of the Waverley crest blazoned on the window above his writing desk. Color has been traditionally mistrusted by those who rule, because a tincture of red or white or blue may impassion and incite the vulgar, but Scott faces down democratic panic with his faith in the composite art of the barred crest: its code conserves regulatory force regardless of the improvisatory quality of the colors.[25] As Scott's introductory tale of the bicker (in which a woman's gift of a green scarf as trophy is sufficient to incite the boys to shed their blood on Edinburgh's streets) suggests, the novel relies on the power of colors to impassion and on the power of lines to regulate, regardless of pedagogical intervention. What goes for ecclesiastics or bearwardens may and probably will go for artisans and novel readers, but such entitlement will occur only on the occasion of a recognition that refers mobility to a precedent, *official* design. *Waverley* is an exercise in pattern recognition, and Scott exerts himself as a would-be historical writer in search of a new paradigm that would not be an old picture. Not Wordsworthian or Hegelian but McLuhanesque is Scott, whose master work aspires toward the cool effectiveness of the icon rather than toward the mere *effect* of the bold thesis or lurid innovation.[26] Not to discern its work, to feel at home in its machinery, is to register its success as an icon of transition from the period of history (called *romance*) to the time of normal change (called *history*).

In the semiotic soup of *Waverley* this array of bars, barriers, and lines has a predominantly spatial orientation — not surprisingly, for under the picture logic of romance time would seem to have no jurisdiction. But there are lines in the novel besides those of loyalty and of duty, lines that communicate an unsettling dynamism to the picture. In his account of the Highland feast, the narrator gives the "long perspective" of the banquet table and beyond, where a "multitude of Highlanders" assemble as guests to partake of the hospitality of their chieftain. Yet the narrator strongly inflects the scene of symbolic expenditure with a diacritical mark. "This hospitality," he remarks, "apparently unbounded, had yet its line of economy" (179). Appearances deceive the participants, for whom this line is unimaginable. Not so the novelist, whose eye, trained in the elementary principles of political economy, sees that the line of economy must be there, even if imperceptible. The novelist sees because he writes from the perspective of a future borne from the past by the dynamism of that bar. He thus heralds the contradiction between the political aspirations of the chieftain and the mode of production that funds his authority. With "line of economy," Scott supplies a name for the virtual horizon of Defoe's exemplary world of the painting-stuffed Wilton House. As a tripwire that triggers the shift from a kind of picturesque description to developmental narration, the "line of economy" describes a virtual ekphrasis of a *moving* picture — of an archaic world always already on its way to commercial society. And thus the historical imagination scarifies the past, incising what Lukacs called a "necessary anachronism": "the writer would allow those tendencies which were alive and active in the past and which in historical reality have led up to the present (but whose later significance contemporaries naturally could not see) to emerge with that emphasis which they possess in objective, historical terms for the product of this past, namely, the present."[27] The "line of economy" is the wound of tendency itself, the bar that prevents the present from continuing on into the future except equivocally, as the stuff of fiction.

If, on its first inscription, the line of economy is imperceptible to the participants at Fergus's feast, on its second it is all but invisible to *Waverley*'s readers. The bar occurs between Charles Edward's brave charge to his troops as he returns to the "line of march" at the end of Chapter 57, "Mais, courage! c'est le grand jeu, apres tout," and the narrator's sober reflection at the beginning of Chapter 59: "The reader need hardly be reminded that, after a council was held at Derby on the 5th of December, the Highlanders relinquished their desperate attempt to penetrate farther into England, and, greatly to the dissatisfaction of their young and daring leader, determined to return northward" (394). Causes stop at the border of England, home of statistics, where the law of large numbers has jurisdiction. Because within the population of the United Kingdom Waverley's apostasy falls within the parameters of the standard deviation, not only Lukacs but the Hanoverian government can safely classify him as merely average.

The unseen line of economy separates the deviant world of romance from the probable world of the novel and cuts off the archaic world of the political, where violent usurpations prevail, from contemporary society, where change is normal and equivocation routinizes conflict. In that respect Scott is at one with the heraldic act that inscribed those bars and which has always already occurred in a prepolitical past, before clans, before the family, when the horizon of their historical being was cannily determined. To pass beyond that horizon is the rare privilege of changeable and wavering minds. The intrusion of the rhetorical into the very heart of the dynastic code tropes chance and change within the social DNA. Because Baron Bradwardine's mind is a medley of codes and rules flitting about among an assemblage of devices and tinctures, he is a suitable candidate to pass over the line that separates the political world of the clan from the social world of domestic reciprocity, private property, and the common law. Steadfast Fergus is immune to such charms: the fluttering of a pennant in the breeze would not touch his dynastic pride or affect his calculation of interest. Although less complimentary than Lukacs in his estimation of Scott's representativeness,

Ruskin was equally acute in his assessment that "the most startling fault of the age being its faithlessness, it is necessary that its greatest man should be faithless. Nothing is more notable or sorrowful in Scott's mind," he adds, "than its incapacity of steady belief in anything. He cannot even resolve hardily to believe in a ghost."[28] Fergus's refusal to tender belief in the mild deceptions of tincture and his scoffing at the courtly literalism of Bradwardine are linked at a level beyond reasoning to the taint of treason and to his superstitious belief in ghosts. Those defined by their loyalty must die or be exiled.[29] Fidelity condemns Fergus and Flora to defeat and, if not to oblivion, then to a fittingly spectral existence as "spirited" figures captured in Waverley's "historical" painting and Scott's historical novel.

Faithlessness is something one cannot, perhaps dare not, teach. But fortunately, faithlessness, like that omnifunctional motive, curiosity, is something one need not teach. If faithlessness is a moral condition, and curiosity the affective drive, then equivocation is the trope appropriate to a society in which apostatic transfers of affection must consistently occur without indictable treason. Equivocation is the form of speech that comes the closest to the pattern in things subject to history. And if Scott's heraldic equivocation does not produce a world picture, it *virtually* does by describing a holding pattern with which British subjects can make do until the final picture coalesces. In Scott, where adherence to any single tendency is subject to the betrayal of history, there is nothing fully to believe in except ghosts. And those who do fondly believe in ghosts, such as Fergus and Flora, will, as penalty for their sentimental fidelity, fail to cross the bar.

Scott's anachronism not only exploits tendencies in the past that were imperceptible to the agents, it also presupposes that there are tendencies in the present whose significance we cannot see. Adherence to a particular tendency involves a risk that may, as it does with Fergus, have fatal consequences. As the readiest device for improvising dynastic fictions, the trope of paranomasia had great utility for the waverley subject in the so-called United Kingdom in 1745, when the primal word *king* itself was antithetically conflicted between de facto and de jure. (115). Although an opponent of canting heraldry, Bradwardine demonstrates the social advantage that his learning in heraldic equivocation gives him over Everhard, who, when saluting the departing Waverley, breaches the form of the toast at the spot where the word *king* should fall and awkwardly substitutes "the Church of England and all constituted authorities" (91). With the suavity of a master of borderline manners, Bradwardine "announced the health of the King, politely leaving to the consciences of his guests to drink to the sovereign de facto or de jure, as their politics inclined" (115). His politics may incline the Whig silently to utter de facto; his politics may incline the Tory internally to pledge faith de jure. By equivocating, men of both camps can observe the formalities of the social occasion. The tactic is hardly antiquarian. As the experience of Coleridge and Thelwall and other radicals and fellow travelers of the 1890s had shown, politic equivocation—often on the occasion of a toast—was a handy device for negotiating the obligation to keep faith with one's heartfelt affiliations and the need to defend one's person against the uncompromising demands of the state.[30]

Jeopardy was clear and pressing during the course of the French wars, when any deviation from the prescribed credal profession could mean prosecution by the state. It is not immediately clear why, in 1814, when repressive pressure on the utterance had waned, Scott, whose aims were not at all subversive, should resolve on a strategy of equivocation. The policy becomes easier to understand when linked with the problem of Waverley's famous passiveness. Considering Waverley's introduction to the prince, George Levine argues that "the entire rhetorical strategy" of the passage is "aimed at exonerating the hero of *Waverley* from the crime of acquiescence in the prince's request."[31] Although the passage does underscore Waverley's powerlessness, a kind of acquiescence nonetheless occurs in the encounter. Morally, Waverley comes up short. If his behavior is pardonable, it is because moral acquiescence is not political consent. There is always a ready eternity for the *augenblick* of moral choice, but there must be real, historical time for consent to count. Acquiescence is passive, consent active. Waverley is beguiled, penetrated, overawed; he acquiesces and submits, but he withholds his consent throughout. He never consents to be ruled, whether by Fergus or his prince. That Waverley does not consent demarcates the politics of Scott's realism, the authentic source of his "resistance and mistrust."

From the perspective of the Stuart prince, of course, Waverley need not consent because a subject's act of consent has no standing before a sovereign who rules by divine right; or, to put it in the language of pre-Humean natural philosophy, the effect does not consent to its cause. From the perspective of the ruling Hanovers, it is crucial that Waverley not consent, most obviously because consent would constitute a deliberate and unforgivable act of treason. But it is also crucial because no more than the Stuarts do the Hanoverians and their adherents wish to ground their claim to the allegiance of their subjects on the Lockean qualification of the consent of the governed. Something more than passive obedience and something less than active consent is called for in a postpolitical world where deeds no longer matter but where interested man proposes and the law of political economy disposes. The middle way, the path sighted by Burke, explored by Benjamin Constant, and mapped by *Waverley*, is the equivocal path of recognition. Equivocation is a policy of accommodation without faith, of lip service without bond. It is a liberal policy that presupposes normal change as the serial production of novelties and a tolerance of inconsequential differences that occur within preordained constraints. No radical, Scott has a politics of reciprocal accommodation that inclines him to endorse the paronomastic equivocation that privatizes political convictions and subordinates them to a recognition of a social code that regulates polite behavior.

The withholding of consent is thus not a resistance to being governed but a shift of grounds to a recognition-based participation in the historical destiny of the nation, the succession of events that decides which tendency embedded in the paronomastic "king" will prevail. The Hanovers, a regime whose legitimacy has unfolded over time, embody that historical destiny and are vehicles of its continuation. If history is the story that winners tell, Scott, like Burke before him, tells us that history itself is Hanoverian: "the course of succession is the healthy habit of the British constitution" (Burke, 109). An allegiance must ultimately be made, but that allegiance is sealed by history, not by the active assertion of individual consent, which is a deed always presupposed. Paronomasia may be cant, but it is the cant of normal change. However illiberal in its professions, *Waverley* is the very pattern of liberalism in its promotion of cant, the language of trade, as the preferred vehicle of political discourse. By imagining nation, market, and household as coextensive, *Waverley* "excludes the possibility of action, which formerly was excluded from the household. Instead, society expects from each of its members a certain kind of behavior, imposing innumerable and various rules, all of which tend to 'normalize' its members, to make them behave, to exclude spontaneous action or outstanding achievement."[32] The heraldic strategy of polite regulation counts on the irrecoverability of an origin beyond the pun, which moots conflict by equivocally managing the antinomy of merit and blood.

Scott's schema answers the problem of teaching someone what in principle she already knows by producing a moment of recognition in which one comes to know what one never needed to learn. But unlike Burke's ancient constitution, with its fabulous origin beyond the veil, the crest has a history. The crest is not engraved in our hearts by our forefathers but devised and displayed by a herald, who, unlike a bard or a minstrel, is no dependent but, crucially, occupies an office. No king, no court, no parliament, no university, no patron underwrites the office of the herald, which capitalizes on the irreducible punning propensity of language, a capital that the herald finds rather than makes. In the worldview of *Waverley*, the herald's office is the formal precondition of *institution*, whether social or state.

Scott's notorious illiberalism thus paradoxically unfolds a higher liberalism—one in accord with the recognition-based polity modeled by such posthistorical liberals as Richard Rorty and Francis Fukuyama. Posthistorical and, in Hannah Arendt's terms, postpublic:

> The public realm, as the common world, gathers us together and yet prevents our falling over each other, so to speak. What makes mass society so difficult to bear is not the number of people involved . . . but the fact that the world between them has lost its power to gather them together, to relate and to separate them. The weirdness of this situation resembles a spiritualist seance where a number of people gathered around a table might suddenly, through some magic trick, see the table vanish from their midst, so that two persons sitting opposite each other were no longer separated but also would be entirely unrelated to each other by anything tangible. (Arendt, *Human*, 52–53)

We may agree with John Dewey's Scottian confidence that "the creation of a *tabula rasa* in order to permit the creation of a new order is so impossible as to set at naught both the hope of buoyant revolutionaries and the timidity of scared conservatives" (Dewey, 162) and yet accept the plausibility of Arendt's scenario, which depends only on the magically induced belief of the erasure of the table as the occasion for the strategic obliteration of the common world. If for Arendt's mysto-Lockean "table" we substitute Pitt's mysto-Satanic "Bonaparte," we capture some of the dismay that prevailed among narrators, dramatists, and gazetteers after 1814, when the artifice of the totality, forged by repression and its minions to simulate the common world that had been lost, suddenly itself lost its raison d'être and hallucinatory coherence.[33] If Byron's *Don Juan* is the classic rendition of what dreams come when the common, tangible world has vanished, *Waverley* takes the long view, which regards that loss as merely an eclipse, one flux of the normal cycle in which the table (call it a world picture or a paradigm) is devised, vended, bought, then replaced by something new. With Scott as our herald of the postmodern consensus we can recognize what Arendt could not: for *intangible*, we are able to substitute *virtual*. The table has been magically erased — all furniture, all the peripheral people and clans, have been cleared away, and we meet on what the novelist calls "the neutral ground" of history (130), there to sample the charms of a new, deliberately vague, and half-formed vocabulary, the virtual ekphrasis of the world picture that is ever about to appear.

More openly than either Rorty or Fukuyama, who exploit but do not reflect on the institutional supports for the postpublic vision, Scott's is an ardently clerical liberalism. In the transition to a recognition-based subject rather than a consent-based citizen, one is "subject" to an office, not a sovereign, to an official who rules and regulates, who is responsible for maintaining the world picture. *Waverley* has been described as accomplishing the transition from deference to status, from the world of patronage to the world of contract. But the more thoroughly modern *Waverley* imagines a state in which "administrative law, rather than contract law, becomes the paradigmatic form of law."[34] Scott does not aim to solve the crisis of authority but to manage it. What makes the genius of *Waverley* so remote from Heidegger's is its oblique but decisive advocacy of the "ascendance of the office over any particular man" (Lustig, 11). *Waverley* is the first bureaucratic novel not just because it was obstetrically delivered from the pigeonhole of an old desk but because in performing its anonymous office, it employs virtual ekphrasis to regulate accommodation to the postponement of a world picture and adjust the British to what Arendt calls the "rule of nobody" (Arendt, *Human*, 45).

Chapter Seven

Using
Romantic Ethics and Digital Media in the Ruins of the University

> Poetry is the first and last of all knowledge — it is as immortal as the heart of man. If the labours of Men of Science should ever create any material revolution, direct or indirect, in our condition, and in the impressions which we habitually receive, the Poet will sleep then no more than at present, but he will be ready to follow the steps of the Man of Science, not only in those general indirect effects, but he will be at his side, carrying sensation into the midst of the objects of the Science itself.
> — William Wordsworth, Preface to *Lyrical Ballads* (1802)

This chapter considers the uses to which Romantic texts and Romantic thinking can be put. In the climate of anti-Romantic ideology that prevails in academic books and journals, in the schools and at the conventions, such a concern for the use, rather than the critique, of Romanticism may appear quaint, and certainly requires justification. I shall not, as is the fashion, develop that justification in terms of paradigm shifts in the geopolitical aesthetic but undertake it in light of my own changing professional commitments, which are bound up with the way I use Romantic texts. In the course of defining a democratic ethics, Ronald Dworkin has urged that we "not just think but . . . live out of what we think."[1] The aim of this chapter is to examine the way my thinking led to the way I live and work now. The end toward which this essay tends is an ethics of Romantic use.

> I have often been asked, how I first came to be a regular opium-eater.
> — Thomas De Quincey, *Confessions of an English Opium Eater*

Roughly ten years ago the School of Arts and Sciences at the Johns Hopkins University was nearly bankrupt — listing under an enormous debt incurred by the construction of a state-of-the-art physics building. That building was planned, contracted, and bricked by administrators in the fond hope that dollars from large grants, each with its healthy chunk of indirect costs, would forever flow from the federal government. From that silver dream, floated on the Fordist belief in large-scale organization and in the cozy stability of the Cold War, Hopkins, like other major research universities, has since awakened to face the downsized reality of increasing costs and diminishing resources.

The deficit crisis prompted a five year plan with a bailout by other divisions. To secure itself for the long term, however, Arts and Sciences was compelled to look for additional sources of revenue. If Hopkins were a corporation in which one could hold shares, it would have recruited investors. But private universities are special kinds of corporations that do not have shareholders; they have alumni, who are expected to give rather than invest. Among private universities, Hopkins has always been something of a special case. Historically the first (in the United States) and traditionally foremost a research institution, Hopkins has not allocated the lion's share of its resources to undergraduate education or cultivated in its undergraduates a sense of their full participation in the intellectual community. At Hopkins the faculty has generally divided the undergraduate population into the "good" undergraduates (that research-oriented core who are future graduate students), the "bad" (premeds, who are imagined to be monocularly focused on admission to medical school), and the "indifferent" (that puzzling segment who pass through on the way to some other career goal).

In the past the system worked. But as federal money slowed, the premed pool softened, and university positions for physics and other disciplines in the natural sciences dwindled, the tendency to treat undergraduates as if they were defective graduate students proved increasingly impractical. Always small and specialized, adherence to its loftily defined research orientation had left Hopkins chronically underendowed (well-heeled alums are almost invariably former undergraduates, usually of the "bad" or "indifferent" variety) and tuition-driven (catering to customers who could not possibly comprehend the "research" product) — more dependent on the consumerist choices of high school students than on ethical obligations developed in its baccalaureates. The near-bankruptcy had the benign, indirect consequence of temporarily focusing Hopkins' attention on the need to take undergraduates seriously as potential alums who would have good reason to reflect with favor on the education they received and to connect whom they have become with where they learned.

The need for reform was generally accepted and indeed trumpeted as the university undertook a major fund-raising campaign targeting dormant alumni with the message of a new commitment to undergraduate education. Nonetheless, it was clear to all that no reform could succeed if it involved transplanting a core curriculum packaged for Ivy League consumption. Any curricular reform would have to proceed directly from individual faculty who would have to respect and exploit the distinctive culture of Hopkins. In the spring of 1994, I helped launch the Johns Hopkins Center for Digital Media Research and Development as an exercise in what Bill Readings has called "institutional pragmatism."[2] My colleague Harry Goldberg and I designed a program that would be project-oriented in the classroom and would target a market beyond: projects within the arts and sciences that would project Arts and Sciences to the world at large. A Romanticist by training, I have no particular computer expertise, but I had developed a scholarly interest in how otherwise ill-assorted individuals, motivated by an elementary social feeling, associate to define and accomplish a common goal. Goldberg, an untenured biophysicist, fit the profile of an ill-assorted individual, with the providential exception that he might as well have been trained by M. H. Abrams (as I was), for he taught me to regard the computer not as a piece of hardware or a determinant technology but as a metaphor, like a mirror or a lamp, which enabled rethinking, reframing, and revision of customary ways of doing things, of envisioning projects. We came to share the view that the craft of digital media development qualifies as a liberal art if in the classroom and the workshop emphasis is placed not on the tools but on the *idea* of a project. We agreed that the historical distinction of the digital arts is that confidence in the imagination entails confidence in the future: if you imaginatively define a digital project, you can devise the tools to accomplish it. First the poem, then the pen.

Goldberg developed courses in which all students were required to arrive on the first day of class with individual projects suitable for multimedia presentation. With responsibility, respect: from the beginning of the term, the students were acknowledged as content experts. A superb teacher, Goldberg assisted students in identifying and mastering the requisite tools to realize their ideas in a multimedia presentation. The class workshopped storyboards, critiqued interface designs, and debated programming strategies. Diversity was the baseline — some came in knowing more about authoring software, some came in as better graphic artists, some came in as better writers, some came in as better geologists. Development was unevenly driven by strange attractions and dialectical leaps. Surmises of what would work, what was elegant, and what was robust were focused on the user — who was that person on the other side of the screen, at the next workstation, hanging out in the dormitory lounge. The final projects were introduced, demonstrated, and defended before a panel of faculty and former students, who appraised them according to the articulated critieria that had guided design and execution. Especially promising projects, those with the potential for use, became the basis for advanced courses in which teams wrote grant applications, sought contracts, made presentations to clients, and collaborated in producing a product to spec and on deadline. Above all, as developed developers the students became capable judges of use.

Hopkins' experiment should be of interest to faculty in public and private research institutions that do not share Hopkins' peculiar traditions, for it is generally pertinent today to ask whether productive, socially valuable research can be understood and undertaken without anchorage in a narrowing professionalist base or without becoming a corporate franchise. What can people use that profit-oriented corporations cannot supply? Is research into use as meritorious as research into structures and forms, causes and combinations? How can the special version of a corporation, the university, make useful products while maintaining the ethos of a liberal arts education?

The prospects for professionals of all stripes have declined drastically over the past decade. Insofar as "the New Federalism" has meant a shift of regulatory authority to the state governments, supposed to be intimately responsive to the popular will, it seems likely that professionalism will come increasingly under attack in the name of the populist ideal of a government without offices, of leaders without training, of de facto without de jure, and of law without regulation. As the ethos of professionalism has lost its social influence, claims to licensing authority have come to look less rational and more nakedly political, impositions to be resisted by the formally unqualified in the political arena where numbers, not credentials, count. Professional codes have begun to take on the aspect of guildlike restrictions of trade. And even professional guilds like the American Medical Association have, in the interest of economic survival, abandoned the professionalist ethos in favor of union cards. Most such attacks have been mounted by the right or by the new corporate patrons of "applied research." Yet identity politics as it is promulgated and practiced in the academy by the left harmonizes with this trend, insofar as the ascription of identity, whether imagined as essentialist or socially constituted, coincides with attacks on the norm of disinterestedness and on the credentializing authority that historically have sustained the progressivist ethos of professionalism.

I do not intend to make a plea for professionalism. Many of the grievances against professional perks and protocols have merit. None-theless, when those grievances become the fuel for demagoguery it would be prudent to respond, if not necessarily resist. On the face of it, it is hard to see how any of the current defenses of professionalism will be widely effective or how they will concretely serve the needs of under-graduates facing careers in a world where attaining a professional iden-tity counts less than developing the versatility to remake oneself accord-ing to projects that one intermittently joins or initiates. There are, of course, those apologists for the way things tend and embrace a conser-vative conception of disciplinarity that, however coherent it may be as an argument (its retreat to a few patent institutional premises guaran-tees that), applies more to the liberal arts degree at Williams or Carleton or Pomona than it does to the research faculty at the University of Texas or Cornell or Johns Hopkins.

Consider the argument of Stanley Fish, as recently represented in an essay in *English Literary Renaissance*. In his familiar terms Fish gives a good account of why English professors should not lament the failure of their attempts to influence public policy — as if such overreaching were a kind of professional hubris that brought its own inevitable punishment — but he has no good account of why practitioners now feel that they should need to exert such influence. He does not analyze what combination of institutional factors provokes fear sufficient to impel professional critics to futile exertions of their political will. Fish wants to understand academics' concern for the "grounds of a disci-pline's possibility" as a theoretically motivated, and therefore false, problem: "In short it is a mistake to believe that because disciplinary intelligibility finally is a function of what exceeds and escapes it — of what it cannot contain — you can get a better purchase on that intel-ligibility by looking beyond it."[3] Fish opposes what he calls a "de-constructive Platonism" (356) with a deconstructive quietism. It is as if Fish wants to forget that the issue is not at all a theoretical one that can be satisfactorily engaged in terms of "intelligibility."

What increasingly impresses disciplinary practitioners in the human-ities department of today is not the theoretical promise of a view of the totality but that the microregulation of their practice is imposed from somewhere outside the so-called discipline (even a private university like Hopkins is unable to add a major without state approval of the curriculum and the numerical designation of the major) or imposed by increasingly interventionist boards of trustees drawn from corporate boardrooms and intent on "rationalizing" university practice according

to corporate models of governance and accountability. In their untutored force, such impositions make the professionalist hypothesis of
disciplinary autonomy little more than a nostalgic fiction for most of
us, its attainment a hollow victory for the rest. Dr. Fish, meet Mr.
Pyrrhus. Insofar as professionalism disavows a social vision broader
than the formal analysis of canonical texts and defensively defines itself
in elitist and parochial (that is, narrow disciplinary) terms, it has ceded
the real social and cultural battleground to its populist adversary and
its corporate patrons.

That might not be a bad thing, were populism a progressive democratic movement rather than a volatile brew of working-class and sectarian resentment stirred by the grand old racist, homophobic, sexist,
and anti-Semitic watchwords and manipulated by the very corporate
system populism professes to attack. Corporate aggressiveness in defining who the people are and what the people want presents a considerable threat to the traditional university not only because corporate
control over the media enables a shaping of that culture in which the
arts and sciences must make their case but also because in the wake of
governmental withdrawal from support of research, corporate America
is, like it or not, the likeliest source for the infusion of capital necessary
for universities to survive and prosper as alternatives to the corporate
model of social organization. Many on the academic left have devoted
themselves to analyzing the mystifications of corporate liberalism and
to theorizing democratic alternatives to the siren song of a new corporate culture that promises to realize the liberal dream of a capitalist
social organization in which "the power of communitarian governance
is synthesized with the pleasure of individual autonomy."[4]

Now whether or not one endorses such a vision, or whether or not,
as the cultural critiquers profess, one can theorize a credible organization of social and economic practices free of corporate sponsorship,
anyone who read the accounts in the business pages during the mid to
late nineties — of brutal layoffs at AT&T, IBM, and NCR, of the wholesale conscription of white-collar staff as strikebreakers at Caterpillar, of
Mitsubishi's mobilization of its workers to protest governmental response to claims of sexual harassment in the workplace, of the spread
of the University of Phoenix's franchises with their squads of academ-
ically indifferent managers and battalions of ill-paid part-time instruc-
tors — ought to suspect that the expressed commitment to such a vision
of blissful integration remains little more than another tactic in the war
of position that the dominant American corporations have conducted
with the administrative state since the 1930s. In the postindustrial era

we have witnessed the mutation of manufacturing sites into "campuses," a transformation that mixes the metaphors of education and business, the conditions of nonprofit and profit, in order to integrate the cultural, social, and economic aspects of its employees' lives under the rubric of corporate sponsorship. Such exercises in liberalizing the conditions of employment have proven to be stratagems in the extension of corporate control,[5] tactical applications of a corporate liberal ideology designed to bind unvested people to strategic goals of production within the corporation, just as advertising campaigns bind populations to strategic goals of consumption outside the corporation — or, increasing the stakes, as identification with corporate trademarks and logos works to erase the distinction between production and consumption, employees and consumers, in favor of a metaclan of fervently unreflecting partisans.

The successful marketing strategies of Microsoft and Nike present distinctly contrasting hegemonic styles. Despite Microsoft's ostensible position on the cutting edge of new digital technologies, its strategy "of intensive accumulation and monopolistic regulation" is substantially more Fordist than Nike's.[6] Even Microsoft's quondam commitment to the campus model of industrial organization bespeaks a Fordist acceptance of those " 'protective frameworks' established in the post-war period." One reason given for the decline of Fordism is that "consumption patterns of the 'affluent worker' have gradually changed; [that is,] a greater variety of use-values is demanded which cannot be satisfied by conventional means of standardized production" (Elam, 65). Bill Gates, CEO of Microsoft, has successfully resisted this differentiation from within the same mass-production ethos as Henry Ford before him by adopting and refining an industrial strategy based on the production of standards that it hopes will be accepted by or imposed on the industry and the public. Gates's commitment to standardization serves his grander strategic repudiation of the heterogeneity of markets in favor of what he calls "the ultimate market," a concept that involves the abolition of use-value altogether in favor of a reduction of all goods and services, including money, into "digital information [which] will be the medium of the new market" — information that is nothing but its exchange.[7]

The Microsoft version of Ford's River Rouge Plant integrates developers, programmers, and testers into an assembly line whose tempo and tone is defined by the overriding imperative of shipping as many products as quickly as possible. Gates goes Ford one better by aiming to conscript consumers into the Microsoft operating system as virtual workers—coopting consumers not only by inducing them to work as testers of product but also by enlisting them as adherents to the Microsoft brand and worldview (which *Windows* is transparently designed to fuse). Moreover, like the original Fordist enterprise, the process has a name and face: the cult of what, in *Microserfs*, Douglas Coupland calls "chairman Bill," who, whether as savior or as demon, embodies the corporation and whose role epitomizes the Fordist formula of "one man, one product, one process."[8]

In *The Road Ahead*, Gates describes his goal as the de facto establishment of *MS/DOS* or *Windows 95* or whatever else comes down the fiberoptic highway from Redmond as an "industry software standard" (44). "Where do you want to go today?" asks the Microsoft commercial, offering *Windows* as the Model T of the millennium. In 1981 Gates candidly explained the corporate advantages of standardization:

> Why do we need standards? . . . It's only through volume that you can offer reasonable software at a low price. Standards increase the basic machine that you can sell into [the market]. . . . I really shouldn't say this, but in some ways it leads, in an individual product category, to a natural monopoly: where somebody properly documents, properly trains, properly promotes a particular package and through momentum, user loyalty, reputation, sales force, and prices builds a very strong position with that product.
> (Cusamano and Selby, 157)

It doesn't take a deconstructionist to detect the armed etymology that connects Gates's insistent use of the adverb "properly" with his implacable insistence on Microsoft's "proprietorial" rights to the software it develops. Given the correspondence between "de facto standards" and "natural monopoly," it is no wonder that Microsoft has a history of confrontations with the antitrust unit of the Justice Department, which has challenged Microsoft's alleged anticompetitive practices in imposing its standards on the computer industry. Although Gates has fiercely resisted government oversight of contractual arrangements and irrational interventions into the efficient operations of the market, Microsoft's success would be inconceivable without federal copyright protection and the ideological commitment of the liberal state to recognize and enforce privately contracted licensing agreements. What Gates calls "friction-free capitalism" remains, even in the best case, rights-based, proprietorial capitalism.[9] The Boolean road of Gates's Internet is every bit as much a chartered street as the labyrinth of Blake's London.

The "pure" market Gates fancies is just another seignorial preserve, protected from poachers by the sheriff.

The perfect market trumps both the public and private spheres; its realization presupposes the legislatively enabled penetration of commerce into all the nooks and crannies of life — a truly neuralized emporium. The notion of a noncommercial space persists as merely a seductive interface in the software package, the pretext for purchase and consumption, not a domain of distinctive practices. In the so-called perfect market, should consumers desire to hear a song or view a video clip, they would pay, download, and play, but would not be free to copy or modify.[10] No re-creation. No sharing. No use. Indeed, Gates's dream of the perfect, friction-free market in which bits and dollars have become identical cannot be realized unless use is reduced to a hypothetical moment, the lure for consumption. Gates has no vision of what lies ahead that does not presuppose the absolute reduction of the social and the political to the economic. Thus the troubling disparity between rich and poor (there are more of the latter than of the former; how do we sell to those with almost no money?) would be overcome (assuming Gingrich's solution of the universal distribution of laptops) simply by allowing the rich to buy products for dollars and the poor to collect advertisements for pennies.[11]

Nike's corporate strategy proceeds from an innovative vision of the social and exploits the spectacular bodies of athletes in order to promote Nike's trademark and, almost incidentally, Nike's actual products. It's not the shoes. It's not the game. It's not even the players. Recall the series of Penny Hardaway commercials in which the NBA player sits on his couch with his robotic double, "Little Penny," watching "himself" perform as pitchman in hyperbolic Nike commercials. No basketball game — the "actual function" by which Hardaway qualifies as the nominal subject of the advertisement — is played or watched. The mockery of the "real" Hardaway by his automaton remarks with surprising frankness on the entirely contingent status of the advertising subject and the plasticity of an actual function that is nothing but its suitability to be symbolized for spectacular consumption.

Nike would have us believe that it has no corporate imaginary. Nike's self-manifestation is fully symbolic, and that symbolization is thoroughly Romantic: it's the swoosh. The company cunningly deploys an updated version of the dehistoricized, interpellative heraldry innovated by Walter Scott — with the significant difference that what is imagined in *Waverley* as a semiotics of self-recognition that would be of use to the emergent and expanding nation has no teleological implications for Nike. Nike need not concern itself with use — because the logic of the spectacle presupposes that use has already been commodified. The slogan "Just Do It" is a command to buy, not to act. The Nike swoosh realizes the apostate poet's chiasmic ideal as what Blake called the limit of contraction or what Stuart Hall has famously called "the aestheticization of the commodity, the commodification of the aesthetic." The dream merger of communitarian governance with the pleasures of individual autonomy has become the "dream team" of individual stars, whose contingent association is bound ónly by the labels they wear. Nike appraises the federal government as just another sponsor whose claims on a citizen's allegiance have no more and no less authority than the corporation's claims on the consumer's brand loyalty.[12]

Hence the controversy surrounding an article by Andrew Levy in the April 1996 issue of *Harper's*, which pointed out the striking resemblance between the logo on a Nike display celebrating the opening of its Niketown store in Chicago and the Nazi swastika. Levy accepts that the conjunction of a "paean to corporate unity" with "the central twentieth-century symbol of the dangers of national unity" was not concretely motivated but persuasively connects its display with "the logic of American business as it is conducted in this decade by multinational corporations like Nike" and attributes the similarity to the corporate deracination of even the most potent symbols of nationalist signification in the name of merchandising.[13] The resemblance is real. Even if unintended, the citation of the resemblance by a writer completing a book on the Holocaust graphically remarks on the limits of the corporate emptying-out of meaning. The apparition of the swastika on Michigan Avenue is not only the sociological extension but also the politically active manifestation of Nike's attempt to bind its customers into an unreasoning allegiance to their products and style. The swastika is thus not an empty signifier but a historically invested icon, overpowering the Nike logo it is meant to serve, evidence that the formalization of symbols can only proceed so far until the repressed social and political content returns to illuminate, however briefly, the corporate unconscious.

The troubles that both Nike and Microsoft have faced in the last couple of years reflect their distinctive corporate identities. Nike's problems have identified a material horizon to the unfettered symbology of the company: journalistic revelations regarding the conditions for workers in the Asian plants where Nike shoes are assembled. Yet even here, where quantifiable issues of pay, hours, and environmental hazards are involved, the real domain is symbolic. It is not the National Labor Relations Board that has been pursuing Nike but Gary Trudeau and Michael Moore. It is not the National Association of Manufacturers that springs to Nike's defense in the halls of Congress but former UN Ambassador Andrew Young, leader of an "independent" fact-finding mission, in a full page ad in the *New York Times*. Asian workers may endure unhealthy working conditions for low pay, but Nike suffers from bad publicity. And what makes the publicity bad is not so much the details of factories in Thailand or Korea but the mere revelation in photos and anecdotes that real people must actually *work* to produce the shoes bearing the logo that elevates the athletes into the ether of universal recognition. Critics of Nike's pricing policy, who decry the wildly inflated prices of Nike shoes, simply miss the material point. Nike has proven to be vulnerable not to the charge that the shoes are worth almost nothing but that they are worth *something*, that embedded in their symbology is a material constituent, that a $149 pair of Air Jordans are actually the materialization of someone's labor rather than an incarnation of Michael Jordan's triumphant will.

Microsoft faces a problem that the twentieth-century history of relations between corporation and the federal government has made familiar: prosecution under the Sherman Antitrust Act. Whatever one thinks of the merits of Microsoft's organicist claims for the seamless unity of its operating system or the charges by the government that Microsoft's integration of *Internet Explorer* constitutes an illegal "tying" of one independent commodity to another, the use of antitrust to arrest or divert Microsoft's corporate strategy has a distinctly Romantic quality. Antitrust prosecutions since the passage of the Sherman Act in 1897 have been sporadic. Even within self-described progressive administrations, such as the first and second New Deal administrations of Franklin Roosevelt, there have been strong ideological disagreements over the use of antitrust prosecution as an instrument of federal economic policy. Although there were those who, following Louis Brandeis, "favored a policy of decentralizing the business structure and enforcing competitive behavior," there were those economic planners, who, according to Hawley, "felt that antitrust action was a hopeless anachronism."[14] The latter view is the position taken by Gates and his supporters.

If a defense of the antitrust suit against Microsoft is to be mounted, it cannot be on grounds that the Sherman Act is *not* an anachronism. Both history and the government's own briefs in the case indicate that a defense of antitrust action on general principles is impossible to mount. As Microsoft has complained, the times and places where it will be applied are impossible to predict. Those activists and critics, such as Ralph Nader and Mark Crispin Miller, who argue that antitrust action is a suitable postindustrial policy for dealing with the conglomeration of the information and entertainment industries are on shaky ground. But just because antitrust is anachronistic does not mean it is hopeless. On the contrary, the government's willingness to launch the suit against Microsoft can be described as Romantic because its antitrust action is a *hopeful* anachronism, a decision to make use of whatever tool is at hand in the face of uncertainties regarding innovation, standardization, and competition in the information industry. Efficiency may suffer, but efficiency defined in terms of obsolescing systems is a secondary consideration in an industry where efficient systems can lead to network lock and technological stagnation.

It is reasonable to ask whether the university system at the end of the twentieth century, whose evolved disciplinary efficiencies increasingly lag behind the mutational effectiveness of emerging corporate forms, has become an obsolescent system. But why ask a question no one can answer? The *pertinent* question for arts and sciences in the contemporary university is this: Can research be understood and undertaken without having a professionalist base or becoming either a ward of the state or a corporate franchise? Can the liberal arts survive and prosper as a hopeful anachronism? More pointedly, what is it that corporations need (though they don't know it), and how can the special version of a corporation, the university, respond to that need while maintaining the ethos of liberal arts? In Gates's lingo, what are the conditions needed for universities to create a "positive spiral" of success in the global market?

That's not a rhetorical question. The current state of multimedia technology favors the university as a corporation not beholden to stockholders. Costs of software development in the private sector are extremely high, for reasons that include the expense of installing and constantly upgrading equipment, the scarcity of talent, and the failure ratio of new titles. Economies of scale favor the huge producer and the small producer: either the corporate conglomerate, which can afford large commitments of venture capital, or the small shop that can risk starting up by managing to keep costs down. The middle cannot hold.[15] As with the film industry before World War II, product recognition and, even more importantly, access to distribution outlets also gives the advantage to large producers. Take the Walt Disney Company as an example. Animation at Disney has historically been an aggressively Fordist enterprise—in which the corporate aim has been to make craftspeople into workers and to make workers interchangeable.[16] But the advent of digital technology has had the paradoxical effect of making it possible for Disney to cut costs and improve product while, at the same time, making Disney incapable of fully controlling creative talent and productivity. *Toy Story* was a big success for Disney but an even bigger success for Pixar, the start-up company that Disney subcontracted for the computer animation.[17]

The university studio or lab can prosper at the artisanal level of multimedia development as long as niche production, niche marketing, and interstitial maneuverability are appreciated tactics in the continued ethical project of finding users. The productions of the media conglomerates on the screen, on the web, and on CD-ROM and DVD cannot stray far from the entertainment model that is the horizon of determination for the mass media. Like part-time programs or continuing studies or summer schools for the gifted and talented, research and development of digital media in the university has an "organic" connection to a population of users inherently more diverse than the masses that consume the pleasures of the entertainment industry; though fewer, its number is still considerable by any other standard than that set by the Hollywood blockbuster. The educational market — especially the humanities — remains largely untapped and untargeted by commercial developers, who have as yet failed to establish distribution networks nuanced and reliable enough to warrant the kind of investments required to introduce titles.[18] Educational users developing software for educational use have a window of opportunity to exploit available talent and favorable economies of scale and establish distribution networks of diverse users in rewarding apposition, if not competitive opposition, to the corporate giants.

Advantage and immunity for the university flow from the tax-exempt status granted to private and public universities as educational institutions. Although profit is less of an incentive for enterprise, the penalty of bankruptcy is far more remote. The tax law makes it possible for a university to do certain things that otherwise would not be done. It is not the fault of the system if universities fail to do them. Take our model project, for example. Our multimedia edition of Ibsen's *A Doll House* edition contains 70 minutes of video recordings of video performances, accessible as annotations to the text or in a separate archive. Some rightsholders bill at a standard $5000-a-minute rate for permission to reproduce such performances. Such a cost (which does not include the permissions for actors and actresses, director and musicians) would ensure that no scholarly edition would make back its investment. But for a product made not for profit and for educational purposes, tax law cuts the costs by as much as 80 percent. Such a discount involves significant marketing restrictions — particularly on distribution (the contracts forbid resale, which means that direct-market sale is required). But such restrictions are tonic challenges to academics to devise their own Internetworks for distribution of educational software. For the university, profit is less important than prestige. Software products produce cultural capital: they advertise the institution as the kind of place where such elegant products are made.

Digital media production answers to the Romantic dream of a craft that would be sensuously pleasurable and socially useful — one that the impatient intellect would not soon be tempted to quit. That dream could not be realized at the beginning of the nineteenth century (for Coleridge, who fell into reflections on surrogates, religious and philosophical, even poetry could not suffice). The best hope for a liberal arts curriculum that engages "corporate culture" on its own terms is to understand undergraduate education as apprenticeship in what the sociologists call "flexible specialization," an "industrial model" that, in the wake of Fordism, is "best capable of producing quality goods for specialist and volatile markets with the minimum of effort, time and cost" (Amin, 20). I call it "apprenticeship," because "related to [flexible specialization] is a broader shift in philosophy concerning the people-machine interface, away from skill substitution and human enslavement by technology, towards the craft idea of machines as tools of work. . . . Flexible specialization promises to *restore* dignity and skills in the workplace, as well as to establish new democratic industrial relations based on cooperation, mutual respect, dialogue and 'studied trust' between employers and employees" (Amin, 21). What makes such a goal Romantic and not nostalgic is that such a restoration *can* happen at any time; always at hand, craftsmanship is unbound to any particular form of social organization; a craft can be effectively practiced regardless of the mode of production, and it can be applied to progressive goals of democracy and autonomy.

The university figures largely in this restoration because the university makes use of what, in the nineteenth century, republican writers called "free labor." According to Michael J. Sandel "free labor referred not to permanent wage labor but to labor that issued ultimately in economic independence."[19] Although Sandel describes a mode of labor that has lapsed not only from the factory and the farm but also from the discourse of political philosophy, students who labor in the university workshop and who are not paid wages — exchangeable for commodities — but credits would seem to be the closest approximation to the republican model of free labor. Credits should not be understood as chits purchased in lots of three or four to be accumulated toward a degree that certifies an overqualified technician as ready to enter into a discipline or an underdetermined manager as ready to enter the corporate hierarchy, but as reliable promises of an expertise that will permit the graduated student to establish him or herself independently of the rules of disciplines and the culture of the corporation and, in concert with other users, to pursue projects under their own rule, governed by themselves.

Flexible specialization involves an applications orientation within a form of organization fundamentally more democratic than laboratory research in chemistry or in the biological sciences. This is not an ideological indulgence but a practical requirement, which, however, ought to be the occasion of some pleasure among those liberal artists who happen to be democrats. By blurring the distinction between the research scientist and the premed, between the scientist and humanist, between the alum and the student, interactive multimedia workshops provide an alternative metaphor and concept to guide teaching and research. It is not interactivity itself that I would choose to highlight. Interactivity, like dialogue, may be one of those things that we are supposed to approve — as opposed to mere activity or mere monologue. And certainly a Romanticist, who has been trained on the critical classics of high Romantic argument — supremely, M. H. Abrams's *Natural Supernaturalism* — which heavily invest in reciprocity between man and nature or man and man, is primed to approve interactivity. Nonetheless, a Romantic ethics, which deliberately blurs the disciplined distinction between Romantic and Romanticist, recognizes that interactivity may be fine under certain circumstances, indifferent in others. I would prefer to focus on the concept of use — which does not serve a prescriptive good but designates an unfolding or developing social practice. In this context, alienation does not mean working on something that someone else owns but working on something you wouldn't or couldn't use. Opportunely, digital technology enables the mode of production to be replicated in the product: users make users. In Romantic and specifically De Quinceyean terms, a user is someone whose power regularly corresponds to his or her wishes.

The humanities user brings to the workshop certain constraints that do not customarily exert force on practitioners in the natural or the computer sciences. A humanities spin on the mission of higher education in a corporatist environment might go thus: every relaxation of the profit imperative entails an increased obligation for reflection on the presuppositions and ends of the project undertaken — its social and political trajectory. Take the Hopkins' "Tour of Baltimore" project, for example. A couple of talented undergraduates undertook to develop a prototype of a tour of Baltimore, using the interface of a bus to permit potential visitors to the city to devise an itinerary based on interest and budget. It soon became clear that engaging a potential user of such a tour meant both understanding what the city is and imagining what it could be. At the most fundamental level there are questions of categorization (restaurant guides and landmarks, surely, but what about neighborhoods?) and evaluation (do we allow restaurants to describe themselves or do we insist on impartial ratings; if we introduce accounts of Baltimore's neighborhoods, do we rate them in terms of safety?). Does packaging require foreclosing exploration? What use would it be to have a section or web link called "Rough Neighborhoods in Baltimore" (or perhaps "The *Homicide* Interface")? Is the university's responsibility in putting together a tour book different from the Chamber of Commerce's or Fodor's? Is there a responsibility to enlighten, even demystify, as well as inform, even if the product will not sell? Is the development of commodities an appropriate vehicle for humanities education? Is there a danger to the liberal arts in describing education so broadly that the distinction between what we do and what anyone can do becomes increasingly ambiguous? When I worry about such issues, am I worrying about my institution, my profession, my career, or my discipline? Or is it just that I'm anxious about developing bad habits?

> I work hard because I love my work. It's not an addiction.
> — Bill Gates, *The Road Ahead*, Afterword

Assuming that you share the liberal values traditionally espoused and occasionally embodied by the university, and assuming that you do not have a non-negotiable commitment to disciplinarity (a larger concession), this chapter has thus far been a narrative of imagined progress: the transition from a world of false oppositions, empty disciplines, and inflexible hierarchy to a more humane world of collaborative labor within a democratically organized workshop — a transition to a livable and workable world where, one hopes, "the power of communitarian governance is synthesized with the pleasure of individual autonomy" (quoted in Amin, 31). In the jargon of the day, such a vision models the university classroom as an empowerment zone where persons are induced to imagine projects and taught to develop the tools to complete them. No doubt I idealize, and I do not apologize for that. Some idealization is necessary to package a set of practices as worthy of emulation. Even so, as the poet of "Alastor" has warned, pursuit of the silver dream can only take us so far until we end in impasse drear.

Romantics, as the very condition of their idealism, should be prepared to heed the poet's warning. But the same admonition applies to the pragmatist, who characteristically idealizes problem-solving as an all-purpose method. For pragmatism too has its romance: a faith in a future that will endlessly unfold as a series of problems to be solved, a faith sustained by a programmatic unwillingness to think the negative. By "negative" I do not mean to signify another problem that must be solved but to invoke that special sort of phenomenon that threatens to undermine the very procedure of problem-solving. Gates's idealization of software as the hero of his market romance is a good example of the programmatic avoidance of the negative. The quintessential pragmatic product of the cybernetic age, software, unlike continually obsolescing hardware, can be fancied to be plastically responsive to altered circumstances and new demands. By adhering to its software origins, Microsoft hopes to prevent any bad consequences that its monopolistic strategy might otherwise provoke. Gates can confidently indulge that hope because software codes the negative as just another bit of information, the "shut" that follows every "open."

For Gates, the perfect market is a great deal like the weather in its pervasiveness and its sudden changes: the cyberflow of a "natural" monopoly. That similarity highlights the illiberal consequences of Gates's vision. Although Gates is fond of invoking the authority of Adam Smith, economic liberal, to legitimate his corporate ambitions, he prudently ignores Smith's doctrinal opposition to monopolism. But there is a potentially more deadly consequence to breathing the Gatesian ether. The discourse of political liberalism from Locke to Constant and from Rawls to Dworkin, which dwells on the question of how the individual can be justly governed by a state system that he or she did not invent and whose necessity is not immediately evident — that tradition is just irrelevant to *The Road Ahead*. People do not consent to the weather. Nor will they have to enroll in Microsoft's electronic environment; consumers, clients, agents will be absorbed into it simply because it will be imposingly, inevitably *there*, a cybernesis administering to their needs, authorizing their desires, and profitably merging needs and desires, public and private space, into a steady stream of electrons that charmingly configure consumable products.[20]

Of course, if immersion in the electrosphere were actually as inevitable as subjection to the wild, west wind, Gates would not have authorized the promotional efforts of *The Road Ahead* and *Business @ the Speed of Thought* (1999) to pacify skeptics and to recruit readers to Microsoft's vision of the cybermarketplace. Gates ardently aspires to influence public policy, an endeavor conveniently unregulated by any conception of what a public might be. Because he still must acknowledge a world where policy has its place, even if only as the troll lurking under the infobahn's projected span over the public interest, Gates must appeal to readers as if they are not yet fully deprived of the power to decide their fate: as a public capable of renouncing a public interest. Despite his indifference to the social and political implications of the Microsoft corporate project, Gates must undertake the political enterprise of rhetorically mobilizing people in the service of a vision of the future. *The Road Ahead* is a rhetorical symptom of unvoiced disturbances in Microsoft's corporate unconscious.

Unvoiced, but not insignificant. Symptoms are telling, and rhetorical ones are especially so. Recall that in the pages of the *Morning Post*, Coleridge considered the rhetorical means by which otherwise atomized individuals were bound toward a common end. He adapted for a postrevolutionary age the Christian triad of the essential virtues of faith, hope, and charity: "fear, hope, and memory," he pronounced, "are the three great agents, both in the binding of a people to a government, and in the rousing them to a revolution."[21] The recollection is apt because Gates employs all three of Coleridge's watchwords: he repeatedly describes himself as an optimist; memory, of course, is the ware he peddles; but the most effective motive in his repertoire is fear. For off-campus audiences Gates may pose as the confident optimist, but he is notorious for cracking the whip of fear—fear of competition, fear of being subjected to one of his vituperative harangues—to motivate his employees to ever greater efforts to ship products, add features, and empower Microsoft to acquire ever greater market control of the personal computer industry. Lester Thurow echoes Gates in speaking of the plight of the worker in the downsized corporation of the future, who, locked into a vassalage that effectively interdicts collective organization, now also finds that even the old-fashioned, individualistic capitalist motive of greed no longer applies: "Without the political threat of socialism or the economic threat of powerful unions, maybe efficiency wages just aren't needed anymore. In the future the motivation for cooperation and effort is not going to be above-market efficiency wages but 'fear'—the fear of being fired into an economy of falling real wages."[22]

If no one seems able to theorize, let alone realize, a practical alternative to multinational capitalism, it might still be useful to search for another motivation for cooperation and effort than fear, which, as Coleridge argued, inevitably has unforeseen consequences. During the suspension of hostilities between England and France wrought by the Treaty of Amiens in 1802, Coleridge's sought to substantialize the socially binding slogans of "hope," "fear," and "memory"—to make them something more than watchwords, the kind of meaningless sounds he associated with the jingle-jangle lures of the sophists, the plausible impersonations of shapers and forgers, and the ideological battle cries of the Jacobins. For Coleridge, such watchwords were rhetorical in the worst sense: mechanical in their operation, transient in their duration, and pernicious in their unforeseen consequences (pernicious *because* unforeseen). Not even the most ardent Jacobin could have known that the tricolor slogan "Liberty, equality, and fraternity" would lead to the denunciations of the National Assembly and the stark exercise in problem-solving called the Terror, but having observed such an effect Coleridge reasoned that it would be prudent to avoid tempting fate by brandishing similarly galvanic abstractions.

The trouble with Coleridge's critique was that the analysis of the liability of signs to the flux of the times could be appreciated, while the moral of the intellectual's social responsibility for his signings could be conveniently ignored. Chief among the unforeseen consequences of Coleridge's cultural criticism was Thomas De Quincey. Observe how De Quincey, an adept in the manipulation of Romantic themes and tropes, deftly rings the changes on the Coleridgean triad as, in the *Confessions of an English Opium Eater* (1821), he makes his peace with the abandoned Ann of Oxford Street: "I sought her, I have said, in hope. So it was for years; but now I should fear to see her. . . . I now wish to see her no longer; but think of her, more gladly as one long since laid in the grave."[23] No doubt De Quincey's ignoble *requiescat* ought to be registered in the roll of examples of the abuse of Romantic themes. And that is all to the good. For one way to avoid the impasse of idealization (believing one is solitary in a world of one's own making) is to take on the burden of the motto "No use without abuse." Just because Gates fails to take abuse seriously as anything more than a figment of the unwired imagination, his version of the pleasures of the road ahead is useless for persons who are not corporations. Fearful of the future toward which he rushes, Gates cannot afford to imagine impasse. It is the Romantic's conviction that those who cannot imagine impasse will surely confront it. And then what? What is to be done if Justice should finally nerve itself to enforce the law? More generally, what is to be done when people continue to perform the motions of solving when there are no more problems; or, to put it in a manner familiar to readers of the mordant contemporary comic strip *Dilbert*, of what use is it for people to go on working when their work is useless?[24]

Such pathologies are not restricted to the funny papers. They occur in the world, even among computer users. You certainly will have heard the rumors of those nightsurfers, solitary and intense, rapt before the infinite unfoldings of cyberspace on the screen before them, obsessively forging an electronic chain, link after link. Those specters have recently been invoked in the pages of the *Chronicle of Higher Education*, where, in a March 1996 article entitled "Snared by the Internet," authorities from several universities express their concern about a new and dangerous phenomenon: "a small but growing number of students who have a problem regulating the amount of time that they spend in front of computers." How small and how quickly growing a number is not specified, but what is clear is that among those officials whose task it is to solve problems that students cannot solve themselves, there is a perception of a new danger, computer addiction. Says Judith Klavens, director of Columbia University's Center for Research on Information Access, "Computer addiction is leaving the nerd crowd and going out to the larger population." The author reports that Ms. Klavens "has met students who spend so much time on the computer that they've forgotten to eat."[25]

So far accounts of this epidemic of computer addiction are merely impressionistic; and those impressions seem to flow less from perceptions of actual behavior than from the institutional motive of normalizing student behavior, which is here fortified not by stories of fraternity hazing or student intoxication but by the X-Files of technophobic lore. Despite efforts to recruit these intellectual creatures into encounter groups where the solvent power of dialogue might be brought to bear on their addiction, the troubled youngsters have so far failed to cooperate by admitting they are indeed addicts. This then is the negative of use, whether real or imagined: an abuse of the tools of software, unregulated indulgence in a solitary practice that masters even biological need: addiction.[26]

When the empirical ground for social analysis dissolves into the apparitional, Romantic anachronisms come into their own. And so, enter Thomas De Quincey, confessed and confessing opium-eater, who asks the same question posed by the apprehensive administrators quoted in the *Chronicle*: "How came any reasonable being to subject himself to such a yoke of misery, voluntarily to incur a captivity so servile, and knowingly to fetter himself with such a sevenfold chain?" De Quincey elected his bondage. Like the creatures of the Internet, he forged his own "subtle links of suffering" (De Quincey, 67). We can responsibly link De Quincey with computer addicts, because in *Confessions* he figures the chain of opium as capable of standing for any bondage that a reasonable person might incur, as opium itself comes to stand for the figurative power of one thing to impersonate another. But though opium is, as De Quincey, announces, "the true hero of the tale," it appears rather late in *Confessions*. De Quincey introduces opium only after an autobiographical account of a series of misadventures that bear a contingent relationship to his discovery of the drug, which occurs (which *must* occur) by accident — one of the few lucky accidents in a narrative that staggers from one unexpected and painful breach to another. If accident is the event that an agent cannot fully prevent, De Quincey's accidental introduction to opium eating is the necessary precondition to the experience of an unanticipated physical and intellectual pleasure that suspends the ethical burden of agency. No one can plan to be an opium user because no one can imagine the pleasure that opium brings. By using opium, De Quincey takes advantage of an accident to insure himself against all further accidents, indeed, against disorder of any kind: "Whereas wine disorders the mental faculties, opium, on the contrary (if taken in a proper manner) introduces amongst them the most exquisite order, legislation, and harmony" (73). Opium will have its sovereign way, but experience teaches that opium only regulates the faculties if you regulate it. De Quincey's distinction between using wine and using opium would thus seem to beg the question, What is the proper manner of use? How regulated? By what rule?

Confessions is almost too explicit in its answer. De Quincey describes in detail how he regulated his use by assessing his resources against the cost of the tincture of laudanum required to produce its pleasurable effects; he recounts how he metered the laudanum itself as, drop by drop, he mixed it with the wine base; he recalls how he carefully scheduled the days of the week when he permitted himself the indulgence. On his first dosage, De Quincey experienced what he hyperbolically describes as "an apocalypse within." But the reliable continuance of that pleasure required that it be economized, measured out in teaspoons.

> I have often been asked, how I first came to be a regular opium-
> eater; and have suffered, very unjustly, in the opinion of my ac-

quaintance from being reputed to have brought upon myself all
the sufferings which I shall have to record, by a long course of indulgence in this practice purely for the sake of creating an artificial
state of pleasurable excitement. This, however, is a misrepresenta-
tion of my case. True it is, that for nearly ten years I did occasionally take opium, for the sake of the exquisite pleasure it gave me:
but so long as I took it with this view, I was effectually protected
from all material bad consequences, by the necessity of interposing
long intervals between the several acts of indulgence, in order to
renew the pleasurable sensations. (35)

De Quincey illustrates how he used opium in an account of the
"debauches" he committed once every three weeks, sometimes on a
Tuesday, sometimes on a Saturday. In tranquility he recollects the intense pleasures of his "Opera nights," spent hanging on the "divine"
choruses and stirred by the "passionate soul" of Grassini. He takes
advantage of the memory to corroborate Sir Thomas Browne's (Wordsworthian) "theory of musical effects": that the pleasure of music is not
had by the passive reception by the ear, but is constructed "by the
reaction of the mind upon the notices of the ear (the *matter* coming by
the senses, the *form* from the mind)." Mounting from theory to epiphany, he celebrates the sublime power of the "chorus, &c. of elaborate
harmony" to display before him, "as in a piece of arras work, the whole
of my past life—not as if recalled by an act of memory, but as if present
and incarnated in the music." And "all this was to be had for five
shillings" (79).

Being in possession of five shillings is not, however, a given in the
world De Quincey haunts. The reader has previously been treated to
the author's account of his impoverished misery during his first, truant
sojourn in London. De Quincey presses the sociological point home as
he continues the narrative of his Saturday night pleasures. From the
lush illustration of the "theory of musical effects" the peripatetic opium
eater, his credentials as an intellectual established, excurses among the
"philosophic" poor, "sympathizing with their pleasures" (80) as they
take their sabbatarian leisure.

Whenever I saw occasion . . . I joined their parties; and gave my
opinion upon the matter in discussion, which, if not always judi-
cious, was always received indulgently. If wages were a little
higher, or expected to be so, or the quartern loaf a little lower, or it
was reported that onions and butter were expected to fall, I was
glad: yet, if the contrary were true, I drew from opium some

means of consoling myself. For opium (like the bee, that extracts its materials indiscriminately from roses and from the soot of chimneys) can overrule all feelings into a compliance with the master key. (81)

As the poor cheerfully submit "to what they consider as irremediable evils, or irreparable losses," so the opium-eater happily complies with the general tenor of opium, easily joins their parties, effortlessly shares in the topics of their discussion — the intellectual as comrade in fatalism. So much for the pleasures of opium.

And what of addiction? There is no story to explain how addiction begins, no representation of some foolish act or some equally foolish failure to act — only the narrator's postulate of a fundamental change:

> This then, let me repeat, I postulate — that, at the time I began to take opium daily, I could not have done otherwise. Whether indeed, afterwards I might not have succeeded in breaking off the habit, even when it seemed to me that all efforts would be unavailing, and whether many of the innumerable efforts which I *did* make might not have been carried much further, and my gradual re-conquests of ground lost might not have been followed up much more energetically — these are questions which I must decline. (87)

No one can plan to become an opium addict because no one can imagine the pain that opium brings. So how does it happen? Uncharacteristically discreet, De Quincey reserves his answer and trumps narrative with a postulate that rescinds the autobiographical compact between author and reader, the promise to attach plausible causes to all improbable effects. The equivalent of the narrated accident that introduced De Quincey to opium is the rhetorical *incident* of the postulate, which interrupts narrative continuity and repudiates any logic except the performative will. "Good logic gave the author no strength to act on it" (114); by the same token the strength to act, to postulate, spites the logic of narrative and of addiction. More than any circumstantial evidence, it is the author's performance of will that proves to the reader that De Quincey, if ever an addict, is one no longer.

Just because De Quincey declines questions does not mean we cannot ask them. It only means that we must supply our own answers. Where does the postulate come from? On whose authority is it imposed? Those questions raise others regarding precedent acts of volition, especially the initial regulation of opium intake appropriate to the continuous production of pleasure. By what rule did De Quincey regulate? The answer to such questions will always be "by Wordsworth's rule" (if, that is, we understand "Wordsworth" as a composite of William Wordsworth, poet, and Samuel Taylor Coleridge, professor).[27] Although Wordsworth does not appear *in propria persona*, he haunts *Confessions*. With wonderful subtlety, Margaret Russett has shown how thoroughly the movements of De Quincey's text are responsive to Wordsworth's poetics, as De Quincey construed them from readings of the *Lyrical Ballads*.

Permit me to adapt Russett to the occasion.[28] At first blush, De Quincey's confessions seem willfully to negate the moralizing tenor of Wordsworth's poetics. His appetite for the spectacle of the opera contradicts Wordsworth's condemnations of "the sickly and stupid German Tragedies." His indulgence in opium for apocalyptic effects and exquisite pleasures — "a degrading thirst after outrageous stimulation" — would seem to bar him from the aristocracy of sensation that Wordsworth imagines when he affirms that "the human mind is capable of being excited without the application of gross and violent stimulants; and he must have a very faint perception of its beauty and dignity who does not know this, and who does not further know, that one being is elevated above another, in proportion as he possesses this capability." De Quincey's investment of a tincture of opium and five measly shillings to procure the sublime pleasures of the opera translates as a materialist's sardonic critique of Wordsworth's Romantic doctrine. Although De Quincey endeavors to persuade his reader that the regulated use of opium does not "blunt" what the poet called the "discriminating powers of the mind," it could hardly be denied that the net effect of his use was an abuse that unfit the mind "for all voluntary exertion [and] . . . reduce[d] it to a state of almost savage torpor."[29]

Even though De Quincey seems hellbent on a systematic inversion of Wordworth's values, in fact this diabolical *imitatio* conscientiously works to demonstrate that the motto "No use without abuse" applies to Wordsworth's dicta. More Romantic than his moral guide, by transferring agency to opium De Quincey deviously enacts the Wordsworthian plot of degradation (while exempting Wordsworth from blame), even to the point of identifying the author with a diseased prostitute. A lesson to all of us potential addicts: stay out of London; don't have accidents; just say no.

But the relation of De Quincey's text to Wordsworth's poetics goes beyond fabulizing its moral. In De Quincey's narrative, addiction occurs with the author's unexplained failure to maintain a "proper manner." But proper according to what rule? Not yet Bill Gates's. By the rule that Wordsworth lays down in the Preface to *Lyrical Ballads*: "The end of poetry is to produce excitement in co-existence with an over-balance of pleasure. . . . But if the words by which this excitement is produced are in themselves powerful, or the images and feelings have an undue proportion of pain connected with them, there is some danger that the excitement may be carried beyond its proper bounds." The master key to the relations between *Confessions* and Wordsworth's Preface is that for De Quincey "opium" can be effectively substituted for "poetry" in Wordsworth's definition. Nothing in their exquisitely pleasurable effects distinguishes the two, except that poetry does not ordinarily lead to addiction, whereas opium does and in doing so leads to that excitement beyond its proper bounds, which De Quincey describes in "The Pains of Opium." What keeps poetry from producing the deleterious effects of opium is not any element intrinsically superior or different (for any pleasurable thing can trigger addiction in De Quincey — addiction is the relapse of pleasure), but that the former is regulated by meter:

> Now the music of harmonious metrical language, the sense of difficulty overcome, and the blind association of pleasure which has been previously received from works of rhyme or metre of the same or similar construction, an indistinct perception perpetually renewed of language closely resembling that of real life, and yet, in the circumstance of metre, differing from it so widely, all these imperceptibly make up a complex feeling of delight, which is of the most important use in tempering the painful feeling which will always be found intermingled with powerful descriptions of the deeper passions. (Wordsworth, 58)

The poet superadds meter to poetry out of sympathy with the reader's own supposed tendency to extend excessive sympathy. Wordsworth ascribes meter's power to restrain the pleasure of poetry within bounds "to small, but continual and regular impulses of pleasurable surprise from the metrical arrangement" (57). We cannot compel Wordsworth to explain what the phenomenon of regular impulses of pleasurable surprise actually *is*, although the impulse is certainly something different from the halt that provokes surmise or the blockage that triggers the sublime. And it is certainly something different from the exacting measurement of drops of laudanum into a glass of wine or the careful scheduling of doses by the calendar.

The deficiency in Wordsworth's explanation of the character and quality of those "regular impulses of pleasurable surprise" was made up, as usual, by Coleridge. As we have seen in his letters from Germany in 1798 and 1799, written just after he and his fellow traveler had split up, Coleridge echoed his collaborator's assertion that the harmony of English verse consists "in the arrangement of pauses & cadences, & not in the even flow of single lines."[30] That formal principle is, as Coleridge perceived, a native distinction of the English tongue, but, as he came to appreciate through the abstract metrical exercises that he scribbled in his notebooks and even more through the passionate exchange of letters with the Wordsworths, English metrical language is also a continuous social act: an intimate breathing together of the poet and the reader (Wordsworth/Coleridge, Coleridge/Wordsworth) in a radical conspiracy that exploits the pretext of the poem to achieve a common ground of pleasure, a tangible understanding.

Addiction appears at precisely that moment when the regulated is transformed into the chronic. From a certain perspective, call it philosophical, the transformation is logical. "Some of these rambles," the epicurean De Quincey fondly recalls, "led me to great distances: for an opium-eater is too happy to observe the motion of time" (81). But time, the stoic knows, does move regardless of our observation. And sooner or later, whether or not the eater wills it, the slow, dull throb of matter will weary the joy right out of pleasure, and he will be recalled to time. Yet even Zeno could not tell us exactly *when* that transformation occurs. If, then, abuse is chronic, the beginning of use is the beginning of regular surprise, which is another way of identifying the manifestation of anachronism, an apparition that mocks time from the self-destined abode of the imagined future. Now we can understand the formal condition of the untimely postulate: it forces the interval at the level of narration missing from the narrative as from the life. The breakdown in the autobiographical contract with the reader which De Quincey's postulate executes indicates what may follow from the application of Wordsworth's rule of regular surprise, but the success of the postulate is due not to Wordsworth's authority but to a post-Wordsworthian conspiracy between the reader and the writer, who secretly agree to revoke all previous agreements. At this pause of the narrative writer and reader conspire to let logic lapse in order to register a fall from opiated pleasure, which, because cadenced, is a vitally formal, that is, poetic pleasure. At the moment of the postulate, the conspiratorial reader discovers that if the regulation of prose is verse, then delinquency from regulation, when self-governed, is, surprisingly, poetry.

The delinquent De Quincey may break Wordsworthian law by relying on the stimulant of opium to produce sublime sensation. Perhaps, as canny plagiarist, he does so to avoid violating an intellectual property in poetry as such to which Wordsworth had laid claim (and which Coleridge did his best to confirm). But in doing so, he preserves the life of his text by subordinating the narrative to the cadences and pauses of poetic composition. The discontinuity at the level of narrative is countered by a narrational meter: what at the logic of the narrative account of addiction appears as a gap, arbitrarily detonated and bridged by a postulate, is at the level of the narration an interval that foregrounds the metrical conventions of the text, which superintend its narrative logic. This benign superintendence by the apparition of form applies not only to the incident of the postulate, but to the numerous falls and pauses that harmonize the disparate episodes of De Quincey's recollected life: from the cascade of his trunkload of books down the stairs of his preceptor's steps as he makes his escape from the chronic boredom of school, to the dying fall of the valediction to Ann of Oxford Street that, descending, opens the preludic interval before the "Pleasures of Opium" chapter.

When confronting the impasse of regulation—when legislation fails and when the egotistical sublime palls—it is the last infirmity of Romantic minds to return reflexively to the problem of writing. What is writing? is so much the same question as What is meter? that for our purposes they can be considered as identical. Writing is the governance of prose to prevent an overbalance of pleasure from producing pain. All writing, anachronistically to paraphrase Coleridge, who genially provided the paraphrase of Wordsworth that created De Quincey, aspires to the condition of poetry. And poetry in the proper manner aspires to compose the mind to endure the pathos of the world. Meter provides the saving limit to sympathy because it formally restricts synchrony. If the chronic reader of *Clarissa* is absorbed in the heroine's correspondingly chronic suffering, it is not because she is a sadist reveling in the heroine's ordeal, but that she has become addicted to the habituating representation of her pain. Reading novels is a habit that some cannot help, even though it may cause them pain. No one reads De Quincey to take pleasure in his pain, because even the most vivid representations of that pain in his militant non-novels are subjected to a mastering meter. The plasticity of the autobiographical text, its susceptibility to endless revision, is the function not of a principle of recovered memory but of a continuous invention that is enabled by the metrical regulation of the text. The continuing potential for substance abuse is continually deferred by what Wordsworth calls the "half consciousness of the unsubstantial existence" that poetic meter confers on all material suitable for narrative representation. To live a life in which those accidents that befall us do not make us despond means scripting a life in which impasse is gentled into regular surprise — a life self-governed by the restorative application of poetic form to what appears as given. Romantic ethics is a Romantic poetics.

But to live a life of willed openness to accident can never be a life alone — a natural monopoly. The Romantic enterprise aspires to restore the common world that has vanished. From the moment it was professed, that aspiration has been contemptuously dismissed by spokesmen for the liberal tradition, who describe it as a rescue fantasy with no consequences that are not illusory or, more forbiddingly, that are not the prelude to the political disaster of tyranny.[31] And there is no doubt that either nothing will happen or that anything can. That common world may or may not be an actual world we have lost; nevertheless, the Romantic concludes, just because it is not *the* world it remains virtually present, a legitimate and worthy object of imaginative re-creation. Since we who can imagine the common world as lost cannot possibly be the same "we" who once occupied what is no longer present to us, the very possibility of our recollection heralds the commonality to which we aspire. If this be but a vain belief, nonetheless the fulfillment of that promise is the goal toward which, in the intervals of our habitual lives, we regularly conspire — with the help of the poets and, yes, the computer.

Romantic use, like poetic meter, is conspiratorial, a portentous and pleasurable breathing together. Such a claim could certainly be illiberal, perhaps even antiliberal, if we take Stephen Holmes's word for it.[32] Conspiratorial thinking and communitarian aspirations are two of the hallmarks of the antiliberal tradition that Holmes energetically dissects in his critique of the wooly-headed political theories of Carl Schmitt, Leo Strauss, and Alasdair McIntyre. But Holmes's opposition between pro- and antiliberalism can only be maintained by reading out of the illiberal tradition legitimate claimants to alternative ethics: the poets, the democrats, and the republicans. Now it is true that there is no guarantee that conspiracy will lead to true community, whatever that may be. The evidence of the careers of De Quincey, Coleridge, Blake, Wordsworth, and John Thelwall — conspirators one and all — would suggest otherwise.

Yet students' addiction attests that sensation has already been carried into the midst of the objects of science, and if poetry has any social use it is to organize that sensation *toward* social use by taking advan-

tage of the fact, put by Bill Readings in a fine De Quinceyean formulation, that we are "addicted to others" (Readings, 190). Indeed, it was in
part in the recognition that what I have called "the elementary form of
social feeling" is very close to the base impulse of addiction, that the
only interdiction in Goldberg's classroom projects was on the development of computer games — not because games were trivial but because
the affect impelling gaming, which is a way of using, not of playing, was
the quantum of sensation he sought to exploit and carry into the midst
of the projects of the class itself. The lesson I take from that successful
teaching is that there is good reason to believe that the aspiration to
community can be put to good use, if not by liberals then by cryptoliberals, obstinately questioning what imposes itself as given, romantically intent on reimagining commercial self-regulation as democratic
self-government. In hard times, modern and postmodern times, conspiracy is the craft of self-government. At other times and under normal
circumstances, a well-wrought ethics does not entail an effective politics — life and the natural monopolies it spawns tend to triumph. As the
poets teach, there is no good reason to believe that the good will win
anything that counts. Nonetheless, in a society such as ours, where
representative man is subject either to enlistment by the corporate
imaginary or enslavement to its pathological Other, conspiratorial man
may find that ethics can serve as venture capital sufficient to launch,
if not sufficient to accomplish, those ends that we cryptoliberals set
for ourselves.

Using De Quincey means using Wordsworth to transform the abject
instance of addiction into a pleasurable social practice, which we are
used to calling poetry or writing but which I am pleased to identify as
the exercise in self-government (surely only one among countless others) called digital media research and development. Earlier, I described
De Quincey's addiction as real or imagined. As scholars have long
known, De Quincey's account of the effects of opium is specious; his
account of his addiction is no more reliable than Ms. Klavens's account
of the "computer addicts" at Columbia University. We can guess why
that description appeared: the impulse to pathologize is normal in a
society where it seems that no form unites a *pluribus*, which is then
represented as a collection of illnesses: from philanderers to gamblers to
pedophiles to alcoholics to romance readers to the working poor — all
are classed as addicts. No matter what motivated the fabrication of a
description of students as computer addicts, however, we ought to be
able to make use of it, because for now we can only be where we are,
queer in a pathological society, where neither prevailing myths nor

professional constraints can any longer guarantee the coherence of individual narratives or the cohesion of the socius. In a society of pathologies, use is managed addiction.[33] We Romantics ought to embrace
an imagined group that has practices, no matter how degraded, in
common. We ought to do so because that group is here among us,
whether discursively or in the flesh. We ought to do so because they
have an unreasoning affinity for something, the kind of affinity that
students formerly had for poetry. Their addiction makes them good
candidates for the cryptoliberal arts, defined as a set of projects emanat-
ing from conspired ideas, designed for use, and formally superintended
by what, after De Quincey, I'll call a Romantic symposiarch. Things
look bad for the addicts among us now, but I postulate that things can
be different.

Notes

Chapter 1: The Romantic Movement at the End of History

A shorter version of this chapter originally appeared in *Critical Inquiry* (Spring 1994), © 1994 by The University of Chicago. Reprinted with permission.

1. Anthony Giddens, *The Constitution of Society: Outline of the Theory of Structuration* (Berkeley: Univ. of California Press, 1984), xxiii.

2. See Edward Said, *Beginnings: Intention and Method* (Baltimore: Johns Hopkins Univ. Press, 1978), 191–97, and Samuel Taylor Coleridge, *Biographia Literaria*, ed. James Engell and Walter Jackson Bate, 2 vols., vol. 7 of *The Collected Works of Samuel Taylor Coleridge*, gen. ed. Kathleen Coburn (Princeton: Princeton Univ. Press, 1983), 1:41 n. Hereafter *BL*.

3. Francis Fukuyama, "The End of History?" *National Interest* (Summer 1989): 3–18, and *The End of History and the Last Man* (New York: Free Press, 1992).

4. Benjamin Constant, *The Spirit of Conquest and Usurpation and Their Relation to Civilization,* in *Political Writings,* ed. Biancamaria Fontana (Cambridge: Cambridge Univ. Press, 1988), 55.

5. Wisely or not, I shall abandon the security provided by the so-called anachronism test, which, contemporary historians of consequence argue, provides an important criterion for determining that the language identified with a historical agent is not the historian's own fabrication. See Quentin Skinner, "Meaning and Understanding in the History of Ideas," *History and Theory* 8:3–53 and J. G. A. Pocock, "Concept of a Language and the *metier d'historien*: Some Considerations on Practice," in *The Languages of Political Theory*, ed. A . Pagden (Cambridge: Cambridge Univ. Press, 1987), 21. Those criteria are explored in the context of interpretations of the language of economics by M. Ali Khan in "On Economics and Language: A Review Article," *Journal of Economic Studies* 20, no. 3 (1993).
    I gladly take the opportunity here to welcome as an ally James Chandler, who in his recent major study *England in 1819* (Chicago: Chicago Univ. Press, 1998) argues for the importance of anachronism as a key to understanding the project of Romanticism. Chandler's

work caps the work of the school of Romantic New Historicism by rightly understanding it as a variant of the historicism of the Romantics themselves. His analysis renders that school of historiography newly intelligible, but at the cost of dismantling its pseudoscientific apparatus of ideology critique. Whether the school of Romantic New Historicism can survive Chandler's discrediting of its pretense both to succeed and to transcend the so-called Romantic ideology is now a matter of precisely academic interest. As a theory of Romantic historiography and as an investigation of the historical genre of the case, Chandler's work diverges from my own, which has long been concerned with Romantic anachronism, although not as a delimited historical case or as a category of historical understanding but as a performative, historicizing trope that is compelling because of its insistently ethical and potentially political import. Romantic anachronism, I have argued, was and is the reiterable positing of "a place where the excluded and extinct can make common cause, eternally renewing their claims in effective apposition to the verdicts rendered by history and achieving thereby a plaintiff immortality" (Jerome Christensen, *Lord Byron's Strength: Romantic Writing and Commercial Society* [Baltimore: Johns Hopkins Univ. Press, 1993], 324).

6.   Fredric Jameson, *Postmodernism: or, The Cultural Logic of Late Capitalism* (Durham: Duke Univ. Press, 1991), 309.

7.   Immanuel Wallerstein, *Unthinking Social Science: The Limits of Nineteenth-Century Paradigms* (Cambridge: Polity Press, 1991), 16–17 Hereafter *USS*.

8.   E. J. Hobsbawm, *Primitive Rebels in Archaic Forms of Social Movement in the Nineteenth and Twentieth Centuries* (New York: Norton, 1959), 151. Hereafter *PR*.

9.   Matthew Arnold, "The Function of Criticism at the Present Time," *Essays in Criticism, First Series*, ed. Sister Thomas Marion Hoctor (Chicago: Univ. of Chicago Press, 1968), 13.

10.   Karl Marx and Friedrich Engels, *The German Ideology*, ed. R. Pascal (New York: International Publishers, 1947), 26. Hereafter *GI*.

11.   Jerome J. McGann, *The Romantic Ideology: A Critical Investigation* (Chicago: Univ. of Chicago Press, 1983), 9.

12.   Louis Althusser, *Lenin and Philosophy and Other Essays,* trans. Ben Brewster (New York: Monthly Review Press, 1971), 82.

13.   Jacques Lacan, "The Freudian Unconscious and Ours," *The Four Fundamental Concepts of Psycho-Analysis,* ed. Jacques-Alain Miller and trans. Alan Sheridan (New York: Norton, 1978), 22.

14.   Paul Ricoeur, *Lectures on Ideology and Utopia,* ed. George H. Taylor (New York: Columbia Univ. Press, 1986), 78.

15.   W. J. T. Mitchell, *Iconology: Image, Text, Ideology* (Chicago: Univ. of Chicago Press, 1986), 169.

16. Coleridge is picking up on Wordsworth's warning to the readers of
     Lyrical Ballads in his 1800 Preface that they might expect "feelings of
     strangeness and awkwardness" in their first encounter with the poetry
     (*Wordsworth: Selected Poems and Prefaces,* ed. Jack Stillinger
     [Boston: Houghton Mifflin, 1965], 445).

17. Maria and Richard Edgeworth, "Essay on Irish Bulls," *Novels and
     Tales,* 18 vols. in 9 (New York: J. Harper, 1834), 1: 102.

18. That children do give us such information is the burden of
     Wordsworth's "We Are Seven" in *Lyrical Ballads* and of Lacan's version
     of the Bull in "The Freudian Unconscious and Ours": "Remember the
     naive failure of the simpleton's delighted attempt to grasp the little
     fellow who declares — *I have three brothers, Paul, Ernest and me.* But it
     is quite natural — first the three brothers, Paul, Ernest and I are counted,
     and then there is I at the level at which I am to reflect the first I, that is to
     say, the I who counts" (20). Lacan takes the Edgeworths' moral, that
     there can be no continuity of identity, and runs with it.

19. J. Laplanche and J. B. Pontalis, *The Language of Psycho-analysis,*
     trans. Donald Nicholson-Smith (New York: Norton, 1973), 457. For a
     subtle discussion of the rhetorical complexity of Freud's concept of
     transference, see Cynthia Chase, "Transference as Trope and
     Persuasion," in *Discourse in Psychoanalysis and Literature,* ed.
     Schlomith Rimmon-Kennen (New York: Methuen, 1987), 211–29.

20. For example: "Sagacious men and *knowing* in their profession they are
     not ignorant that even diseases may prove convenient: they remember
     that Demosthenes, a state-physician, when he wished to finger a large
     fee from Harpalus, yet was expected by his former connections to
     speak out according 'to the well-known tendency of his political
     opinions' found a *sore-throat* very serviceable; and they have learnt
     from their own experience how absolutely necessary in point of 'selfish
     policy' is a certain political palsey in the head, 'omnibus omnia
     annuens' " (*Lectures 1795 on Politics and Religion,* ed. Lewis Patton
     and Peter Mann, vol. 1 of Coburn, ed., *Collected Works,* 326–27; see
     also 207). For an important exception to this programmatic
     derogation, see Coleridge's letter home from Germany in March 1779,
     in Chapter 4 below.

21. J. G. A. Pocock, "Virtues, Rights, and Manners: A Model for
     Historians of Political Thought," *Virtue, Commerce, and History*
     (Cambridge: Cambridge Univ. Press, 1985), 43–45.

22. Commitment to a rights-based liberalism in which rights are conceived
     as fundamentally transferable has led liberal theorists to countenance
     the possibility that liberal society presupposes an individual's right to
     enter into a transaction that would result in his or her enslavement.
     See Robert Nozick, *Anarchy, State, and Utopia* (New York: Basic
     Books, 1974), 331, and the critique of Nozick's rights-based model in
     David Johnston's *The Idea of a Liberal Theory: A Critique and
     Reconstruction* (Princeton: Princeton Univ. Press, 1994), 48–58.

23.   C. B. Macpherson, *Democratic Theory: Essays in Retrieval* (Oxford: Clarendon Press, 1973), 3–12.

24.   Sigmund Freud, "The Dynamics of the Transference," trans. James Strachey, in *Therapy and Technique*, ed. Philip Rieff (New York: Macmillan, 1963), 113–14.

25.   Michael Oakeshott, *On Human Conduct* (Oxford: Oxford Univ. Press, 1975), 78–79.

26.   Benedict Anderson, *Imagined Communities: Reflections on the Origin and Spread of Nationalism* (London: Verso, 1983), 75.

27.   Francis Horner, one of the founding editors of the *Edinburgh Review,* comments on the difficulty of acquiring a comprehensive knowledge of the manual arts: "A knowledge of the arts, as they are practised in different parts of the country, is what I am desirous to possess on many accounts; but especially the subserviency of such knowledge to the study of political economy. To collect information from workmen is a matter of some address, for they are in general mere machines, and not unfrequently more ignorant, literally speaking, than the tools which they employ" (*Memoirs and Correspondence of Francis Horner*, ed. Leonard Horner, 2 vols. [Boston: 1853], 1:112–13).

28.   My account of the vernacular is intended to be more astringent than that of Olivia Smith in her admirable *The Politics of Language 1791–1819* (Oxford: Oxford Univ. Press, 1984). Smith describes contestation over the status of language in the period as conflict between a hierarchized, idealist, and socially exclusive distinction of refined from vulgar and a materialist, reformist, and more radical advocacy of the clarity, force, and flexibility of the vernacular. Although I do not dispute her general account, I employ the term *demotic* to designate a kind of wild, popular utterance that even reformers like the etymologists and the grammarian William Cobbett, programmatically committed as they were to the standards of perspicuity, coherence, and correctness found unacceptable. Both the refined and the vernacular speech appeal to principles of propriety: the former to propriety of social class, high versus low; the latter to propriety of native place, English rather than Latin or Greek or French. Because the demotic can be spoken or signed by anybody, it is hard to place and therefore neither vulgar nor refined, familiar nor alien.

29.   Not least in my own writing, where, I confess, this is the third time I have pulled out this particular plum.

30.   Coleridge, "Once a Jacobin Always a Jacobin," *Essays on His Times,* ed. David V. Erdman, 3 vols., vol. 3 of Coburn, ed., *Collected Works,* 1:368.

31.   This unlinking attempts to break with the paranoid logic of political debate in the 1790s. For reformers, radicals, and loyalists "much of the argument and rhetoric of the decade revolve[d] around the presence or absence of a link between principles and practice in

France," according to Mark Philp ("The Fragmented Ideology of Reform" in *The French Revolution and British Popular Politics*, ed. Mark Philp [Cambridge: Cambridge Univ. Press, 1991], 58–65).

32. John Bohstedt, *Riots and Community Politics in England and Wales 1790–1810* (Cambridge, Mass: Harvard Univ. Press, 1983), 4–5.

33. The various investments are in display in Philp, *French Revolution*.

34. See Roger Wells, *Insurrection: The British Experience 1795–1803* (Gloucester: Alan Sutton, 1983), passim. The list comes from Hobsbawm, *Primitive Rebels*, 160.

35. Susan Stewart, "*Ceci Tuera Cela*: Graffiti as Crime and Art," in *Life after Postmodernism: Essays on Value and Culture*, ed. John Fekete (New York: St. Martin's Press, 1987), 169. Stewart stands in for a vast range of research in cultural studies on the capacity for resistance in contemporary popular culture, most of it indebted to the paradigmatic work done at the Birmingham Centre for Contemporary Cultural Studies and responsive to the intellectual initiatives of Raymond Williams and Stuart Hall. For a fine critical account of the history and of the controversies surrounding the theory and practice of cultural studies, see Jim McGuigan, *Cultural Populism* (Routledge: London, 1992), especially his chapter "Trajectories of Cultural Populism," 45–85.

36. Edgeworth and Edgeworth, "Essay on Irish Bulls," 100.

37. "Where no other organization existed, as after the defeat of a revolutionary movement, masonic lodges were very likely to become the refuge of the rebels" (*PR*, 163).

38. See Stephen Jay Gould, *Wonderful Life: The Burgess Shale and the Nature of History* (New York: Norton, 1989), 45–52.

39. Mike Davis, *City of Quartz: Excavating the Future in Los Angeles* (New York: Vintage, 1992), 297.

40. Fredric Jameson, *The Political Unconscious* (Ithaca: Cornell Univ. Press, 1981), 20.

41. A cipher called *individualism*. On the distinction between individualism and individuality, see William E. Connolly, *Identity | Difference: Democratic Negotiations of Political Paradox* (Ithaca: Cornell Univ. Press, 1991), 72–74.

42. Richard E. Flathman, *Willful Liberalism: Voluntarism and Individuality in Political Theory and Practice* (Ithaca: Cornell Univ. Press, 1992), 139. See Part 2 of that volume (123–223) for the full development of Flathman's argument.

43. John Horne Tooke, *Diversions of Purley* (1786–98), revised and corrected, Richard Taylor (London: William Tegg and Co., 1857), 33.

44. Letter to John Murray, Byron's publisher, 3 November 1821; quoted in Truman Guy Steffan, *Lord Byron's* CAIN (Austin: Univ. of Texas Press, 1968), 9. Hereafter *LBC*.

45. Slavoj Žižek, *The Sublime Object of Ideology* (London: Verso, 1989), 61.

46. Hannah Arendt, *On Violence* (New York: Harcourt Brace Jovanovich, 1970), 64.

47. Leigh Hunt, *Examiner* (June 2, 1822); quoted in *Byron: The Critical Heritage*, ed. Andrew Rutherford (New York: Barnes and Noble, 1970), 224–25.

48. *Gentleman's Magazine*, Supplement, Jan. 1821; quoted in *The Romantics Reviewed — Byron*, 5 vols., ed. Donald H. Reiman (New York: Garland, 1972), 3:1125.

Chapter 2: The Color of Imagination and the Office of Romantic Criticism

1.   Coleridge, *Collected Marginalia*, ed. George Whalley, vol. 1 of *The Collected Works of Samuel Taylor Coleridge*, gen. ed., Kathleen Coburn (Princeton: Princeton Univ. Press, 1980), 1:5466.

2.   William Wordsworth, Preface to *Lyrical Ballads* (1802), in *Literary Criticism of William Wordsworth*, ed. Paul M. Zall (Lincoln: Univ. of Nebraska Press, 1966), 40.

3.   Coleridge, *Biographia Literaria*, vols., ed. James Engell and W. Jackson Bate, vol. 7 of Coburn, ed., *Collected Works*, 2:5.

4.   Quoted in John Gage, *Colour in Turner: Poetry and Truth* (London: Studio Vista, 1969), 48.

5.   David Hume, *Essays Moral, Political, and Literary,* ed. Eugene F. Miller (Indianapolis: *Liberty* Classics, 1985), 220.

6.   *The Hermetic and Alchemical Writings of Paracelsus*, ed. Arthur Edward White, 2 vols. (1894; rpt., Berkeley: Shambala, 1976), 1:55.

7.   *Quarterly Review* 12 (July 1816): 399–400.

8.   *The Notebooks of Samuel Taylor Coleridge*, 4 vols., ed. Kathleen Coburn (Princeton: Princeton Univ. Press, 1973), 3:4414.

9.   *The Collected Writings of Thomas De Quincey*, ed. David Masson, 16 vols. (London, 1897), 9:136.

10. Arden Reed, *Romantic Weather* (Hanover, N.H.: Univ. Press of New England, 1983), 194–95; 199.

11. Paul D. Sheats, *The Making of Wordsworth's Poetry, 1785–1798* (Cambridge, Mass.: Harvard Univ. Press, 1973), 59–62.

12. Alexander Nisbet, *A System of Heraldry, Speculative and Practical, with the True Art of the Blazon, According to the Most Approved Heralds in Europe*, 2 vols. (1722; 2d ed., Edinburgh 1804), 16.

13. *Collected Letters of Samuel Taylor Coleridge*, ed. Earl Leslie Griggs, 6 vols. (Oxford: Clarendon Press, 1956–71), 1:394–98.

14. *Hazlitt's Works: Sketches and Essays,* ed. W. Carew Hazlitt (London, 1902), 55.

15. Alan Liu, " 'Shapeless Eagerness': The Genre of Revolution in Books 9–10 of *The Prelude*," *Modern Language Quarterly* 43, (1982): 5–6. I want to acknowledge the contribution of a seminar paper by Steven Newman to the development of this argument.

16. James Chandler's capstone to the New Historicist project, *England in 1819* (Chicago: Univ. of Chicago Press, 1998), may be excepted from this generalization, as it is responsive to the theoretical implications of any form of periodization and recognizes the historicist dimensions of the Romantics' own literary projects. Consult Liu's subsequent analysis "of the acute embarrassment that is the New Historicism" in "The Power of Formalism: The New Historicism" (*ELH* 56 [winter 1989]: 721–72), which concludes by calling for a "rhetorical notion of literature as text-cum-action performed by historical subjects on other subjects" (756) — a project in which these essays participate.

17. That appetite for failure is one vestige of the de Manian ethos on Liu's New Historicism. The other is in the selection of his key terms, *enactment* and *epitaphic*, which translate de Man's *performative* and *constative*.

18. Fredric Jameson, *Postmodernism, or The Cultural Logic of Late Capitalism* (Durham: Duke Univ. Press, 1991), 21.

19. David Simpson, "What Bothered Charles Lamb about Poor Susan?" *SEL* 26 (1986), 589–612; Marjorie Levinson, "Insight and Oversight: Reading 'Tintern Abbey' " in *Wordsworth's Great Period Poems: Four Essays* (Cambridge: Cambridge Univ. Press, 1986), 14–57.

20. Fredric Jameson, *The Political Unconscious* (Ithaca: Cornell Univ. Press, 1981), 105.

21. Neil Hertz, *The End of the Line* (New York: Columbia Univ. Press, 1985), 218.

22.

> In a well-known passage Marx powerfully urges us to do the impossible, namely, to think of this development positively *and* negatively all at once; to achieve, in other words, a type of thinking that would be capable of grasping the demonstrably baleful features of capitalism along with its extraordinary and liberating dynamism simultaneously within a single thought, and without attenuating any of the force of either judgment. We are somehow to lift our minds to a point at which it is possible to understand that capitalism is at once and the same time the best thing that has ever happened to the human race, and the worst. The lapse from this austere dialectical imperative into the more comfortable stance of the taking of moral positions is inveterate and all too human; still, the urgency of the subject demands that we make at least some effort to think the cultural evolution of late capitalism dialectically, as catastrophe and progress all together (*Postmodernism*, 47).

Urging to think, to achieve, to "make at least some effort" — aspiring to avoid moralism — Jameson inexorably, if poignantly, falls back on ethical injunctions to a reader who cannot be explained *as* reader, let alone counted on as part of anything more than a rhetorical "we."

23.   In the 1850 *Prelude* the poet revises the passage thus:

> I crossed the square (an empty area then!)
> Of the Carrousel, where so late had lain
> The dead, upon the dying heaped. (10:55–57)

The revision eliminates the depiction of the square as monchromatic, insisting instead on its emptiness, moves the parenthetical description of the square from its position as virtual object of the crossing, and splits square from carousel, with the effect of disassembling the paradox of the squared circle.

24.   Arthur C. Danto, *After the End of Art* (Princeton: Princeton Univ. Press, 1997), 154.

Chapter 3: *Ecce Homo*

An earlier version of this chapter appeared in *Contesting the Subject*, ed. William H. Epstein, © 1991 Purdue University Press.

1.   François Furet, *Interpreting the French Revolution*, trans. Elborg Forster (Cambridge: Cambridge Univ. Press, 1981), 48.

2.   *Collected Letters of Samuel Taylor Coleridge*, ed. Earl Leslie Griggs, 6 vols. (Oxford: Clarendon Press, 1956–71), 1:527. Hereafter *CL*. Coleridge anticipates Furet's characterization of revolutionary politics in the first of his letters "To Mr. Fox" published in the *Morning Post* in November 1802. "Let a free country be, or be supposed to be, in danger," he writes, "and Jacobinism is the necessary consequence. All men promiscuously, not according to rank or property, but by the superiority of popular talents, and the impulse of superior restlessness, will take an active part in politics. And this is itself Jacobinism, a political disease." (*Essays on His Times*, ed. David V. Erdman, vol. 3 of *The Collected Works of Samuel Taylor Coleridge*, gen. ed. Kathleen Coburn [Princeton, N.J.: Princeton Univ. Press, 1978], 1:382).

3.   Edmund Burke, *Reflections on the Revolution in France* (London: Penguin, 1968), 211.

4.   *The Correspondence of Edmund Burke*, 10 vols., ed. T. L. Copeland et al. (Cambridge: Cambridge Univ. Press, 1958–78), 6:25. Hereafter *CEB*.

5.   On Burke's application of the sublime and its associated oedipal scenario to the French Revolution, see Ronald Paulson, *Representations of Revolution* (1789–1820) (New Haven: Yale Univ. Press, 1983), 57–73. For a discussion of the place of theatricality in Burke's work, see Paul Hindson and Tim Gray, *Burke's Dramatic Theory of Politics* (Aldershot: Avebury, 1988).

6. "Our principles are antijacobin. We cannot be neuter. We are on the Stage: and cannot occasionally jump into the Pitt or Boxes to make observations on our brother actors" (*CEB*, 7:461).

7. John Brewer, *The Sinews of Power: War, Money and the English State, 1688–1783* (New York: Knopf, 1988), 3–24 and passim.

8. On the recognition of the biographical subject, see William H. Epstein, *Recognizing Biography* (Philadelphia: Univ. of Pennsylvania Press, 1988), 71–89.

9. See J. C. D. Clark, *English Society: 1688–1832* (Cambridge: Cambridge Univ. Press, 1985), 38–45.

10. "Four Letters on the Proposals for Peace with the Regicide Directory of France," Letter 1, *Selected Writings of Edmund Burke*, ed. Walter J. Bate (New York: Random House, 1960), 476.

11. Ibid., 486.

12. Sigmund Freud, "Mourning and Melancholia," *General Psychological Theory: Papers on Metapsychology*, ed. Philip Rieff (New York: CollierBooks, 1963), 170.

13. For a useful discussion of the poem, see Nicholas Roe, *Wordsworth und Coleridge: The Radical Years* (Oxford: Clarendon Press, 1988), 263–68.

14. For a comprehensive account of the importance of the threatened invasion to the mobilization of the British citizenry and the formation of a modern nation state through an allegiance based on the public ritual of oath-taking, see Linda Colley, *Britons: Forging the Nation 1707–1837* (New Haven: Yale Univ. Press, 1992), 3 and 283–319. See especially her account of the effect of the Defence of the Realm Act of April 1798, 289–90.

15. For a discussion of the Test Act in the context of political turmoil during the 1790s, see Clark, *English Society*, 341–46.

16. On the general importance of oath-taking to the government and to its adversaries, see Colley, *Britons*, 308–12; Robert Hole, *Pulpits, Politics and Public Order in England: 1760–1832* (Cambridge: Cambridge Univ. Press, 1989), 105; Roger Wells, *Insurrection: The British Experience 1795–1803* (Gloucester: Alan Sutton, 1986), 198 and passim.

17. See Colley, *Britons*, for an account of the disrespect shown by Leicester women in September 1798 toward the militiamen, on their homeward march through the county, who had refused to fight in Ireland, "the logical jumping-off spot for any French invasion force aimed at the British mainland" (257).

18. Samuel Taylor Coleridge, *Lectures 1795 on Politics and Religion*, ed. Lewis Patton and Peter Mann, vol. 1 of Coburn, ed., *Collected Works*, 1:52. Hereafter *LPR*.

19. On this function of romance, see Fredric Jameson, *The Political*

Unconscious: Narrative as a Socially Symbolic Act (Ithaca: Cornell Univ. Press, 1981), 115–19.

20. Quoted in Colley, *Britons,* 312. See also Colley's discussion of the "corrosive" effects of the requirement that, in order to defeat the French, the British had to mobilize the mass of the people on the French model (318).

21. Theodor Adorno, *Aesthetic Theory,* trans. C. Lenhardt (London: Routledge and Kegan Paul, 1970), 48.

22. *The Salisbury Plain Poems of William Wordsworth,* ed. Stephen Gill (Ithaca: Cornell Univ. Press, 1975), 125.

23. For the best discussion of the various transactions that occur in Wordsworth's poem, see Karen Swann, "Public Transport: Adventuring on Wordsworth's Salisbury Plain," *ELH* 55 (winter 1988): 811–34.

24. Short for "Ecce Iterum Crispinus!" from Juvenal's *Satire* 4 (1. 1). As Leslie Marchand translates it: "Lo, Crispin again (I revert to the topic I have mentioned so often before)." *Byron's Letters and Journals,* 12 vols. (Cambridge, Mass.: Harvard Univ. Press, 1973–82), 1:194 n.

25. There is, however, the curious fact that in Hamburg Coleridge found himself lodged — by Wordsworth's arrangement — at "Der Wilder [sic] Man i.e. The Savage — an hotel not of the genteelest Class" (*CL,* 1:433).

26. Walter Jackson Bate, *Coleridge* (New York: MacMillan, 1968), 88, 95.

27. This outcome is represented, although not fully dramatized, in act 3 of Coleridge's *Osorio: A Tragedy (The Complete Poetical Works of Samuel Taylor Coleridge,* ed. E. H. Coleridge, 2 vols. [Oxford: Oxford Univ. Press, 1912], 2:554–56). Cf. the pictorialism of Coleridge's suburban cottage in "Reflections on Having Left a Place of Retirement."

28. In De Quincey's version of the scene, Wordsworth is dragged back within the oedipal orbit: "happening to look down at Klopstock's swollen legs, and recollecting his age, [Wordsworth] felt touched," according to De Quincey, "by a sort of filial pity for his helplessness" ("Samuel Taylor Coleridge," *De Quincey's Collected Writings,* ed. David Masson, 14 vols. [London, 1896], 2:170).

29. The literary model for this paratragical scene is Pope's translation of the passage in book 24 of the *Iliad,* where the venerable Priam appears before Achilles to plead for the corpse of Hector. The scene ends awash in tears. Burke's citation of the passage in his *Enquiry* had made it a touchstone for discussions of sublimity (see Burke, *A Philosophical Enquiry into the Origin of Our Ideas of the Sublime and Beautiful* [Notre Dame, Ind.: Univ. of Notre Dame Press, 1968], 64; for commentary, see Thomas Weiskel, *The Romantic Sublime: A Study in Transcendance* (Baltimore: Johns Hopkins Univ. Press, 1976), 89, and

Jerome Christensen, " 'Thoughts That Do Often Lie Too Deep for Tears': Toward a Romantic Concept of Lyrical Drama," *Wordsworth Circle* 12 [winter 1981]: 54–56).

30.   James Clifford, *The Predicament of Culture: Twentieth-Century Ethnography, Literature, and Art* (Cambridge, Mass.: Harvard Univ. Press, 1988), 9. Coleridge sums it up: "They call him the German Milton—a very German Milton indeed!" (*CL*, 1:445).

31.   *The Notebooks of Samuel Taylor Coleridge*, ed. Kathleen Coburn, 4 vols. (Princeton: Princeton Univ. Press, 1957), 1:372, 373.

32.   For a fuller account of the advantages that Coleridge characteristically finds in falling, see Jerome Christensen, " 'Like a Guilty Thing Surprised': Coleridge, Deconstruction, and the Apostasy of Criticism," *Critical Inquiry* (summer 1986), 769–87.

33.   A similar suspicion attaches to Coleridge's scene. How is it that Coleridge, who spoke no French, could have imagined he had audited Wordsworth's prosodic instruction of Klopstock, which was conducted in French? The crucial prosodic instruction does not appear in Coleridge's detailed account of the interview in his notebooks (*Notebooks*, 1:339). Did Coleridge's recollection improve during the composition of the letter? Or did he ventriloquize Wordsworth?

34.   On Samuel Johnson's "characteristically Augustan (and aesthetically, rather than paradoxical) failure to feel accents strongly [as an] explanation of his customary deprecation of blank verse," see Paul Fussell, Jr., *Theory of Prosody in Eighteenth-Century England* (1954; rpt., Hamden, Conn.: Archon Books, 1966), 155. Fussell credits Coleridge's experimentation with accentual verse in "Christabel" as being the watershed in the "Discovery of the Force of English Accent," (151–53). It is clear that "Christabel," although (or perhaps because) unpublished, was the most powerful poetic precedent of 1798—its meter signally influencing and deforming the poetic enterprises of Scott, Byron, and Southey, as well as Wordsworth and Coleridge himself. Wordsworth's remarks explaining his decision to exclude "Christabel" from the 1800 *Lyrical Ballads* are well known: "I found that the Style of this Poem was so discordant from my own that it could not be printed along with my poems with any propriety" (quoted in *CL*, 1:643). Wordsworth's exclusion registers the threat that Christabel represented as *text* (and, in the character of Geraldine, as performative theory of the rhetorical power of texts) to the *Lyrical Ballads* as book—an exclusion that was in fact the echo of Coleridge's own attempt to make "Fears in Solitude" a book by quarantining dangerous romance in the unpublished "Christabel." But, alarmingly, "Christabel" kept coming back: it is disseminated throughout "Fears" and its companion poems, as well as throughout the writings of Coleridge's contemporaries. A full account of the postrevolutionary and non-Miltonic line of "Christabel"'s metrical influence remains to be written. The two essays most attentive to the unsettling "style" of

"Christabel," Karen Swann's superb " 'Christabel': The Wandering Mother and the Enigma of Form" (*Studies in Romanticism* 23 [winter 1984]: 533–53) and her "Literary Gentlemen and Lovely Ladies: The Debate on the Character of 'Christabel' " (*ELH* 52 [spring 1985]: 397–418), disregard meter in favor of generic issues involving the supernatural, male literary culture, and the feminine. A supplementary account would build on John Hollander's illuminating remarks about meter as a "curiously strong indication or emblem of genre" in order to argue the way in which the irregularity of "Christabel" at once announces what Hollander calls a "metrical contract" and disables the contract form (John Hollander, *Vision and Resonance: Two Senses of Poetic Form* (New York: Oxford Univ. Press, 1975), 192–96.

35. I rely on Hollander's fine discussion of the ethos of the hexameter in *Vision and Resonance*, 190–91. Paul Magnuson illuminatingly discusses Coleridge's "attempt to recover the audibility of a natural language" in *Coleridge and Wordsworth: A Lyrical Dialogue* (Princeton: Princeton Univ. Press, 1988), 188.

36. The theoretical implications of this hope for a kind of transference without trope are referred to a de Manian and psychoanalytic vocabulary and analyzed with exemplary subtlety by Cynthia Chase in her essay " 'Transference' as Trope and Persuasion," in *Discourse in Psychoanalysis and Literature,* ed. Schlomo Rimmon-Kennan (New York: Methuen, 1987), 211–33.

37. Hollander remarks that "it is with Romantic poetry that we begin to get a poetic confrontation of the realms of the two reigning senses." His historical analysis suggests that Coleridge's momentous engagement with Greek hexameters is at once a unique confrontation and the repetition of a struggle that has always occurred at the articulation of modernity with the classical Greek: "The superimposition of schemata for the poetry of one language upon the hostile realities of another engender[s] grave complexities. . . . It was with the adaptation of Greek meters to Latin that poetry, originally inseparable from music, began to grow away from it. And it was then that poetry began to develop, in its meter, a seeming music of its own" (*Vision and Resonance*, 23, 11).

38. Philippe Lacoue-Labarthe, "The Echo of the Subject," in *Typography: Mimesis, Philosophy, Politics*, ed. Christopher Fynsk (Cambridge, Mass: Harvard Univ. Press, 1989), 175. For a remarkable and graphic synthesis of this dynamism in "The Boy of Winander" passage, see Neil Hertz, *The End of the Line* (New York: Columbia Univ. Press, 1985), 217–19. The graphic dimension of Hertz's analysis is discussed in Chapter 2.

39. Having completed his inquiries, Coleridge did duly report on the function of professing in Germany. "A Professor," he wrote, "is one who has received from the Government & University that especial Degree which authorizes him to teach publickly in the particular

department or faculty, of which he is Professor" (*CL*, 1:477).
Unfortunately, Coleridge's letter survives only in fragmentary form.

40. For a critique of liberalism as requiring a "net transfer of powers," see
C. B. Macpherson, "The Maximization of Democracy," in *Democratic Theory: Essays in Retrieval* (Oxford: Clarendon Press, 1973), 3–23.

Chapter 4: The Dark Romanticism of the *Edinburgh Review*

An earlier version of this chapter appeared in *South Atlantic Quarterly* (summer 1996) © 1996 Duke University Press.

1. See Robert Hole, *Pulpits, Politics and Public Order in England, 1760–1832* (Cambridge: Cambridge Univ. Press, 1989), 151. Henceforth quotations from the October 1802 *Edinburgh Review* will appear in the text, noted as *ER*.

2. See Immanuel Wallerstein, *Unthinking Social Science: The Limits of Nineteenth-Century Paradigms* (Cambridge: Basil Blackwell, 1991), 17–18. For Furet's deployment of Tocqueville, see part 1 of his *Interpreting the French Revolution*, trans. Elborg Forster (Cambridge: Cambridge Univ. Press, 1981).

3. Written by Francis Jeffrey, the lead review, like all those published in the *Edinburgh Review* appeared anonymously, thereby implying a corporate voice.

4. Sir George Cornewall Lewis, *Essays on the Administrations of Great Britain from 1783 to 1830 Contributed to the* Edinburgh Review (London, 1864), 216.

5. For an account of the popular response, see Roger Wells, *Insurrection: The British Experience, 1795–1803* (Gloucester: Alan Sutton, 1986), 225.

6. Lewis, *Essays*, 221.

7. Charles Dauben, *A Guide to the Church, in Several Discourses* (London, 1798), p. 456; quoted in J. C. D. Clark, *English Society: 1688–1832* (Cambridge: Cambridge Univ. Press, 1985), 273.

8. Benedict Anderson, *Imagined Communities: Reflections on the Origin and Spread of Nationalism* (London: Verso, 1983), 16.

9. Linda Colley, *Britons: Forging the Nation 1707–1837* (New Haven: Yale Univ. Press, 1991), 287.

10. For the application of this tropology to the truce of Amiens, see Samuel Taylor Coleridge, *The Friend*, ed. Barbara Rooke, 2 vols., vol. 4 of *The Collected Works of Samuel Taylor Coleridge*, gen. ed. Kathleen Coburn (Princeton: Princeton Univ. Press, 1969), 2:300–301.

11. Adam Seligman, *The Idea of Civil Society* (New York: Macmillan, 1992), 33.

12. *Memoirs and Correspondence of Francis Horner*, ed. Leonard Horner, 2 vols. (Cambridge, 1843), 1:96.

13. See the reviewer's description of the mutual trust that subsists among commercial men and its connection to the transformation of verbal obligations to promissory notes to bills of exchange to currency (*ER*, 175).

14. See P. G. M. Dickson, *The Financial Revolution in the Development of Public Credit, 1688–1756* (New York: St. Martin's Press, 1967).

15. F. H. Hinsley, *Sovereignty*, 2d ed. (Cambridge: Cambridge Univ. Press, 1986), 152.

16. Ernesto Laclau and Chantal Mouffe, *Hegemony and Socialist Strategy: Towards a Radical Democratic Politics* (London: Verso, 1985), 7.

Chapter 5: Romantic Hope

1. *Essays on His Own Times*, ed. David V. Erdman, 3 vols., vol. 3 of *The Collected Works of Samuel Taylor Coleridge*, gen. ed. Kathleen Coburn (Princeton: Princeton Univ. Press, 1978), 1:312. Hereafter *EOT*.

2. For two recent accounts of how the British were formed into a national people willing to be taxed and to take arms against a common enemy in the eighteenth and early nineteenth centuries, see John Brewer, *The Sinews of Power: War, Money, and the English State, 1688–1783* (New York: Knopf, 1989), and Linda Colley, *Britons: The Forging of a Nation, 1707–1837* (New Haven: Yale Univ. Press, 1992).

3. *EOT*, 1:337. Coleridge had only recently changed his tune: in the spring of 1800 he was reporting that "Bonaparte has addressed the people of France on the wisdom and duty of preparing for war, by personal enthusiasm and financial sacrifices; and uses as motives of inducement, not the ordinary appeals to terror or indignation, but the more sublime and humane excitement of hope" (*EOT*, 1:215).

4. Donald H. Reiman, "The Beauty of Buttermere as Fact and Romantic Symbol," *Criticism* 26, no. 2 (spring 1984), 144. In his account of the episode, De Quincey, who accused Coleridge of being "bitter — almost vindictive" in his remembrance of Hatfield's letters, comments that "the few, and simple neighbours, who had witnessed her imaginary elevation, having little knowledge of worldly feelings, never for an instant connected with her disappointment any sense of the ludicrous, or spoke of it as a calamity to which her vanity might have co-operated. They treated it as unmixed injury, reflecting shame upon nobody but the wicked perpetrator" (*Recollections of the Lakes and the Lake Poets*, ed. David Wright [Harmondsworth: Penguin, 1970], 70–71).

5. De Quincey notes that the inn was so remote from the traffic of strangers that it was probably operated "more, perhaps, for the sake of gathering any little local news, than with much view to pecuniary profit" (ibid., 68). That is, it was a center of intelligence, not commerce.

6.   *Collected Letters of Samuel Taylor Coleridge*, ed. Earl Leslie Griggs, 5 vols. (Oxford: Clarendon Press, 1956), 2:1121. Hereafter *CL*.

7.   Reiman, "The Beauty of Buttermere," 145. Reiman's essay gives a full account of the literature in which Mary Robinson appeared both before and after the events of 1802 — an important contribution, for Coleridge overlooked and De Quincey denied that the secluded cottage had been the object of curiosity before the arrival of Hatfield. For an account of the investment of Wordsworth in the purity of the Maid of Buttermere, see Mary Jacobus, *Romanticism, Writing, and Sexual Difference* (Oxford: Clarendon Press, 1989), 208–12.

8.   Benedict Anderson, *Imagined Communities: Reflections on the Origin and Spread of Nationalism*, 2d ed. (London: Verso, 1991), 33.

9.   For an example of poetic enterprise of this kind, see Wordsworth's "Lines Written at a Small Distance from My House," from the 1798 *Lyrical Ballads,* which lyrically promotes an affectional community self-determined by a "living calendar" that is implicitly counterposed to the calendar of the Jacobin republic.

10. See Jerome Christensen, *Coleridge's Blessed Machine of Language* (Ithaca: Cornell Univ. Press, 1981), Chapters 4 and 5, for an account of this figure.

11. Roger Wells, *Insurrection: The British Experience, 1795–1803* (Gloucester: Alan Sutton, 1983), 220–52.

12. Norman Bryson, *Word and Image: French Painting of the Ancien Régime* (Cambridge: Cambridge Univ. Press, 1981), 40.

13. *The Works of Thomas Love Peacock*, ed. H. F. B. Smith and C. E. Jones (London, 1861; rpt., New York: AMS Press, 1967), 5:6.

14. See Plato, *The Sophist*, in *Parmenides and Other Dialogues*, trans. John Warrington (London: J. M. Dent, 1961), 160–61.

15. On pikes, see David V. Erdman, *Commerce des Lumieres: John Oswald and the British in Paris* (Columbia: Univ. of Missouri Press, 1986).

16. Claude Lefort, *Democracy and Political Theory* (Cambridge: Polity Press, 1988). On Continental social movements, both political and "prepolitical," see Eric Hobsbawm, *Primitive Rebels: Studies in Archaic Forms of Social Movement in the Nineteenth and Twentieth Centuries* (1959; rpt., New York: Norton, 1965).

17. *Lectures 1795: On Politics and Religion,* ed. Lewis Patton and Peter Mann, vol. 1 of Coburn, ed., *The Collected Works of Samuel Taylor Coleridge,* 10.

18. Coleridge, *Biographia Literaria,* ed. James Engell and Walter Jackson Bate, 2 vols., vol. 7 of Coburn, ed., *Collected Works,* 281.

19. See Erdman's note 8, *EOT*, 1:415.

20. E. P. Thompson, *The Making of the English Working Class* (New York: Norton, 1964), 832.

21.   Marjorie Levinson, "Insight and Oversight: Reading 'Tintern Abbey'"
        in *Wordsworth's Great Period Poems: Four Essays* (Cambridge:
        Cambridge Univ. Press, 1986), 43.

Chapter 6: Clerical Liberalism

1.   Daniel Defoe, *A Tour Through England and Wales,* 2 vols. (1724; rpt.,
        London: Dent, 1928), 1:193.

2.   I rely on the definition of *ekphrasis* as "the verbal representation of
        visual representation," proposed by James Heffernan in "Ekphrasis
        and Representation," *New Literary History* 22, no. 2 (spring 1991):
        297–316.

3.   Oliver Goldsmith, *The Vicar of Wakefield* (1766; rpt.,
        Harmondsworth: Penguin, 1982), 99–100.

4.   Walter Scott, *Waverley* (1814; rpt., London: Dent, 1969), 80.

5.   Hannah Arendt, "What Is Authority?" in *Between Past and Future:
        Eight Exercises in Political Thought* (New York: Penguin, 1961), 92. I
        am indebted to Charles Dove for this reference.

6.   Kim Ian Michasiw, "Nine Revisionist Theses on the Picturesque,"
        Representations, no. 38 (Spring 1992), 85. On pictures in *Waverley,*
        see also P. D. Garside, "*Waverley*'s Pictures of the Past," *ELH* 44, no. 4
        (1977): 659–82.

7.   Wendy Steiner, *Pictures of Romance: Form against Context in
        Painting and Literature* (Chicago: Univ. of Chicago Press, 1988), 50.

8.   Alexander Welsh makes the case forcefully in "Patriarchy, Contract,
        and Repression in Scott's Novels," *The Hero of the Waverley Novels
        with New Essays on Scott* (Princeton: Princeton Univ. Press, 1992),
        213–41.

9.   For a recent account of the way the name *Waverley* figures the
        development of the main character's identity, see David Glenn Kropf,
        Authorship as Alchemy (Palo Alto: Stanford Univ. Press, 1994),
        109–30.

10.   Carl Schmitt, *Political Romanticism,* trans. Guy Oakes (Cambridge,
        Mass.: MIT Press, 1986), 17.

11.   Edmund Burke, *Reflections on the French Revolution* (1790;
        Harmondsworth: Penguin, 1969), 121.

12.   Richard Rorty, *Contingency, Irony, and Solidarity* (Cambridge:
        Cambridge Univ. Press, 1989), 9.

13.   John Dewey, *The Public and Its Problems* (1927; rpt. with afterword,
        Athens, Ohio: Swallow and Ohio Univ. Press, 1954), 200.

14.   On the difference, see Coleridge's "Essay on Method" in the 1818
        Friend, ed. Barbara Rooke, 2 vols., vol. 4 of *The Collected Works of
        Samuel Taylor Coleridge,* gen. ed. Kathleen Coburn, 2 vols.
        (Princeton: Princeton Univ. Press, 1969), 1:436–46.

15. Coleridge applies the phrase in the second of his 1802 news articles in the *Morning Post* on the suspicious marriage of the Maid of Buttermere, *Essays on His Times*, ed. David V. Erdman, 2 vols., vol. 3 of Coburn, ed., *Collected Works*, 1:374.

16. The pastness of the Pretender's own claims to being recognized as sovereign is represented by his dependence on such accessories as the tartan and the mirror in which Edward admires himself — the pattern of the tartan and the reflection are charming, they are not the man. Peter Murphy's *Poetry as an Occupation and an Art in Britain, 1760–1830* (Cambridge: Cambridge Univ. Press, 1993) superbly revives the category of the charming as a token of exchange between high and popular culture.

17. Norman Bryson, *Word and Image: French Painting of the Ancien Régime* (Cambridge: Cambridge Univ. Press, 1981), 19–20.

18. Michael Baxendall, *Patterns of Intention: On the Historical Explanation of Pictures* (New Haven: Yale Univ. Press, 1985), 42.

19. Dugald Stewart, "On Taste," *Philosophical Essays* (London, 1811), 321.

20. Preface to *Lyrical Ballads* (1802), *Literary Criticism of William Wordsworth*, ed. Paul M. Zall (Lincoln: Univ. of Nebraska Press, 1966), 40.

21. Thomas De Quincey, *Confessions of an English Opium Eater*, ed. Alethea Hayter (1821; rpt., Harmondsworth: Penguin, 1971), 106. I am indebted to Margaret Russett's provocative reading of De Quincey's rhetorical strategy in the Piranesi episode in *De Quincey's Romanticism: Canonical Minority and the Forms of Transmission* (Cambridge: Cambridge Univ. Press, 1997), 164–70.

22. John Gibson Lockhart, *Memoirs of Sir Walter Scott*, 5 vols. (New York: Macmillan, 1900), 2:332.

23. For a discussion of the ecclesiastical employment of *des armes parlantes*, see Thomas Robson, *The British Herald, or Cabinet of Armorial Bearings of the Nobility and Gentry of Great Britain and Ireland, from the Earliest to the Present Time* (Durham, 1830), 26.

24. For the distinction between discourse and figure, see Bryson, *Word and Image*, 1–28.

25. During a leadership struggle in the Conservative Party in Great Britain in the summer of 1995, the *Guardian* indicated that one Tory M.P. had made his money as an investment banker in part by "refusing to lend money to any country with green in its flag." On this improvisation and the use of colors in heraldry in general, see John Gage, *Color and Culture: Practice and Meaning from Antiquity to Abstraction* (Boston: Little, Brown, 1993), 81–90.

26. For Marshall McLuhan's discussion of the "inclusive form of the icon," as well as of "cool forms" in general, see his book

Understanding Media: The Extensions of Man (1964; rpt., Cambridge, Mass.: MIT Press, 1994), 12–24.

27.   George Lukacs, *The Historical Novel,* trans. Hannah Mitchell and Stanley Mitchell (Harmondsworth: Penguin, 1969), 68.

28.   *The Works of John Ruskin,* ed. Edward Cook and Alexander Wedderburn, 39 vols. (London: G. Allen, 1903–12), 5:336.

29.   Talbot is a special case, but he proves himself unfaithful, that is, commercial, by the transfer of affections from his own dead child to Waverley.

30.   See Jerome Christensen, "Once an Apostate Always an Apostate," *Studies in Romanticism* 21, no. 3 (fall 1982): 461–64.

31.   George Levine, *The Realistic Imagination: English Fiction from Frankenstein to Lady Chatterley* (Chicago: Univ. of Chicago Press, 1981), 99.

32.   Hannah Arendt, *The Human Condition* (Chicago: Univ. of Chicago Press, 1958), 40.

33.   For a fuller discussion of the Napoleonic aftermath, see Jerome Christensen, *Lord Byron's Strength: Romantic Writing and Commercial Society* (Baltimore: Johns Hopkins Univ. Press, 1993).

34.   R. Jeffrey Lustig, *Corporate Liberalism: The Origins of Modern American Political Theory, 1890–1920* (Berkeley: Univ. of California Press, 1982), 25.

Chapter 7: Using

1.   Ronald Dworkin, Thallheimer Lectures, Johns Hopkins University, March 12, 1996.

2.   Bill Readings, *The University in Ruins* (Cambridge, Mass.: Harvard Univ. Press, 1996), 168.

3.   Stanley Fish, "What It Means to Do a Job of Work," *English Literary Renaissance* 25, no. 3 (autumn 1995): 357.

4.   Quoted by Ash Amin, "Post-Fordism: Models, Fantasies and Phantoms of Transition," in *Post-Fordism: A Reader,* ed. Ash Amin (Oxford: Blackwell, 1994), 41.

5.   Although Microsoft is renowned for its hacker ethos, its policy of vesting employees in the company through stock options, and its policy of promoting its management from its own teams of programmers, rapid expansion has demanded an organization rigidly hierarchical in structure and less loosely fraternal in style than in the early days. Mark Walker, a developer hired out of college by Microsoft in the mid-1980s, comments: "The feel of the company has changed quite a bit in just the three years since I've started. . . . Now it seems to be going the direction of more traditional organizations, where you move up when somebody leaves and you wait for attrition and that kind of thing" (quoted in Michael A. Cusamano and Richard W. Selby,

Microsoft Secrets: How the World's Most Powerful Software Company Creates Technology, Shapes Markets, and Manages People [New York: Free Press, 1995], 120. For a more optimistic view of the prospects of the new corporate culture, see Avery Gordon, "The Work of Corporate Culture: Diversity Management," *Social Text* 44 (fall/winter 1995): 3–30.

6. Mark Elam, "Puzzling out the Post-Fordist Debate: Technology, Markets and Institutions," in Amin, ed., *Post-Fordism*, 63.

7. Bill Gates, *The Road Ahead* (New York: Viking, 1995), 6.

8. Douglas Coupland, *Microserfs* (New York: Regan Books, 1995), passim. Mark Smith, *Making the Modern: Industry, Art, and Design in America* (Chicago: Univ. of Chicago Press, 1993), 87.

9. For a cogent argument regarding the paradox rights-based liberalism returns to because of its commitment to the perfection of the market and its need to insist on rights to intellectual property, see James Boyle, *Shamans, Software, and Spleens: Law and the Construction of the Information Society* (Cambridge, Mass.: Harvard Univ. Press, 1996).

10. See Gates, *The Road Ahead*, 175–76.

11. Gates's message is egalitarian to the extent that he represents all people as consumers, but social differentiation emerges starkly in conjunction with his radical extension of the powers of targeting advertising, which hard-headedly confronts the economic fact that not all consumers are equal.

> Some of the billions of dollars now spent annually on media advertising . . . will instead be divvied up among consumers who agree to watch or read ads sent directly to them as messages.
> Mailings offering this sort of paying advertisement could be extremely effective because they can be carefully targeted. Advertisers will be smart about sending messages worth money only to people who meet appropriate demographics. . . . Advertisements and messages from unknown people could be sorted by how much money was attached to them. There would be a group of 1-cent messages, a group of 10-cent messages, and so forth. (*The Road Ahead*, 174)

12. For a brilliant and not, I think, inadvertent trope of this relationship and of Nike's triumph over the national trademark, see the cover of the summer 1996 special edition of *Time*, which features track star Michael Johnson, Nike swoosh emblazoned on his chest, hands on hips, and standing astride a dais draped with the American flag.

13. Andrew Levy, "The Swastikas of Niketown," *Harper's Magazine*, 292, no. 1751 (April 1996): 32–33.

14. Ellis W. Hawley, *The New Deal and the Problem of Monopoly: A Study in Economic Ambivalence* (1966; rpt., New York: Fordham Univ. Press, 1995), 12–13.

15. In a *Wired* interview, organizational psychologist Karl Weick responded to the question posed by John Gierland, "What organizations will be like in the future?": "I think you're going to lose middles. People talk about the disappearing middle class; there's no more middle management; and midsize organizations really don't exist anymore." John Gierland, "Complicate Yourself," *Wired*, April 1996, 137.

16. See Marc Eliot, *Walt Disney: Hollywood's Dark Prince* (New York: Harper, 1993), 127–64, for history of labor disputes at Disney in the 1930s.

17. Disney executives and Imagineers have disputed this account with the claim that if Pixar was responsible for the technological toys, it was Disney which, at a late stage in the production of a very iffy project, contributed the story.

18. An exception may be Disney, which has established the Disney Institute in Orlando as a site for educational seminars in a resort atmosphere. But insofar as it remains an onsite experience, such an experiment would seem to be limited in scope and transitional in status.

19. Michael J. Sandel, *Democracy's Discontent: America in Search of a Public Philosophy* (Cambridge, Mass.: Harvard Univ. Press, 1996), 179.

20. Here's Dave Maritz, former tank commander in the Israeli army and manager of Microsoft's MS-DOS/Windows testing group:

    > In the military, when I was in tank warfare and I was actually fighting in tanks, there was nothing more soothing than people constantly hearing their commander's voice come across the airwaves.... When you don't hear [the commander's voice] for more than fifteen minutes to half an hour, what's happened? Has he been shot? Has he gone out of control? Does he know what's going on? You worry. And this is what Microsoft is. These little offices, hidden away with the doors closed. And unless you have this constant voice of authority going across the e-mail the whole time it doesn't work. Everything that I do here I learned in the military.... You can't do anything complex unless you have structure.... And what you have to do is make that structure as unseen as possible and build up this image for all these prima donnas to think that they can do what they like. (Cusamano and Selby, 18–19)

21. Samuel Taylor Coleridge, *Essays on His Times*, ed. David V. Erdman, 3 vols, vol 3 of *The Collected Works of Samuel Taylor Coleridge*, gen. ed. Kathleen Coburn (Princeton: Princeton Univ. Press, 1978), 1:337.

22. Lester Thurow, *The Future of Capitalism* (New York: William Morrow, 1996), 27–28.

23. Thomas De Quincey, *Confessions of an English Opium Eater*, ed. Alethea Hayter (1821; rpt., Harmondsworth: Penguin, 1971), 65.

24. See Scott Adams, *The Dilbert Principle: A Cubicle's-Eye View of Bosses, Meetings, Management Fads, and Other Workplace Afflictions* (New York: Harperbusiness, 1997).

25. Thomas J. DeLoughry, "Snared by the Internet," *The Chronicle of Higher Education*, March 1, 1996, A25.

26. Cf. Fredric Jameson's description of postmodernism as a "cultural form of image addiction which, by transforming the past into casual mirages, stereotypes or texts, effectively abolishes any practical sense of the future." Frederic Jameson, *Postmodernism or, The Cultural Logic of Late Capitalism* (Durham: Duke Univ. Press, 1991), 46.

27. I stipulate those two for early texts, because, as John Barrell shows, the later De Quincey of *Suspiria de Profundis* and the essays shifts his ground to a composite of individual psychology and imperial ambitions (*The Infection of Thomas De Quincey: A Psychopathology of Imperialism* [New Haven: Yale Univ. Press, 1991]).

28. See Margaret Russett, *De Quincey's Romanticism: Canonical Minority and the Forms of Transmission* (Cambridge: Cambridge Univ. Press, 1997).

29. William Wordsworth, Preface to *Lyrical Ballads* (1802), in *Literary Criticism of William Wordsworth*, ed. Paul M. Zall (Lincoln: Univ. of Nebraska Press, 1966), 44.

30. *Collected Letters of Samuel Taylor Coleridge*, ed. Earl Leslie Griggs, 6 vols. (Oxford: Clarendon, 1956–71), 1:442.

31. See Stephen Holmes, *The Anatomy of Antiliberalism* (Cambridge, Mass.: Harvard Univ. Press, 1993), 187–200.

32. Ibid.

33. To some extent, Bill Gates's industrial policy has anticipated me here. Jim Conner, a program manager for Microsoft Office, observes: "That's one of the things I respect about Microsoft. They're outstanding at hiring workaholics. . . . You get weird cases where people literally move into their offices. I used to have problems when I was a test manager; I would have to order people to go home because they were exhausted. They'd work for three or four days straight. . . . They were just compulsive about it. And I think that's how Microsoft makes the strategy work" (Cusamano and Selbuy, 95).

Index

Library of Congress Cataloging-in-Publication Data

Christensen, Jerome, 1948–
    Romanticism at the end of history / Jerome Christensen.
        p.   cm.
    Includes bibliographical references (p.   ) and index.
    ISBN 0-8018-6319-8 (alk. paper)
        1. English literature — 19th century — history and criticism.   2. Literature and
history — Great Britain — History — 19th century.   3. France — History — Revolution,
1789–1799 — Literature and the revolution.   4. Napoleonic Wars, 1800–1815 —
Literature and the wars.   5. English literature — French influences.   6. Romanticism —
Great Britain.   I. Title.
PR468.H57C47   2000
820.9′358 — dc21
                                                                                        99-43278
                                                                                        CIP

Lightning Source UK Ltd.
Milton Keynes UK
UKOW02f1612110716

278121UK00001B/254/P